To Evelyn

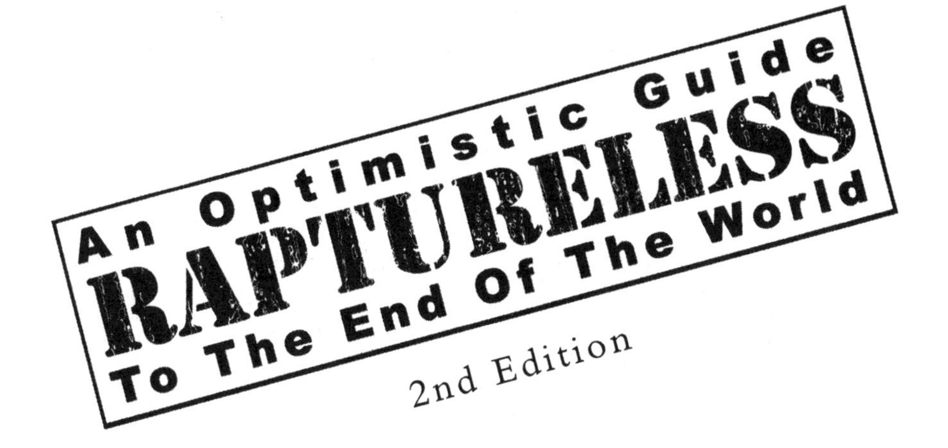

Including The Art of Revelation

JONATHAN WELTON

Praise for *Raptureless*

In our ministry to women and children in prostitution on the streets of Brazil, we see people living every day in what I would describe as hell on earth. Children as young as eight are sold for sex ten to twenty times a night, women are locked away as sex slaves, and constant streams of men look for girls of all ages. We see much tribulation in the lives of these precious ones on the streets of Brazil. As I travel I often hear comments such as this, "Wow, that is horrible, and the world is only going to get worse before Jesus comes back."

The problem with this false eschatology—which has been so glamorized by products like *Left Behind*—is that it creates an excuse within the minds of Christians to just leave it to Jesus to clean up the mess. However, He already paid the price to clean up the mess, and He put the broom in our hands and said, "Go into all the world!" I am so appreciative of my friend Jonathan Welton for having the passion and courage to write this book. Although some will call it controversial, I consider it a breath of fresh air! Simple biblical truths, a constant in *Raptureless*, keep controversy at bay, allowing us to thoroughly discover what the Bible really says about the endtimes and discern the current age. Jonathan has been given a gift of understanding the Scriptures, and he puts in the hours and hard work to refine and strengthen that gifting. This is very evident in this book, and I am sure you will be challenged and blessed as you read *Raptureless.*

NIC BILLMAN
Shores of Grace Ministries
Recife, Brazil
www.shoresofgrace.com

Jonathan Welton is a fresh author whose ministry that is bringing to light historical truth concerning end-time eschatology in our day. He has taken bold steps to confront the fear-based theology that has paralyzed the Church concerning "end of the age" mentality, and he has brilliantly composed what I believe to be one of the most biblically and historically correct perspectives on eschatology to date.

If we want to fully move into our personal and corporate destiny, it's crucial we understand *who* we are and *where* we stand biblically in human history. *Raptureless* holds the view that many, if not most, Church Fathers have held—including John Calvin, Charles Spurgeon, John Wesley, and Jonathan Edwards. I highly endorse *Raptureless* by Jonathan Welton. I believe it will be used as a textbook to transform generations to come.

JEFF JANSEN
Senior Leader, Global Fire Church & Global Connect
Global Fire Ministries International
Kingdom Life Institute & Global Fire School of Supernatural Ministry

Jonathan Welton is a voice to the rising Church. We need his teaching gift stirring the Body of Christ to action. Here in *Raptureless*, Jonathan has revealed his scholarship and ability to communicate on subjects pertinent to the issues facing today's Church. Read it and be challenged. With this much evidence, the reader must make a decision!

HAROLD EBERLE
President, Worldcast Ministries and Publishing
Author, *Victorious Eschatology* and *Who Is God?*

Jonathan Welton has taken a bold step in confronting one of the greatest "sacred cows" of our day: end-time theology! The fear created by the expectation of a coming antichrist and a great tribulation are keeping many believers in bondage. Many believe that defeat is the future destiny of the Church. As Jesus said, human traditions make void the Word of God. In his easy-to-read presentation, Jonathan dismantles many of the popular ideas in the Church about the endtimes.

JOE MCINTYRE
Word of His Grace Church & the Healing Centre
Empowering Grace Ministries
Kenyon's Gospel Publishing Society

Jonathan Welton's new book, *Raptureless*, is a must-read. While he covers some ground that has been covered by others before him, he does so in a fresh, crisp, and concise manner. But he also has new insights on various passages of Scripture. His arguments are scriptural and lucid, and they are simply and powerfully presented. In addition, Jonathan provides fresh historical background for a number of the historical sources that he has quoted, such as Flavius Josephus. The true significance of these sources establishes the truths presented in *Raptureless.*

GEORGE KOURI
Chancellor of the Apostles Theological Seminary
Presiding Apostle of the Communion of Apostolic Churches
Senior Pastor of the King's Church
Jacksonville, Florida

Although I've only known Jonathan Welton a short time, I have a huge value for our growing relationship. Jonathan communicates with a skill and an insight beyond his years. His passion for the Word and the truth and his deep knowledge of history put a rare weight on his teaching. Beyond his transformational truths, I have found Jonathan to be humble, relational, accountable, and passionate for our King and His Kingdom. I have personally benefited from Jonathan's teachings and greatly value him as a gift to our generation.

DAN MCCOLLAM
Director, Sounds of the Nations
Bethel School of the Prophets & School of Supernatural Worship
Deeper School of Supernatural Life
The Mission, Vacaville, CA

Whenever the prophets of the Bible saw God's people facing difficult times, they acknowledged the problem but pointed people to a brighter future where God would right all wrongs, do "a new thing" in the earth, and offer a new and better way. Jesus did the same—He pointed out the destruction that was facing Jerusalem but also pointed to the brave new world, the Kingdom of God that would grow in our midst, making all things new. Today, Jonathan Welton is one of the people continuing that prophetic tradition. He acknowledges the mess that much of the Church has made (mainly due to faulty theology), but instead of "doom and gloom," he offers faith-filled optimism and clear, biblical theology. I highly recommend this book!

MARTIN TRENCH
Co-author, *Victorious Eschatology*

Raptureless, An Optimistic Guide to the End of the World is an amazing new prophetic view that will surely encourage you to be part of what God is doing on earth today!

DOUG ADDISON
Author, *Understand Your Dreams Now*
http://dougaddison.com

Raptureless, by Jonathan Welton, is not just another book about the endtimes; it is a field manual for the twenty-first century that brings fresh hope to a generation who has otherwise lost hope because of the deceptions of end-times madness! Welton has successfully penned a manifesto that puts an end to the false teachings that so many of us have inherited from our families and churches.

If you are not satisfied with the subjective ideologies that have been imbedded into your mind, making you unsure about what tomorrow may hold, read this book. You may just find that tomorrow holds something genuinely good! This book is destined to transform the mentality of a whole new generation of leaders, and it will change *your* life forever!

SHANE MASON
Preacher, author, and founder of Shane Mason Ministries

Jonathan's new book is long overdue. His clear and detailed teaching exposes numerous myths about the rapture theory and the endtimes. This thought-provoking book will challenge every serious believer who is seeking truth.

GARY OATES
Author, *Open My Eyes, Lord*
International conference speaker

I so appreciate the thought-provoking, well-studied, forthright, and optimistic arguments put forward in Jonathan Welton's *Raptureless*. No matter what your end-time theological inclinaiton is or what you believe about the rapture, the antichrist, and the end-time events, *Raptureless* will give you something to think about. For those who have been around the eschatological block, if you have an appreciation for thoughtful, well-researched discussion and if you have an appreciation for early church perspectives, you will not be disappointed. If you are just cutting your teeth on all this, you will also not be disappointed. *Raptureless* is both intriguing and profoundly accessible to even the newest of biblical students. Thank you, Jonathan, for giving us such a well-researched document and presenting these perspectives for honest discussion in the Body. There is never a time when honest, honoring discussion among genuine truth seekers is not enriching. Thank you, Jonathan, for giving us all a lot to think about and talk about. What I most appreciate about *Raptureless*, however, is not the discussion points but rather the heart to see the Church of Jesus Christ get up and get on with the work of bringing His love, glory, and truth to a world that needs that love right now.

FAYTENE GRASSESCHI
Director, TheCRY Movement, MY Canada, & V-Kol Media

I believe we are in an epoch season during which God is bringing reformation and a new wineskin to the Church. Jonathan is one of many voices who are bringing revelatory insight and a fresh perspective to His people. I have personally observed as a friend the heart of this man to bring truth and break wrong mindsets that have encamped themselves in the Church. He is constantly studying out the Scriptures and is the ultimate learner who is searching out the Scriptures to bring abundant life. I would strongly encourage you to dive in and immerse yourself in the book *Rapturless*. There is a fresh anointing in these pages for God to kill any sacred cows in your life and theology.

CHAD DEDMON
Global Legacy
Bethel Church, Redding, CA

Sometimes it can be hard to find prophetic ministries who truly represent Jesus Christ as He is. One day I was in a small meeting where I believe a true vessel of the voice of Jesus Christ gave me this word: "Jesus says to you, 'I will remove your doomsday mentality and give you a message of hope for My people. I encourage you to give some attention to the topic of the endtimes because My Spirit will teach you about this.'" I was puzzled that the Lord said I had a doomsday mentality. *Did I?*

I bought every possible book and video about the endtimes I could find. Eventually, I threw it all away. Frustrated, I said, "Lord, if you want to show me the truth about the endtimes and give me hope for the future, You will have to do it, because everything I have read, listened to, and watched so far is (sorry for the messengers) one big mess."

Years later, God opened my eyes, transformed my thinking, and showed me how gloriously bright the future of planet earth and humankind is. When the Lord started revealing this to us, I thought I was pretty alone and crazy. But God always speaks to a multitude of wild guys in the desert who are willing to pay the price of listening more to His voice than to the many other voices that yell at us, even (especially?) in the Christian world. So when I discovered Jonathan Welton's book, I was excited and encouraged. God is indeed speaking to many that the future is not dark and gloomy but bright and glorious. Jesus Christ is not the dusk; He is the dawn. *"The path of the righteous is like the light of dawn, that shines brighter and brighter until the full day"* (Prov. 4:18 NASB).

For some readers, it can be quite shocking to read what Jonathan writes. But I encourage you to be brave and trust the Spirit of Truth who leads you into all truth and who does not lie. If this book is full of deception, the Spirit of God will show you. If Jonathan speaks liberating truth that will bring forth much fruit, the Spirit of Truth will be a witness to you, and His truth will set you free. Do not let fear guide you, but let Him guide you. I believe a brand new insight awaits you. After you have struggled your way through fear, confusion, and questions, you will have a tremendous revelation of Jesus Christ, who is right here with us in His glory and who wants to bring His glory into all the earth, not one day—later—but right now, through you and me, His glorious Bride.

David Sorensen
Soundofheaven.info

Raptureless is a must-read! Jonathan Welton does an amazing job of bringing a fresh yet biblical perspective on the endtimes as well as the days we are living in as a Church. This *Kingdom now* book offers a fresh perspective about the victorious Church and Bride whom God is raising up in this hour. Read as Jonathan demystifies and unlocks a lot of the unanswered questions about the endtimes and brings a clear reality to the revelation of Jesus Christ.

Jerame Nelson
Living At His Feet Ministries
Author, *Burning Ones, Activating Your Spiritual Senses,* and *Activating Your Dream Language*

This rogue, Jonathan Welton, got me—hook, line, and sinker—"caught up" in reading *Raptureless!* Rarely have I come across a book that is so compelling and engrossing, a genuine, un-put-downable, page-turner. How often does one say that about a theology book? But, though it is detailed and scrupulous in its historical insight and scriptural analysis, this is no mere dry academic treatise. No! This is an essential manual for the victorious Church written by someone who loves the Word and the Spirit.

As a prophetic people and a prophetic Church, it is so important to have the right script inside of us. After all, we prophesy according to our faith. This book will go a long way to help you ensure you have the right faith script inside you—a biblical script with a victorious, glorious final act in which we all have parts to play. That includes you! It's time for you to play your part in advancing the Kingdom!

Jonathan's clear and engaging writing takes the reader on a crescendo of hope, building our faith in the presently increasing Kingdom of Jesus Christ here on earth. *Raptureless* puts the optimistic eschatological view of revivalists and reformers like Wesley, Edwards, and Spurgeon back on the table and is a must-read for all the Word-loving, Spirit-filled Church. You will be encouraged, strengthened, and galvanised as you consume the pages of this book!

David Stark
Co-director, International Network of Prophetic Centres at Glasgow Prophetic Centre
Scottish Regional Coordinator, Christian International Europe

Jonathan Welton is a prophetic vessel who has a fresh and heavenly perspective that is both cutting-edge and anointed. I have read a couple of Jonathan's books, and I have been challenged and riveted by both his revelation and authenticity. *Raptureless* is a *now* word that addresses one of the most needed messages of the endtimes—hope. Darkness has delighted every time a believer sucks on the bottle of despair, but *Raptureless* feeds the mentality of an end-time revivalist for the glory of God to be released and for the harvest to be unleashed. I'm convinced that any eschatology that is worth anything is one that inspires you to get up in the morning to fulfill the Great Commission, and Jonathan's book definitely does that!

Sean Smith
Author, *I Am Your Sign*
www.seansmithministries.com
@revseansmith

Jonathan's book, *Raptureless*, boldly exposes the fallacies surrounding much of the contemporary teaching on the endtimes. He presents an understanding of the future that is biblically robust and consistent with the greater part of Church history. Jonathan is masterful in slaying sacred cows and destroying misconceptions that have kept God's people shackled by fear and foreboding. Instead, he brings enlightenment to many Bible passages that have been previously misapplied, especially through the distorting lens of dispensational teaching. He affirms the presence, influence, and growth of God's Kingdom in the here and now—releasing optimism regarding the future. *Raptureless* is a clarion call to biblical perspectives about our present and our future.

Ian Rossol
Co-author, *Win the World or Escape the Earth*

RAPTURELESS
AN OPTIMISTIC GUIDE TO THE END OF THE WOLRD
2ND EDITION

Cover design by Benjamin Valence
Layout design by Renee Evans

ISBN: 978-0-9911510-0-4
Library of Congress Cataloging-in-Publication Data:
www.WeltonAcademy.com

I would like to acknowledge the authors David Chilton, Gary DeMar, Kenneth Gentry, Milton Terry, and N.T. Wright. I have learned so much from your amazing works. I have pulled together many of the things in this book from what I have learned by standing on your shoulders. Thank you for being pioneers, and thank you for being brave.

I want to also acknowledge my friends in the group "An Optimistic End-Time View"; without your thoughtful input and debate, this book would have been ever so boring to write. Thank you.

JONATHAN WELTON
August 1, 2013

Raptureless 2nd Edition

The Art of Revelation

FOREWORD

Seeing, feeling, tasting, and experiencing the future have their setbacks. One of them is a disdain for futureless people. They've always been around, and they frustrated even the Son of God. When Jesus pronounced to Simon Peter that He had given him the keys of the Kingdom based on His revelation that Jesus was the Son of the living God, Simon must have been overjoyed. However, it took only a few minutes of expanding that revelation to draw out the voice of satan from that same instrument. Jesus showed *how* the magnificent Son of God would raise up His Kingdom on the earth,

> *From that time Jesus began to show to His disciples that He must go to Jerusalem, and suffer many things from the elders and chief priests and scribes, and be killed, and be raised the third day. Then Peter took Him aside and began to rebuke Him, saying, "Far be it from You, Lord; this shall not happen to You!" But He turned and said to Peter, "Get behind Me, Satan! You are an offense to Me, for you are not mindful of the things of God, but the things of men"* (Matthew 16:21–23 NKJV).

Whenever there are crises, tribulations, attacks, and persecutions upon the Church as a whole or Christians personally, the cream of the defeatist crap arise, declaring it's the end and finding absolutely no reason to believe this is the prelude to yet another resurrection, another victory, another occupation. And then there's the issue of tribulation and the Great

Tribulation. Read what Jonathan writes, and I know you'll agree with me that this book is not only an answer to prayer but a light for a generation that quite simply needs no further encouragement to run from the Church.

> While many fictional authors speculate at what the Great Tribulation is going to be like in the future, the truth is that the events of the AD 70 destruction of Jerusalem fulfilled the prophecy of the Great Tribulation and fortunately shall never be repeated. There is no future Great Tribulation. Yes, there will continue to be trials, tribulations, and persecutions, but the Great Tribulation or "the Time of Jacob's Trouble," as prophesied by Jesus, has already happened just as He said it would and within the generation timeframe that He declared (see Matt. 24:34).

As you can see in this excerpt from his book, *Raptureless*, Jonathan has hit at the heart of the theological lie of escapism, a defeatist dogma that has rendered so many of God's people useless in today's troubled world.

You want a rapture? How about worshiping God? You'll be raptured. It's true. I experience it every day of my life.

Kim Clement

INTRODUCTION

My parents both graduated from a Pentecostal Bible College in the early 1970s. They attended classes during the era of the Jesus People Movement, the Vietnam War, and the epically bestselling *Late Great Planet Earth* by Hal Lindsey. During those turbulent times, my parents met and married. After they had my two older siblings, I was born into their family in 1983. This was an era of much speculation and fear regarding the endtimes, which many believed had already begun. My parents had heard all the confusing and conflicting points of view regarding the endtimes, and instead of becoming obsessed with figuring it all out, they made a choice.

They determined to raise godly children who would raise godly grandchildren. They chose to think long-term and invest in their future and the future of their children. They didn't have all the answers regarding a "perfect theology of the endtimes," but they knew better than to buy into the hype. When their friends quit their jobs, bought boats, and racked up credit card debt "because the end of the world is around the corner and we won't have to pay it back," my parents called this irresponsible and unChristlike behavior.

Growing up, I never knew what my parents really thought about the "end of the world." When I pressed them for an answer, they would say, "We are pan-millennial," which was a humorous way of saying that it will all "pan out" in the end! This left me with a lot of questions in my teen years when the *Left Behind* series became a raging bestseller.

Since I was not force-fed a particular point of view by either my parents or my church while growing up, I had the full ability to think freely. I began to dig into studying the endtimes and very quickly realized that this study was going to be deep, complex, and scary.

It didn't take long for me to become thoroughly confused. At that point, I felt the Holy Spirit speak to my heart. He said to me, *"Jonathan, please set aside your study of the endtimes. It is not the right season for you to study this. If you will trust Me, I will guide you to a right understanding in the future, but now is not the time. Wait on Me to give you a green light."* So for the next two and half years, I chose to read nothing regarding the endtimes; I didn't watch the *Left Behind* movies (sorry Kirk Cameron); I didn't even read the Book of Revelation!

One day, as I was browsing a used book sale, I saw a book on the endtimes, and I heard the Holy Spirit say to me, "Buy that book; it is time to begin to reveal the truth to you." It has now been over ten years since that day, and what the Holy Spirit has taught me about the endtimes has been some of the most wonderful revelation that I have received from His Word.

Plenty of books about the endtimes have been written based on personal visions or wild interpretations of Scripture. This is not one of those books. I have a Masters Degree in Biblical Studies. I am a student of Church History. I am *not* going to fill this book with subjective visions and fantasies regarding private interpretations of the endtimes. Enough of those books already exist, and the Holy Spirit had me avoid them for two and half years so that He could prepare my heart for what He wanted to show me.

Here are my starting points:

- Every part of the gospel is simple, including the teaching regarding the endtimes. If something is too complex for the average person to grasp, then it is being taught *wrongly*.
- Our view of the future should not cause fear. No part of the gospel (which literally means "good news") ever causes fear.
- Our understanding of the endtimes determines how we live our lives and whether we plan long-term, build a legacy, prepare

> our children for a lifetime of service to the Lord, and so forth. A correct view of the endtimes will set us free from fear. It will cause us to have a renewed passion for Jesus rather than an obsession with the antichrist.

Since many of you did not grow up in "pan-millennial" households, it is possible that you have been force-fed a particular point of view for many years. I would ask you to lay down what you have heard all your life and consider opening your heart to hear a fresh understanding from the Holy Spirit. In trade, I as the author promise to write simply. I will choose not to use large theological terms. I will not waste your time; I will respect your time as my reader. I can promise you that I will not try to coerce you into agreement with me, but I will share with you what the Holy Spirit has shown me, and you can *test all things and hold fast that which is good* (see 1 Thess. 5:21).

Thank you for investing your time in this book; it will be worth it.

HOW DID WE GET HERE?

When I was in my early teens, my brother worked at a Christian bookstore. He would often bring home the latest Christian movie releases, and we would enjoy getting to watch them long before others could. I remember when *Veggie Tales* first came out; what an amazing new era that brought. Finally the Battle of Jericho included slushies! This was a huge step forward from the *Superbook* and *McGee and Me* videos I grew up with, but I digress.

I remember when my brother brought home the videocassette of *The Thief in the Night.* That was a bit much for a fourteen-year-old! For many years, I had one clip from the movie stuck in my memory. In this memory clip, a big guy who looked like Santa and was wearing overalls had a giant end-times chart covered with dragons and beasts from Revelation. I recently re-watched the whole *Thief in the Night* movie series on YouTube (Santa, dragons, and all), and my memory wasn't that far off.

Although it isn't as common today, the end-times chart used to be a standard way of communicating about the end of the world. Each pastor and teacher had his or her own views mapped out on personal charts. Most famous are the antique *Clarence Larkin's Charts* (from the early 1900s).

In retrospect, I am very glad my family didn't celebrate Christmas with the Santa Claus tradition; otherwise, I would have been thinking of the big guy from the end-times movie coming down my chimney with his dragon and beast wall charts.

Years later, the Holy Spirit began to reveal the truth about the endtimes to me. Considering my weird background of a "pan-millenial" ("It will all pan out...") family and scary Christian movies, I wonder if He chuckled to Himself, knowing He really had a piece of work on His hands!

I began my study of the endtimes by studying the history of the many end-time views. To understand a belief system, it is very helpful to start by researching the history behind it. Through my study, I found that, throughout Church history, the majority of Bible teachers and theologians held to a similar view of the endtimes. Yet, in the last century, the western Church has fractured into teaching many differing views. Simply stated, from AD 30 to the 1500s, the majority of the Church had an optimistic view of the future—that the Kingdom of God was growing in the earth and would continue to do so until the final return of Christ.

The fragmentation of viewpoints began in the reformation of the 1500s. This eventually led to the modern Church believing in:

- The rapture
- A one-world "antichrist" ruler
- A seven-year global tribulation

Before the 1500s, none of these three points were understood the way that they are taught today. Through study, I came to understand that the modern understanding is based more on a tradition from the 1800s than from a historical and biblically orthodox view. As I will show, the Church fathers of the first 1500 years had a biblical understanding that is very different than the modern understanding.

So where did the two roads diverge?

The Historical Development

The Reformation of the 1500s changed a lot of things, and unwittingly it eventually affected the end-time beliefs of much of the Church. In the early 1500s, Martin Luther railed against the Roman Catholic Church, and in his passion, he called her the Whore of Babylon and the Beast. Gary DeMar gives us a big-picture view of this time period:

> The Reformers, almost without exception, believed that the papal system was the antichrist, with the individual popes reflecting the spiritual application of Paul's description of the Man of Lawlessness of 2 Thessalonians 2. The papal antichrist view was written into the confessions of that era. The Westminster Confession of Faith (1643–47) declared that "There is no other head of the Church but the Lord Jesus Christ; nor can the Pope of Rome in any sense be head thereof; but is that Antichrist, the son of perdition, that exalteth himself in the Church against Christ, and all that is called God" (25.7).[1]

To counter this, in 1585 a Jesuit priest by the name of Francisco Ribera published a 500-page work that placed Daniel 9:24–27, Matthew 24, and Revelation 4–19 in the distant future. This was the first teaching of this kind, and it is the foundation of many modern end-time views.[2] The significance of this new interpretation is that, rather than seeing these passages as fulfilled, now Ribera was saying they were still future.

Historically speaking, Ribera's new view did not gain momentum. In fact, his writing was lost until 1826, when Samuel Maitland, librarian to the Archbishop of Canterbury, rediscovered Ribera's forgotten manuscript and published it for the sake of public interest and curiosity.

When the book resurfaced, a small group of ultra-conservatives, led by John Darby, began to take Ribera's book seriously and came under the influence of this thinking. John Darby and his contemporary, Edward Irving, became extremely vocal about their new theology of the endtimes and began to attract many followers. Their most important follower was C.I. Scofield, who later published these concepts in his famed Scofield Reference Bible.

The Scofield Bible was the most popular of its time because it was one of the earliest Bibles to contain a full commentary. It quickly became a standard for seminary students of the time. This continued unchallenged until the 1948 Latter Rain movement, which disagreed with the Scofield Reference Bible's claims that the spiritual gifts had ceased. The Pentecostals pushed back against these portions of the commentary, but still swallowed Ribera's end-time teachings without realizing the error.[3]

Then in 1961, Finis Dake published the Dake's Annotated Reference

Bible, which continued to promote the same Darbyism as the Scofield Bible, and the Ryrie and MacArthur Study Bibles have continued this tradition of Darbyism.

Thus we see that when Martin Luther railed against the Roman Catholic Church, one priest reacted by writing a new doctrine. This began the belief that certain prophecies in the Bible have not yet been fulfilled!

The Timing of the New Doctrine

It is also important to consider the timing of John Darby's teaching ministry. During the 1830s, the Holy Spirit, through the Second Great Awakening, was stirring American churches to life with great fervor. At the same time, satan was hard at work releasing distortions and false teachings into the earth. From the late 1700s to the late 1800s, a multitude of major false teachings were released into the Church. For example:

- Joseph Smith founded Mormonism in 1830 (in Palmyra, New York, a suburb of Rochester, New York, where Charles Finney was having his revival meetings at the same time).
- Charles Taze Russell founded the Jehovah's Witnesses in the late 1870s.
- The Fox Sisters founded Spiritualism in 1848 (which later became the foundation of the New Age Movement).
- The first Unitarian church began in Boston in 1785.
- Mary Baker Eddy founded the cult named Christian Science in 1879 (which was a blending of Swedenborgism, Mesmerism, and Metaphysics).[4]

During this time period, John Nelson Darby also brought forth his new end-time teachings. Since C.I. Scofield published Darby's beliefs in his Bible commentary notes, Darbyism has become the mainstream end-time teaching of many modern teachers. Yet many have never even considered where these beliefs came from.

The Last One Hundred Years

After the Scofield Reference Bible was published in 1909, the earth went through a deeply traumatic season: World War I, the Great Depression, and World War II. By the time this period of thirty-one years was over, pessimistic Scofield-ism had deeply rooted itself in American thinking.

In fact, Darbyism led to apathy among the European churches when Hilter and Mussolini arose. Darbyism basically taught people to believe, "These men could be the antichrist; therefore, we should let them rise in power because this will lead to our soon rapture." For example, a booklet published in 1940 identified Mussolini as the antichrist, stating that he fulfilled forty-nine prophecies of the antichrist.[5] Gary DeMar says of this era:

> Many will recall widespread preaching during the World War II era that Mussolini or Hitler was the Antichrist. Since the slogan VV IL DUCE was widely used by Mussolini, and because the Roman numeral value of the slogan/title is 666, many were sure of positive identification.[6]

Dwight Wilson, author of *Armageddon Now!*, convincingly demonstrates that dispensational premillennialism (essentially Darbyism) advocated a "hands off" policy regarding Nazi persecution of the Jews during World War II. Since, according to dispensational views regarding Bible prophecy, "the Gentile nations are permitted to afflict Israel in chastisement for her national sins," there was little that should be done to oppose it. He continues:

> Another comment regarding the general European anti-Semitism depicted these developments as part of the on-going plan of God for the nation; they were "Foregleams of Israel's Tribulation." Premillennialists were anticipating the Great Tribulation, "the time of Jacob's trouble." Therefore, they predicted, "The next scene in Israel's history may be summed up in three words: purification through tribulation." It was clear that although this purification was part of the curse, God did not intend that Christians should

> participate in it. Clear, also, was the implication that He did intend for the Germans to participate in it (in spite of the fact that it would bring them punishment) and that any moral outcry against Germany would have been in opposition to God's will. In such a fatalistic system, to oppose Hitler was to oppose God....
>
> Pleas from Europe for assistance for Jewish refugees fell on deaf ears, and "Hands Off" meant no helping hand. So in spite of being theologically more pro-Jewish than any other Christian group, the premillenarians also were apathetic—because of a residual anti-Semitism, because persecution was prophetically expected, because it would encourage immigration to Palestine, because it seemed the beginning of the Great Tribulation, and because it was a wonderful sign of the imminent blessed hope.[7]

Then in 1948, Israel regained its independent statehood, which caused many to say Matthew 24:32–33 indicated when Israel became a state again the end was near.

> *Now learn this lesson from the fig tree: As soon as its twigs get tender and its leaves come out, you know that summer is near. Even so, when you see all these things, you know that it is near, right at the door* (Matthew 24:32–33).

In the next verse, it says, *"Truly I tell you, this generation will certainly not pass away until all these things have happened"* (Matt. 24:34). Since the Bible teaches that a generation is forty years, this led millions of Christians to believe and teach the rapture would occur in 1988. Thus, Edgar Whisenant sold 4.5 million copies of his book, *88 Reasons Why Jesus Will Return in 1988*. Whisenant was quoted as saying, "Only if the Bible is in error am I wrong; and I say that to every preacher in town," and "If there were a king in this country and I could gamble with my life, I would stake my life on Rosh Hashanah in 1988."[8]

Whisenant's predictions were taken seriously in some parts of the evangelical Christian community. As the great day approached, regular programming on the Christian Trinity Broadcast Network (TBN) was interrupted to provide special instructions on preparing for the rapture.[9] When the predicted rapture failed to occur, Whisenant followed up with later books with predictions for various dates in 1989, 1993, 1994, and 1997.

At this point, some of the modern teachers have started to redefine what *generation* means. They say that the clock started at 1948, but since a forty-year generation is wrong, they are now saying a generation is seventy or even 100 years.

In 1970, Hal Lindsey wrote *The Late Great Planet Earth*. He sold approximately 35 million copies and deeply affected a generation of pastors and leaders growing up in the Jesus People Movement of the early 1970s. The lasting fruit of this book has created a generation that believes more in Lindsey's mythology than understanding what the Bible and history actually teach. In his book, Hal Lindsey concluded that, since the United States was not mentioned in Daniel or Revelation, it would not be a major player on the world scene when the Great Tribulation happened. Based on his interpretation of various biblical texts, he also presumed that the European Economic Community (now the European Union) would become what he termed the "United States of Europe." This union would have ten members and would become, according to Lindsey, the revived Roman Empire, ruled by the antichrist, needed to fulfill Bible prophecy. At the time of this publication, the European Union has twenty-eight members.

Later, Hal Lindsey released another book titled *The 1980s: Countdown to Armageddon*, implying that the battle of Armageddon would happen soon. He even went so far as to say, "The decade of the 1980s could very well be the last decade of history as we know it,"[10] and he suggested that the United States would be destroyed by a surprise Soviet attack. Not surprisingly, because of Lindsey's adamant insistence that the 1980s would usher in the Great Tribulation, the book was quietly taken out of print in the early 1990s. Lindsey, however, would not give up. In the early 1990s, he published *Planet Earth—2000 A.D.*, which warned Christians that they should not plan to still be living on earth by the year 2000.

Throughout his several books, Lindsey assumed that the Cold War would continue until the end and, in fact, play a significant part in the unfolding of end-time events. He even named Russia as the famous Gog of Revelation 20:8. Likewise, Lindsey believed the hippie culture of the 1960s and '70s would become the dominate culture in the United States, ultimately leading to the immorality and false religion "prophesied" to arise in the endtimes by various Bible passages. Clearly, none of these prophecies have come to pass, and many have been proven wrong due to the dates ascribed to them, yet Lindsey is still lauded by many Christians as a great modern prophet.

Then in 1995, the first of the mega-bestselling book series, *Left Behind*, was released. Due to the paranoia and fear regarding Y2K, Christians were primed for rapture fever. When all was said and done, Y2K was all hype, and 60 million copies of *Left Behind* had been sold (as well as three terrible feature length films that were similar in nature and theology to the *Thief in the Night* movie series of the 1970s).

Now we are in the new millennium, and it is high time that we begin to deeply question the modern end-time views. If a teacher has been proclaiming that the end of the world is coming soon for over forty years, we should stop paying attention. If a teacher has proclaimed over forty different people to be the antichrist, we should ignore him. The fact that these teachers wear suits and are on TV doesn't make them any less wrong than the crazy guy on the street corner wearing a sandwich board sign that reads, "The end is near!" If a teacher was a paranoid alarmist regarding Y2K, we shouldn't be concerned about that teacher's other futuristic proclamations.

In summary, the teaching that Jesus' words in Matthew 24, the prophecies of Daniel, and the Book of Revelation are all referring to future events is a *new concept*, which came as a reaction to the Reformation. It has become deeply imbedded in the American evangelical community, but it does not have the support of Church history or Scripture, as we shall see.

Angry Letters

Since my first edition of *Raptureless*, I have found that there is almost nothing more contentious than writing history. History should be static truth, but since there are so many perspectives, this isn't the case. Therefore, rather than just writing the truth of history, I will intentionally quote from dispensational leaders so as to confirm that what I have written is accurate. (What I have described as Darbyism is theologically known as dispensationalism.)

Charles Ryrie, renowned dispensational theologian and author of the 1966 classic, *Dispensationalism*, writes:

> Dispensationalists recognize that as a *system* of theology it is recent in origin.[11]

He then argues that some pieces or elements that eventually were systematized into dispensationalism were present in the writing of early Church fathers. After giving a few examples, he writes:

> It is not suggested, nor should it be inferred, that these early church fathers were dispensationalists in the later sense of the word. But it is true that some of them enunciated principles that later developed into dispensationalism, and it may be rightly said that they held to primitive or early dispensational-like concepts.
>
> From this time [the 1100s] until after the Reformation [1500s], there were no substantial contributions to that which was later systematized as dispensationalism.[12]

Clearly, though Ryrie tries to connect dispensationalism to the historical teachings of the Church, that connection is very tenuous. As he admits, for over 400 years, not one of our Church fathers wrote anything that could be aligned with dispensational thought. My point is this: As a system of biblical interpretation, dispensationalism holds little weight historically.

In the words of the great commentator F.F. Farrar:

> There have been three great schools of apocalyptic interpretation: 1. The Preterists, who regard the book as having been mainly fulfilled 2. The Futurists, who refer it to events, which are still wholly future.

> 3. Those [Historicists] who see in it an outline of Christian history from the days of St. John down to the End of all things. The second of these schools—the Futurists—has always been numerically small, and at present may be said to be non-existent.[13]

Even Thomas Ice, the executive director of the Pre-Tribulation Research Center on the campus of Liberty University in Lynchburg, Virginia, recognizes Darby as the starting point and sees that people are coming full circle and moving back to an optimistic view (preterism). This he wrote clearly in several letters to the preterist author John Bray:

> Thomas Ice, in a letter to me [John Bray] dated September 20, 1989, said: "Many are moving toward a preterist interpretation of the Olivet Discourse and Revelation in our day. It is coming full cycle since the days of Darby. I have a very large collection of literature advocating that view, which was a very prominent view among both liberals and evangelicals 100-150 years ago." And then he added in a letter of November 30, 1989, "I do think that dispensationalism will continue to grow increasingly unpopular as we head into the 1990's." (These statements do not mean that Dr. Ice himself is changing from a Dispensationalist—far from it; but they simply indicate that he recognizes the reality of what is going on today among those who are studying eschatology.)[14]

From this we can see that dispensationalism has been, at best, a fad that began with Darby in the mid-1800s and is already beginning to wane. Even leaders in the movement have noticed that the momentum has shifted toward the more biblical, historical, and optimistic view. If that is not enough proof, here are some simple evidences against dispensationalism based on Jesus' mandate to judge the fruit.

Judge Fruit

Jesus told us to judge the messages of various prophets by examining the fruit of their lives and the fruit of their prophetic words (see Matt.

7:15–20). With this in mind, now that we have seen that this modern end-time teaching is a new phenomenon, we must also ask ourselves, *What fruit is coming from it?*

Twelve Fruits I Have Witnessed:

1. Love usually takes the back seat, while fear is emphasized. Sometimes the fear is covered over by a rapture escape or by divine protection from coming wrath.
2. All long-term thinking becomes limited. It becomes impossible to even prophesy beyond a few decades because of the supposed "any minute return" of Christ.
3. It creates a fear of technology because that new GPS, computer, smartphone, laptop, or whatever might be used as the "mark of the beast."
4. It harbors a fear of politics because the antichrist could be right around the corner.
5. It breeds an anti-culture view—to the point of irrelevancy. Yet, even the apostle Paul was able to quote from the popular culture of his own day (see Acts 17:28).
6. It discourages people from pushing forward in health, medicine, the environment, or technology because they reason, "Why would one work for the good of a world that is going to burn?"
7. It has created a bizarre form of Christian racism. Many have become pro-Israel to the point that no political thought is exercised. For example, if Israel were to mistreat her surrounding nations, many modern Christians would give them a free-pass because they are God's "chosen people." Christians have literally accepted a new form of pro-Israel and anti-Arab racism. Also, it breeds a suspicion toward other countries, producing anti-Russian and anti-Chinese attitudes among many Christians. This Christian racism is rooted in a wrong understanding of the endtimes.
8. Hope is narrowed down to a rapture escape.
9. This end-time view is the seedbed of many cults and militias.

10. Many have turned to extended hours of fasting and prayer, to quick evangelism, and to looking for the rapture or the "signs of the times," rather than studying and training for a lifetime of advancing the Kingdom.
11. This view doesn't take the time texts of Scripture seriously or literally (for example, Matt. 23:36; 24:34).
12. It has birthed many silly conspiracies; it fits perfectly with those who believe in the Illuminati, the New World Order, and other secret society theories.

Welton's Wager

The mathematician, physicist, and Catholic philosopher, Blaise Pascal (1623–1662), proposed a famous wager that has become known as Pascal's Wager or Pascal's Gambit. I will paraphrase: *What if you chose to believe in God and live as if He exists? If you are right, then wonderful! But if you are wrong and you find out that you simply lived a healthy moral life, but were wrong about God, what have you lost?*[15]

To counter the twelve negative fruits of dispensationalist beliefs, I would like to propose my own Welton's Wager, based on the same logic Pascal used. What if you chose to believe optimistically about the endtimes, raise godly kids, plan long-term, reject thoughts of fear, and work as a member of the Bride making herself ready (see Rev. 19:7)? Even if you are wrong and suddenly get raptured out, what have you lost? You will have been a good steward of what God put in your hands rather than sitting on your hands, burying your talents, and waiting for a rapture that may not come in your lifetime! If you spend your life in fear, trying to figure out dates and guess who the antichrist is, you will be held accountable for all that wasted living.

A final thought. Some say that having a fearful future motivates evangelism. Actually most non-Christians just think we are nuts and don't want to join us. In fact, some famous atheists (for example Christopher Hitchens) say that Jesus was a false prophet because His prophecy didn't happen in the first century (see Matt. 24:34).[16] This is based on the popular dispensational belief that the events of Matthew 24 will happen in the future. Even when some people do get saved out of fear for the future, this is not the gospel of the Kingdom; Jesus never said to preach the endtimes. Many have been brought into Christianity through fear of hell, judgment, or rapture; they then have had to spend years untangling their spiritual walk from the fear into which they were birthed.

It is time to change our thinking.

CHAPTER POINTS

- The belief in a future rapture, antichrist, and Great Tribulation are new ideas that arose from a reaction against the Reformation in the 1500s.
- John Darby reintroduced this view, and C.I Scofield popularized it in his Scofield Reference Bible in the early 1900s. Thus it became mainstream belief among evangelical and charismatic Christians.
- The appearance of many new cults in that same era and the worldwide negative impact of World War I, The Great Depression, and World War II firmly rooted a negative view of the end in much of the Christian community.
- End-time predictors such as Hal Lindsey and Edgar Whisenant sold millions of copies of predictive books that have been proven to be false prophecy, yet their teachings are still heeded by many Christians.
- This new end-time view consistently bears bad fruit in its adherents.
- It would be wiser to live with a long-term, optimistic view (and end up being wrong and suddenly raptured out) than to live with a rapture-focused, short-term view (and end up being wrong and ultimately held accountable for not working to advance the Kingdom in your lifetime).

DISCUSSION QUESTIONS

1. Give each person a few minutes to summarize their end-time theology as they understand it from growing up.

2. How much influence would you say Darby has had in your thinking?

3. What fruit have you witnessed from your end-time upbringing?

4. Are you willing to consider other views about the endtimes?

5. What would it cost you personally to take up the "Welton Wager"?

THE RAPTURE

I used to be a counselor at an all-male Christian summer camp. The greatest prank of all time was the year when we raptured everyone! Well, not really, but that was the goal. As staffers, we had schemed and plotted that if the Camp Director ever left the campground long enough, the counselors would take the campers into the woods and stage an elaborate rapture prank.

When the Director returned to the camp, he would see random clothes littered about the soccer field, swimming trunks floating by themselves in the pool, a random camper sitting in the grass crying about how all his bunkmates had disappeared in the rapture, and so forth. Although this would have been epic, we never managed to pull it off during the six summers I was on staff. Every summer the idea would resurface, but it never came to fruition.

It was about this same time that I began studying the history of the modern view of the endtimes. As I did, I learned that the whole concept of the rapture, as it is commonly taught, cannot be found in Church history before the 1800s and that it comes from a few deeply misunderstood Scriptures.

The Rapture

As I discussed in the previous chapter, John Darby and C.I. Scofield spread their teachings through the Scofield Reference Bible. One of the main teachings was that of the rapture.

The concept of the rapture is that on any day in the future, Jesus will secretly snatch away His followers to Heaven. This will be followed by the antichrist rising and seizing rule of the entire planet. He will rule from a revived Roman Empire and sit on a throne inside a rebuilt Temple in Jerusalem (some hold the view that the rapture will happen halfway through the antichrist's seven-year rule). Then God will pour out His wrath upon the wicked in the earth, finally culminating in what will be called the Battle of Armageddon. This is a general summary of what Darby taught. Essentially, none of these teachings were widely taught before the 1830s.

Rather than belabor my point about the short history of these teachings, in this chapter, I shall examine what the Bible says about the rapture. Four main passages are used to teach the rapture concept. I will examine them one at a time.

Passage #1: 1 Thessalonians 4:13-18

> *Brothers and sisters, we do not want you to be uninformed about those who sleep in death, so that you do not grieve like the rest of mankind, who have no hope. For we believe that Jesus died and rose again, and so we believe that God will bring with Jesus those who have fallen asleep in him. According to the Lord's word, we tell you that we who are still alive, who are left until the coming of the Lord, will certainly not precede those who have fallen asleep. For the Lord himself will come down from heaven, with a loud command, with the voice of the archangel and with the trumpet call of God, and the dead in Christ will rise first. After that, we who are still alive and are left will be caught up together with them in the clouds to meet the Lord in the air. And so we will be with the Lord forever. Therefore encourage one another with these words* (1 Thessalonians 4:13-18 NIV).

The Thessalonian church was a church surviving under tremendous persecution. We see this in Paul's encouragement to them: *"Therefore, among God's churches we boast about your perseverance and faith in all the persecutions and trials you are enduring"* (2 Thess. 1:4). Because of this persecution, many of their members had been put to death. This is the context in which Paul wrote the above passage. Paul did not hint in any way that a coming Great Tribulation, under the one-world ruler called the antichrist, must be avoided and that God would rapture Christians two thousand years after he wrote this letter. In fact, he made it clear that he was writing words of clarification and comfort, for his first-century readers, regarding what would happen to those who had died. This is the context of verse 13: *"But I do not want you to be ignorant, brethren, concerning those who have fallen asleep, lest you sorrow as others who have no hope."*

In the next verses, we see that those who have died will be resurrected as Jesus was resurrected:

> *For we believe that Jesus died and rose again, and so we believe that God will bring with Jesus those who have fallen asleep in him. According to the Lord's word, we tell you that we who are still alive, who are left until the coming of the Lord, will certainly not precede those who have fallen asleep* (1 Thessalonians 4:14-15 NIV).

Paul continued to encourage his listeners not to despair about those who had died, saying that they would actually be resurrected and transformed even before the living are! *"For the Lord Himself will descend from heaven with a shout, with the voice of an archangel, and with the trumpet of God. And the dead in Christ will rise[1] first"* (1 Thess. 4:16 NKJV).

Prior to the invention of the rapture doctrine in the 1830s, all published commentators interpreted First Thessalonians 4:13–18 as referring to the resurrection. For example, Matthew Henry's commentary on this passage, written in 1721, says:

> They shall be raised up from the dead, and awakened out of their sleep, for God will bring them with him, v 14. They then are with God, and are better where they are than when they were here; and when God comes he will bring them with him. The doctrine of the resurrection and the second coming of Christ is a great antidote against the fear of death and inordinate sorrow for the death of our Christian friends...[2]

Matthew Henry, along with nearly all other commentators prior to John Darby, saw the obvious intention of this passage as referring to the resurrection of the dead at the final coming of Christ, not to a secret rapture seven years prior to the resurrection.

This is the same resurrection that Paul spoke of in First Corinthians 15:51–54:

> *Listen, I tell you a mystery: We will not all sleep, but we will all be changed—in a flash, in the twinkling of an eye, at the last trumpet. For the trumpet will sound, the dead will be raised imperishable, and we will be changed. For the perishable must clothe itself with the imperishable, and the mortal with immortality. When the perishable has been clothed with the imperishable, and the mortal with immortality, then the saying that is written will come true: "Death has been swallowed up in victory."*

First Thessalonians 4:17–18 are the most quoted two verses when speaking of the rapture concept:

> *Then we who are alive, who are left, will be caught up together with them in the clouds to meet the Lord in the air, and so we will always be with the Lord. Therefore encourage one another with these words* (NIV).

Yet, the context in this passage did not change. Paul was still comforting a first-century church under persecution. He was still instructing them regarding their dead friends and relatives; he had not begun to explain a secret rapture two thousand years in the future. It is clear Paul was talking about the final resurrection and how we will all be caught up together with the Lord, after which the books will be opened for the final judgment.

The famous commentator Adam Clarke gives a clear summary to this passage to the Thessalonians:

> The Lord himself—That is: Jesus Christ shall descend from heaven; shall descend in like manner as he was seen by his disciples to ascend, i.e., in his human form, but now infinitely more glorious; for thousands of thousands shall minister unto him, and ten thousand times ten thousand shall stand before him; for the Son of man shall come on the throne of his glory: but who may abide the day of his coming, or stand when he appeareth?

With a shout—Or order, εν κελευσματι· and probably in these words: Arise, ye dead, and come to judgment; which order shall be repeated by the archangel, who shall accompany it with the sound of the trump of God, whose great and terrible blasts, like those on mount Sinai, sounding louder and louder, shall shake both the heavens and the earth!

Observe the order of this terribly glorious day:

1. Jesus, in all the dignity and splendor of his eternal majesty, shall descend from heaven to the mid region, what the apostle calls the air, somewhere within the earth's atmosphere.

2. Then the *κελευσμα,* shout or order, shall be given for the dead to arise.

3. Next the archangel, as the herald of Christ, shall repeat the order, Arise, ye dead, and come to judgment!

4. When all the dead in Christ are raised, then the trumpet shall sound, as the signal for them all to flock together to the throne of Christ. It was by the sound of the trumpet that the solemn assemblies, under the law, were convoked; and to such convocations there appears to be here an allusion.

5. When the dead in Christ are raised, their vile bodies being made like unto his glorious body, then,

6. Those who are alive shall be changed, and made immortal.

7. These shall be caught up together with them to meet the Lord in the air.

8. We may suppose that the judgment will now be set, and the books opened, and the dead judged out of the things written in those books.

9. The eternal states of quick and dead being thus determined, then all who shall be found to have made a covenant with him by sacrifice, and to have washed their robes, and made them white in the blood of the Lamb, shall be taken to his eternal glory, and be for ever with the Lord. What an inexpressibly terrific glory will then be exhibited! I forbear to call in here the descriptions, which men of a poetic turn have made of this terrible scene, because I cannot trust to their correctness; and it is a subject which we should speak of and contemplate as nearly as possible in the words of Scripture.[3]

From this examination, we can clearly see that there is no secret pre-tribulation rapture in First Thessalonians 4, but there is a clear presentation of the resurrection of the dead before the final judgment.

Passage #2: Matthew 24:40-41

Then two men will be in the field: one will be taken and the other left. Two women will be grinding at the mill: one will be taken and the other left (Matthew 24:40-41 NKJV).

This passage refers to the random killings perpetrated by the Romans at their siege of Jerusalem in AD 70. In fact, the entirety of Matthew 24 is about the destruction of Jerusalem in AD 70. First Jesus declared the destruction of the Temple (see Matt. 24:2–3). Then Jesus told them in AD 30 that within a generation (forty years) the destruction would come (see Matt. 24:34). I will address Matthew 24 further in a different chapter, but suffice it to say this passage does not imply a secret rapture. Jesus was prophesying the way in which the Roman soldiers would arbitrarily kill the Jews.

Passage #3: Revelation 4:1

After these things I looked, and behold, a door standing open in heaven. And the first voice which I heard was like a trumpet speaking with me, saying,

> *"Come up here, and I will show you things which must take place after this"* (Revelation 4:1 NKJV).

This verse *is not* a metaphor; it is a record. John *was not* telling his readers that they would be sucked up before the throne but that he was! John was not speaking of the rapture. Many have said that John was speaking of the rapture because the Church is not mentioned anymore in Revelation 4–19.

Gary DeMar does a great job dissecting this worn out argument that the Church must be raptured in Revelation 4:1 because the word *church* doesn't reappear in chapters 4–19 of Revelation. He starts by pointing out that the saints are referred to over eleven times in Revelation 4–19 (see Rev. 5:8; 8:3–4; 11:18; 13:7,10; 14:12; 16:6; 17:6; 18:24; 19:8), and then he demolishes this interpretation by applying it to the rest of the New Testament:

> Let's continue by applying [Hal] Lindsey's hermeneutical logic to other passages. The words church and churches appear just once in the Book of Hebrews (12:23) and twice in 2 Corinthians (1:1 and 2:14). The church is not mentioned as such in Mark, Luke, John, 2 Timothy, Titus, 1 Peter, 2 Peter, 1 John, 2 John, or Jude, and not until chapter 16 of Romans. Unless we are prepared to relegate large chunks of the NT to a limbo of irrelevance to the Church, we cannot make the mention or omission of the term 'church' a criterion for determining the application of a passage to saints of the present age.[4]

Similarly, even John Walvoord, an avid teacher of the secret pre-tribulation rapture of the Church, writes of Revelation 4:1:

> It is clear from the text that this is not an explicit reference to the Rapture of the church, as John was not actually translated [raptured]; in fact he was still in his natural body on the island of Patmos. He was translated into scenes of heaven only temporarily. Though there is no authority for connecting the Rapture with this expression, there does seem to be a typical representation of the order of events,

namely, the church age first, then the Rapture, then the church in heaven.[5]

Passage #4: Revelation 12:5

She bore a male Child who was to rule all nations with a rod of iron. And her Child was caught up to God and His throne (Revelation 12:5 NKJV).

The context of this reference is the ascension of Christ, not the rapture of the Church. The word *Child* is capitalized because it refers to Christ. Also, He is the one who rules all nations with a rod of iron (see Ps. 110). He is the one who ascended to God and sits on His throne in Heaven. This is not a reference to a secret rapture of the Church.

Additional Thoughts

Since we have addressed all the passages used to teach the rapture concept, I would like to approach this topic briefly from another angle. First Thessalonians 4:17 says we will meet the Lord in the air. That statement begs the question, *Where is the air?* According to the Greek root word translated as "air," this is a reference to the air that surrounds us on the earth. Many have taken this to mean that we will meet the Lord in the sky, but actually, there is less and less air the higher one goes. It makes more sense that we would meet Him here, in the atmosphere.

The Thessalonian passage also says that we will *meet* the Lord (see 1 Thess. 4:17), the Greek word translated as "meet" is used several times in the New Testament. It always has the meaning of *welcoming* someone, especially like welcoming a king or dignitary. We are going to be welcoming King Jesus to earth when He returns.

This passage also speaks of being *caught up* (see 1 Thess. 4:17). The Scripture teaches that Jesus has been resurrected and given His glorious body. I suggest that this means that if I am "caught up," it would be similar to what would happen if Jesus and I were in a footrace, He had run twenty miles, and I had only run two miles. If Jesus were to stop and wait for me, once I had run an additional eighteen miles, I would be "caught up."

Like the apostle John said, *"...We know that when Christ appears, we shall be like him"* (1 John 3:2). We have not been resurrected and given our glorious bodies yet; presently, there is a great disparity between Jesus and us. We must get "caught up!" Christ will be equally yoked to His Bride, the Church (see 2 Cor. 6:14–16). When He appears, we will instantly be caught up to His likeness in the twinkling of an eye (see 1 Cor. 15:52). Tying this all together, we see that *when Jesus returns to earth, we shall meet* (welcome) *Him in the air* (atmosphere) *and be caught up* (in His likeness) *together.* It's important to note here that I technically believe in the rapture of the Church, in that there will be a day in the future when we are all changed in the twinkling of an eye. This will be when we receive our glorious bodies. However, I do not believe in the rapture as it is commonly taught.

Lastly, it is important to note that the very leaders who teach the secret rapture doctrine have admitted that they have no scriptural foundation for their doctrine. For example:

> One objection to the pre-Tribulation Rapture is that no one passage of Scripture teaches the two aspects of His Second Coming separated by the Tribulation. This is true. But then, no one passage teaches a post-trib or mid-trib Rapture, either. —Timothy LaHaye[6]

> It is scarcely to be found in a single book or sermon through the period of 1600 years! If any doubt this statement, let them search... the remarks of the so-called Fathers, both pre and post Nicene, the theological treaties of the scholastic divines, Roman Catholic writers of all shades of thought, the literature of the Reformation, the sermons and expositions of the Puritans, and the general theological works of the day. He will find the "mystery" conspicuous by its absence. —Henry Ironside[7]

Until Darbyism in the 1830s, the modern concept of the rapture was not taught, believed in, or even conceived of. Even after its advent, the rapture teaching didn't gain major traction until the Scofield Bible came out in 1909. It then became deeply ingrained in western thinking simply because it would be much nicer to be raptured than to live through another World War I, Great Depression, and World War II. The rapture fever spread, not because it is biblical, but because it was enticing to those who desired an escape from the trauma of the early 1900s.

It is time to re-think and re-examine some of these long-held beliefs. Considering that even the leaders of the pre-tribulation rapture movement have admitted that they have no scriptural foundation for their doctrine, it is time to move on. It is time to recognize the testimony of Scripture and Church history. I agree with the first 1,800 years of Christian history that there is no secret rapture but that Paul was writing about the final return of Jesus, the resurrection, and judgment day.

CHAPTER POINTS

- The rapture doctrine is a new teaching that was popularized in the early 1900s.
- First Thessalonians 4:13–18 was written to a church in persecution, comforting them regarding what had happened to their martyred friends after death and telling them of the future resurrection of the dead at the final coming of Christ.
- Matthew 24:40–41 speaks of the random killings that happened at the hands of the Roman soldiers during their attack on Jerusalem leading up to its destruction in AD 70.
- Revelation 4:1 is a record of John's actual experience, not a prophecy of coming events.
- Revelation 12:5 speaks of the ascension of Christ, not a rapture of the Church.
- The meaning of the original language in First Thessalonians 4:17 clearly shows that *when Jesus returns to earth, we shall meet* (welcome) *Him in the air* (atmosphere) *and be caught up* (in His likeness) *together.*

DISCUSSION QUESTIONS

1. How do you imagine the rapture?

2. Do you have any personal or funny tales about the rapture?

3. Could First Thessalonians 4 actually be speaking about the resurrection on the final day? Why or why not?

4. How did you feel when you first read the quote from Timothy LaHaye regarding the lack of biblical evidence for a secret rapture?

THE GREAT TRIBULATION

Over the last few years of traveling and teaching in many churches, I have heard some amazing stories. I remember one lady telling me that she was not able to shower without wearing a towel because she didn't want to be raptured while naked. Another told me that she wouldn't travel on airplanes for missions and such because, if the antichrist suddenly arose, she might not be able to get back home to her husband.

Then there's my friend who told me she had nightmares for years about the scene in *Thief in the Night* when the red balloon floats into the sky while people below are being beheaded by guillotines. Perhaps you have heard similar stories or experienced fears like these yourself. Clearly, the idea of a future seven-year, hell-on-earth type of Great Tribulation has created terror in the imaginations of Christians for the last two centuries.

The main passage that is used to paint this picture comes from the prophecy of Jesus in Matthew 24. Most scholars agree that the Book of Revelation is a parallel to the words of Jesus in Matthew 24, but because I am writing a simple introduction and because of lack of space, I will not be addressing Revelation in this book. (My forthcoming book will be a follow-up entitled, *Revelation Simplified*.) Matthew 24 is the passage that predicts earthquakes, famines, plagues, false teachers, and Jesus' coming on the clouds.

However, as I studied Matthew 24, I discovered that, throughout Church history, most Christians believed the whole chapter of Matthew 24 occurred at the destruction of Jerusalem in AD 70. In fact, many of the well-known Church leaders have taught this. Here are quotations from a few:

> All this occurred in this manner in the second year of the reign of Vespasian [A.D. 70], according to the predictions of our Lord and Saviour Jesus Christ. —Eusebius[1]

> Thousands and thousands of men of every age who together with women and children perished by the sword, by starvation, and by countless other forms of death...all this anyone who wishes can gather in precise detail from the pages of Josephus's history. I must draw particular attention to his statement that the people who flocked together from all Judaea at the time of the Passover Feast and—to use his own words—were shut up in Jerusalem as if in a prison, totaled nearly three million. —Eusebius[2]

> This was most punctually fulfilled: for after the temple was burned, Titus the Roman general, ordered the very foundations of it to be dug up; after which the ground on which it stood was ploughed by Turnus Rufus...this generation of men living shall not pass till all these things be done—The expression implies that a great part of that generation would be passed away, but not the whole. Just so it was; for the city and temple were destroyed thirty-nine or forty years after. —John Wesley[3]

> You will preach everywhere....Then he added, "This gospel of the kingdom will be preached throughout the whole world, as a testimony to all nations; and the end will come." The sign of this final end time will be the downfall of Jerusalem. —John Chrysostom[4]

> There was a sufficient interval for the full proclamation of the gospel by the apostles and evangelists of the early Christian Church, and for the gathering of those who recognized the crucified Christ as the true Messiah. Then came the awful end which the Saviour foresaw and foretold, and the prospect of which wrung from His lips and

heart the sorrowful lament that followed his prophecy of the doom awaiting his guilty capital.

The destruction of Jerusalem was more terrible than anything that the world has ever witnessed, either before or since. Even Titus seemed to see in his cruel work the hand of an avenging God. Truly, the blood of the martyrs slain in Jerusalem was amply avenged when the whole city became a veritable Aceldama, or field of blood. —Charles Spurgeon[5]

Hence it appears plain enough that the foregoing verses [Matt. 24:1-34] are not to be understood of the last judgment, but, as we said, of the destruction of Jerusalem. There were some among the disciples (particularly John), who lived to see these things come to pass. —John Lightfoot[6]

And *Verily I say unto you;* and urge you to observe it, as absolutely necessary in order to understand what I have been saying, *That this generation of men now living shall not pass away until all these things be fulfilled*, for what I have foretold concerning the destruction of the Jewish state is so near at hand, that some of you shall live to see it accomplished with a dreadful exactness. —Phillip Doddridge[7]

It is to me a wonder how any man can refer part of the foregoing discourse [Matt. 24] to the destruction of Jerusalem, and part to the end of the world, or any other distant event, when it is said so positively here in the conclusion, *All these things shall be fulfilled in this generation.* —Thomas Newton[8]

This chapter contains a prediction of the utter destruction of the city and temple of Jerusalem, and the subversion of the whole political constitution of the Jews; and is one of the most valuable portions of the new covenant Scriptures, with respect to the *evidence* which it furnishes of the *truth* of Christianity. Every thing which our Lord foretold should come on the temple, city, and people of the Jews,

has been fulfilled in the most correct and astonishing manner....
—Adam Clarke[9]

Christ informs them, that before a single generation shall have been completed, they will learn by experience the truth of what he has said. For within fifty years the city was destroyed and the temple was razed, the whole country was reduced to a hideous desert.
—John Calvin[10]

If Jesus and the early church used the relevant language in the same way as their contemporaries, it is highly unlikely that they would have been referring to the actual end of the world, and highly likely that they would have been referring to events within space-time history which they interpreted as the coming of the kingdom.
—N.T. Wright[11]

In this discourse [Matthew 24] Jesus predicts the destruction of the temple, the destruction of Jerusalem, and the dispersion of the Jews, all of which took place in A.D. 70. The uncanny accuracy of these predictions is embarrassing to higher critics.... —R.C. Sproul[12]

The Fulfillment of Matthew 24

As an author, this is my fourth book. In all of my writing, I have never written anything like what I have in this chapter. I feel the need to literally warn you.

In this chapter, I will share with you the historical account of the fulfillment of Matthew 24 in the AD 70 destruction of Jerusalem. George Peter Holford wrote a small booklet in 1805 about the AD 70 destruction. It is incredibly graphic and heart-wrenching, but it is accurate to what actually took place. The first time I read Holford's work, I publically had tears streaming down my face as I flew on an airplane.

While many fictional authors speculate at what the Great Tribulation is going to be like in the future, the truth is that the events of the AD 70 destruction of Jerusalem fulfilled the prophecy of the Great Tribulation and *fortunately* shall never be repeated. There is *no* future Great Tribulation. Yes, there will continue to be trials, tribulations, and persecutions, but the Great Tribulation or "the Time of Jacob's Trouble," as prophesied by Jesus, has already happened just as He said it would and within the generation timeframe that He declared (see Matt. 24:34).

Before you read this chapter, please stop reading and pray. Ask the Holy Spirit if you are ready to read the contents of this chapter. I also recommend not reading this chapter before you go to bed at night. If you are *not* ready to read to this chapter, please skip to the next chapter and know that the great church leaders, such as Charles Spurgeon, John Calvin, John Wesley, John Chrysostom, and Eusebius taught that there is no further, future Great Tribulation. This is the necessary presupposition for reading the remainder of the book.

The Context

In Matthew 23, Jesus unleashed the harshest of His recorded sayings. He declared a whole chapter's worth of woes upon the religious leaders and denounced them publically. He ended by saying,

> ***And so upon you*** *will come all the righteous blood that has been shed on earth, from the blood of righteous Abel to the blood of Zechariah son of Berekiah, whom you murdered between the temple and the altar.* ***Truly I tell you, all this will come on this generation****. Jerusalem, Jerusalem, you who kill the prophets and stone those sent to you, how often I have longed to gather your children together, as a hen gathers her chicks under her wings, and you were not willing. Look, your house is left to you desolate* (Matthew 23:35–38).

This was clearly stunning to Jesus' disciples, who followed Him away from the Temple to ask Him follow-up questions.

> *Jesus left the temple and was walking away when his disciples came up to him to call his attention to its buildings. "Do you see all these things?" he asked. "Truly I tell you, not one stone here will be left on another; every one will be thrown down."*

> *As Jesus was sitting on the Mount of Olives, the disciples came to him privately. "Tell us," they said, "when will this happen, and what will be the sign of your coming and of the end of the age?"* (Matthew 24:1–3)

Jesus declared that the Temple and its buildings would be destroyed, and the disciples, no doubt enthralled, asked Him to tell them *"when will this happen?"* Jesus replied with eight signs of the coming destruction:

1. False messiahs and false prophets (see Matt. 14:4– 5,11,23–26)
2. Wars and rumors of wars, nation rising against nation (see Matt. 24:6–7)
3. Famines (see Matt. 24:7)
4. Earthquakes (see Matt. 24:7)
5. Persecution of believers (see Matt. 24:9)
6. Falling away from the faith (see Matt. 24:10)
7. Love growing cold (see Matt. 24:12)
8. Gospel preached in the whole world (see Matt. 24:14)

We will examine each of these signs in depth in this chapter. In order to do that, I will share with you George Peter Holford's booklet, *The Destruction of Jerusalem*. His work is drawn mostly from the earlier works of Josephus. I will supplement Holford's writing with my own notes, set apart as: [Author's notes:]

Last chance to skip this chapter….

The Destruction of Jerusalem by George Peter Holford[13]

Such were the questions of the disciples, in answer to which our Lord gave them a particular account of the several important events that would precede, as well as of the prognostics that would announce the approaching desolations, including suitable directions for their conduct under the various trials to which they were to be exposed. He commences with a caution: "Take heed that no man deceive you; for many shall come in my name, saying, I am Christ, and shall deceive many" (Matt. 24:4–5).

The necessity for this friendly warning soon appeared. Within one year after our Lord's ascension, Dositheus the Samaritan arose, who had the boldness to assert that he was the Messiah of whom Moses prophesied, while his disciple Simon Magus deluded multitudes into a belief that he, himself, was the *"great power of God."*

About three years afterward, another Samaritan impostor appeared and declared that he would show the people the sacred utensils, said to have been deposited by Moses, in Mount Gerizim. Induced by an idea that the Messiah, their great deliverer, had now come, an armed multitude assembled under him, but Pilate speedily defeated them and slew their chief.

While Cuspius Fadus was procurator in Judea, another deceiver arose, whose name was Theudas. This man actually succeeded so far as to persuade a very great multitude to take their belongings and follow him to Jordan, assuring them that the river would divide at his command. Fadus, however, pursued them with a troop of horses and slay many of them, including the impostor himself, whose head was cut off and carried to Jerusalem.

Under the government of Felix, deceivers rose up daily in Judea and persuaded the people to follow them into the wilderness, assuring them that they should there behold conspicuous signs and wonders performed by the Almighty. Of these, Felix, from time to time, apprehended many and put them to death. About this period (AD 55), Felix the celebrated Egyptian impostor arose, who collected thirty thousand followers and persuaded them to accompany him to the Mount of Olives, telling them that from thence they should see the walls of Jerusalem fall down at his command—as a prelude to the capture of the Roman garrison and to their obtaining the sovereignty of the city. The Roman governor, however, apprehending this to be the beginning of revolt, immediately attacked them, slew four hundred of them, and dispersed the rest, but the Egyptian escaped.

In the time of Porcius Festus (AD 60), another distinguished impostor seduced the people by promising them deliverance from the Roman yoke if they would follow him into the wilderness. But Festus sent out an armed force, which speedily destroyed both the deceiver and his followers. In short, impostors to a divine commission continually and fatally deceived the people, at once both justifying the caution and fulfilling the prediction of our Lord.

If it be objected that none of these impostors, except Dositheus, assumed the name of Messiah, we reply, that the groveling expectations of the Jews was directed to a Messiah who should merely deliver them from the Roman yoke and *"restore the kingdom to Jerusalem,"* and such were the pretensions of these deceivers. This expectation, indeed, is the only true solution of these strange and reputed insurrections, which will naturally remind the reader of the following prophetic expressions of our Lord:

> *"I am come in my Father's name, and you receive me not; if another shall come in his own name, him you will receive." "If they shall say unto you, 'Behold he is in the desert!' go not forth. They will show (or pretend to show) great signs and wonders."* [See Matthew 24:23–26.]

Wars and Rumors of Wars

Our Savior thus proceeded:

> *And ye shall hear of wars, and rumors of wars; see that ye be not troubled: for all these things must come to pass, but the end is not yet, for nation shall rise up against nation and kingdom against kingdom, and great earthquakes shall be in divers places, and famines, and pestilences: all these are the beginnings of sorrows* (Matthew 24:6-8; Luke 21:11).

"Wars and rumors of wars." These commotions, like distant thunder, that forebodes the approaching storm, *"At first heard solemn o'er the verge of heaven,"* were so frequent from the death of our Lord until the destruction of Jerusalem that whole interval might, with propriety, be appealed to in illustration of this prophecy. One hundred and fifty of the copious pages of Josephus, which contain the history of this period, are everywhere stained with blood. To particularize a few instances: About three years after the death of Christ, a war broke out between Herod and Aretas, king of Arabia Petraea, in which the army of the former was cut off. This was *"kingdom rising against kingdom."*

Wars are usually preceded by rumors. It may, therefore, appear absurd to attempt a distinct elucidation of this part of the prophecy; nevertheless, it ought not to be omitted that, about that time, the emperor Caligula, having ordered his statue to be placed in the Temple of Jerusalem, and the Jews having persisted to refuse him, the whole nation was so much alarmed by the mere apprehension of war that they neglected even to till their lands! The storm, however, blew over.

About this period, a great number of Jews, on account of a pestilence that raged at Babylon, removed from that city to Seleucia, where the Greeks and Syrians rose against them and destroyed of this devoted people more than five myriads! "The extent of this slaughter," says Josephus, "had no parallel in any former period of their history." Again, about five years after this dreadful massacre, there happened a severe contest between the Jews at Perea and the Philadelphians, regarding the limits of a city called Mia, and many of the Jews were slain. This was *"nation rising up against nation."*

Four years afterward, under Cumanus, a Roman soldier offered an indignity to the Jews within the precincts of the Temple. This they violently resented, but upon the approach of the Romans in great force, their terror was so excessive and their flight so disorderly that not less than ten thousand Jews were trodden to death in the streets. This, again, was *"nation rising up against nation."* Four years more had not elapsed before the Jews made war against the Samaritans and ravaged their country. The people of Samaria had murdered a Galilean, who was going up to Jerusalem to keep the Passover, and the Jews thus revenged it.

At Caesarea, the Jews had a sharp contention with the Syrians for the government of the city, and an appeal was made to who decreed it to the Syrians. This event laid the foundation of a most cruel and sanguinary contest between the two nations. The Jews, mortified by disappointment and inflamed by jealousy, rose against the Syrians, who successfully repelled them. In the city of Caesarea alone, upwards of twenty thousand Jews were slain. The flame, however, was not now quenched; it spread its destructive rage wherever the Jews and Syrians dwelt together in the same place: throughout every city, town, and village, mutual animosity and slaughter prevailed. At Damascus, Tyre, Ascalon, Gadara, and Scythopolis, the carnage was dreadful. At the first of these cities, ten thousand Jews were slain in one hour, and at Scythopolis, thirteen thousand treacherously in one night.

At Alexandria, the Jews, aggrieved by the oppressions of the Romans, rose against them. But the Romans, gaining the ascendancy, slew of that nation fifty thousand persons, sparing neither infants nor the aged. And after this, at the siege of Jopata, not less than forty thousand Jews perished.

While these destructive contests prevailed in the East, the western parts of the Roman Empire were rent by the fierce contentious of Galba, Otho, and Vertellis. Of which three emperors, it is remarkable that they all, together with Nero, their immediate predecessor, died a violent death within the short space of eighteen months. Finally, the whole nation of the Jews took up arms against the Romans, King Agrippa, etc. and provoked that dreadful war which, in a few years, deluged Judea in blood and laid its capital in ruins.

If it be here objected that, because wars are events of frequent occurrence, it would be improper to refer to supernatural foresight in a successful prediction respecting them, I would here reply that much of this objection will be removed by considering the incompetency of even statesmen themselves in foretelling the condition, only for a few years, of the very nation whose affairs they administer. It is a well-known fact that the present minister of Great Britain, [at the time of authorship, 1805, the Prime Minister was William Pitt] on the very eve of the late long and destructive war with the French Republic, held out to this country a picture of fifteen successive years of peace. Indeed, the points on which peace and war often depend baffle all calculations from present aspects, and a rumor of war that is so loud and so alarming as even to suspend the operations of farming may terminate, as we have just seen, into nothing but rumor.

Further, let it be considered that the wars to which this part of our Lord's prophecy referred were to be of two kinds and that the events corresponded accordingly. They occurred within the period to which he had assigned them, and they fell with the most destructive severity on the Jews, to whom the prophecy at large chiefly related. Further, the person who predicted them was not a statesman, but a carpenter's son! On this subject, more in another place.

Author's note: Jesus declared *"wars and rumors of wars"* during the *Pax Romana,* the "Roman Peace," which was the only time in history when war had essentially ceased because the empire had conquered all of its enemies. At any other time in history, wars would have been a poor "sign of the times" because wars are always happening.

Earthquakes

"And great earthquakes shall be in divers places." Of these significant emblems of political commotion, there occurred several within the scene of this prophecy, and as our Savior predicted, they happened in divers places. In the reign of Claudius, there was one at Rome and another at Apamea in Syria, where many of the Jews resided. The earthquake at the latter place was so destructive that the emperor, in order to relieve the distresses of the inhabitants, remitted its tribute for five years. Both these earthquakes are recorded by Tacitus. There was one also, during the same reign, in Crete. This is mentioned by Philostratus in his *Life of Apollonius*, who also says that there were others "at Smyrna, Miletus, Chios, and Samos; in all which places Jews had settled."

In the reign of Nero, there was an earthquake at Laodicea. Tacitus records this also. It is likewise mentioned by Eusebius and Orosius, who add that Hieropolis and Colose, as well as Laodicea, were overthrown by earthquakes. There was also one in Campania during this reign (of this both Tacitus and Seneca speak) and another at Rome in the reign of Galba, recorded by Suetonius. To all those may be added the earthquakes that happened on the dreadful night when the Idumeans were excluded from Jerusalem, a short time before the siege commenced. Josephus says, "A heavy storm burst on them during the night; violent winds arose, accompanied with the most excessive rains, with constant lightnings, most tremendous thunderings, and with dreadful roarings of earthquakes. It seemed as if the system of the world had been confounded for the destruction of mankind; and one might well conjecture that these were signs of no common events!"

Author's note: There are many records regarding this time period having an incredible amount of earthquakes in the localized region.

Theologian and author, J. Marcellus Kirk wrote:

> And as to earthquakes, many are mentioned by writers during a period just previous to 70 AD. There were earthquakes in Crete, Smyrna, Miletus, Chios, Samos, Laodicea, Hierapolis, Colosse, Campina, Rome, and Judea. It is interesting to note that the city of Pompeii was much damaged by an earthquake occurring on February 5, 63AD.[14]

Another Bible scholar, Henry Alford, wrote about the earthquakes of this period:

The principle earthquakes occurring between this prophecy and the destruction of Jerusalem [in 70AD] were, (1) a great earthquake in Crete, A.D. 46 or 47; (2) one at Rome on the day when Nero assumed manly toga, A.D. 51; (3) one at Apamea in Phrygia, mentioned by Tacitus, A.D. 53; (4) one at Laodicea in Phrygia, A.D. 60; (5) one in Capania.[15]

Commentator Edward Hayes Plumptre wrote:

Perhaps no period in the world's history has ever been so marked by these convulsions as that which intervenes between the Crucifixion and the destruction of Jerusalem.[16]

The famed philosopher Seneca also wrote of this phenomenon:

> How often have cities in Asia, how often in Achaia, been laid low by a single shock of earthquake! How many towns in Syria, how many in Macedonia, have been swallowed up! How often has this kind of devastation laid Cyprus in ruins! How often has Paphos collapsed! Not infrequently are tidings brought to us of utter destruction of entire cities.[17]

Many earthquakes are mentioned in the New Testament, including at Jesus death (see Matt. 27:51–52) and again at His resurrection (see Matt. 28:2). Earthquakes also happened when the building was shaken in Acts 4:31 and when Paul and Silas were freed from prison in Philippi (see Acts 16:26).

Famines

Our Lord predicted *"famines"* also. Of these, the principal one was that which Agabus foretold would happen in the days of Claudius, as related in the Acts of the Apostles. It begun in the fourth year of his reign and was of long continuance. It extended through Greece and even into Italy, but was felt most severely in Judea and especially at Jerusalem, where many perished for want of bread. This famine is recorded by Josephus also, who relates that "an assaron of corn was sold for five drachmae" [about a week's wages]. It is likewise noticed by Eusebius and Orosius. To alleviate this terrible calamity, Helena, queen of Adiabena, who was at that time in Jerusalem, ordered large supplies of grain to be sent from Alexandria, and Izates, her son, consigned vast sums to the governors of Jerusalem to be applied to the relief of the more indigent sufferers. The Gentile Christian converts residing in foreign countries also sent, at the instance of Saint Paul, liberal contributions to relieve the distresses of their Jewish brethren (see 1 Cor. 16:3).

Dion Cassius relates that there was likewise a famine in the first year of Claudius that prevailed at Rome and in other parts of Italy. And in the eleventh year of the same emperor, there was another famine mentioned by Eusebius. To these may be added the famines that afflicted the inhabitants of several of the cities of Galilee and Judea, which were besieged and taken previous to the destruction of Jerusalem, where the climax of national misery, arising from famine and every other cause, was so awfully completed.

Author's note: The famine predicted by Agabus and discussed above is mentioned in the Book of Acts 11:28-30 and in First Corinthians 16:1-3.

Pestilences

Our Savior adds *"pestilences"* (see Luke 21:11), likewise. Pestilence treads upon the heels of famine; it may, therefore, reasonably be presumed that this terrible scourge accompanied the famines, which have just been recounted above. History, however, particularly distinguishes two instances of this calamity that occurred before the commencement of the Jewish war. The first took place at Babylon about AD 40, and it raged so alarmingly that great multitudes of Jews fled from that city to Seleucia for safety, as has been hinted at already. The other happened at Rome in AD 65, and it carried off prodigious multitudes. Both Tacitus and Suetonius also record that similar calamities prevailed during this period in various parts of the Roman Empire.

After Jerusalem was surrounded by the army of Titus, pestilential diseases soon made their appearance there to aggravate the miseries and deepen the horrors of the siege. They were partly occasioned by the immense multitudes that were crowded together in the city, partly by the putrid emanations that arose from the unburied dead, and partly from the spread of famine.

Heavenly Signs

Our Lord proceeded, *"And fearful sights and great signs shall there be from heaven"* (Luke 21:11). Josephus has collected the chief of these portents together and introduces his account by a reflection on the strangeness of that infatuation that could induce his countrymen to give credit to impostors and unfounded reports, while they disregarded the divine admonitions that were confirmed, as he [Josephus] asserts they were, by the following extraordinary signs:

1. "A meteor, resembling a sword, hung over Jerusalem during one whole year." This could not be a comet, for it was stationary, and was visible for twelve successive months. A sword too, though a fit emblem for destruction, but ill represents a comet."
2. "On the eighth of the month Zanthicus, (before the feast of unleavened bread) at the ninth hour of the night, there shone round

about the altar, and the circumjacent buildings of the temple, a light equal to the brightness of the day, which continued for the space of half an hour." This could not be the effect of lightning, nor of a vivid aurora borealis, for it was confined to a particular spot, and the light shone uninterrupted for thirty minutes.

3. "As the High Priest were leading a heifer to the altar to be sacrificed, she brought forth a lamb, in the midst of the temple." Such is the strange account given by Josephus. Some may regard it as a "Grecian fable," while others may discern in this prodigy a miraculous rebuke of Jewish infidelity and impiety, for rejecting the antitypical Lamb, who had offered Himself as an atonement "once for all" and who, by thus completely fulfilling their design, had virtually abrogated the Levitical sacrifices. However this may be, the circumstances of the prodigy are remarkable. It did not occur in an obscure part of the city, but in the Temple; it did not at an ordinary time, but at the Passover—the season of our Lord's crucifixion—in the presence, not of the vulgar merely, but of the High Priests and their attendants, and when they were leading the sacrifice to the altar.
4. "About the sixth hour of the night, the eastern gate of the temple was seen to open without human assistance." When the guards informed the Curator of this event, he sent men to assist them in shutting it, and with great difficulty they succeeded. This gate, as has been observed already, was of solid brass and required twenty men to close it every evening. It could not have been opened by a "strong gust of wind," or a "slight earthquake" for, as Josephus says, "It was secured by iron bolts and bars that were let down into a large threshold, consisting of one entire stone."
5. "Soon after the feast of the Passover, in various parts of the country, before the setting of the sun, chariots and armed men were seen in the air, passing round about Jerusalem." Neither could this portentous spectacle be occasioned by the aurora borealis, for it occurred before the setting of the sun; nor could it have been merely the fancy of a few villagers, gazing at the heavens, for it was seen in various parts of the country.
6. "At the subsequent feast of Pentecost, while the priests were going,

by night, into the inner temple to perform their customary ministrations, they first felt, as they said, a shaking, accompanied by an indistinct murmuring, and afterwards voices as of a multitude, saying, in a distinct and earnest manner, 'let us depart hence'." This gradation will remind the reader of that awful transaction that the feast of Pentecost was principally instituted to commemorate.

First, a shaking was heard; this would naturally induce the priests to listen. An unintelligible murmur succeeds it; this would more powerfully arrest their attention, and while it was thus awakened , they heard, says Josephus, the voices, as of a multitude, distinctly pronouncing the words, "let us depart hence." And accordingly, before the period for celebrating this feast returned, the Jewish war had commenced, and in the space of three years afterward, Jerusalem was surrounded by the Roman army, the temple converted into a citadel, and its sacred courts streaming with the blood of human victims.

7. As the last and most fearful omen, Josephus relates that one, Jesus—the son of Ananus, a rustic of the lower class—during the Feast of Tabernacles, suddenly exclaimed in the temple, "A voice from the east a voice from the west—a voice from the four winds—a voice against Jerusalem and the temple—a voice against bridegrooms and brides—a voice against the whole people!" These words he incessantly proclaimed aloud, both day and night, through all the streets of Jerusalem for seven years and five months together. He began at a time (AD 62) when the city was in a state of peace and was overflowing with prosperity, and he ceased amidst the horrors of the siege.

This disturber, having excited the attention of the magistracy, was brought before Albinus the Roman governor, who commanded that he should be scourged. But the severest stripes drew from him neither tears nor supplications. As he never thanked those who relieved him, so neither did he complain of the injustice of those who struck him. And no other answer could the governor obtain to his interrogatories, but his usual denunciation of "Woe, woe to Jerusalem!" which he still continued to proclaim through the city, but especially during the festivals, when his manner became more

> earnest and the tone of his voice louder. At length, on the commencement of the siege, he ascended the walls and, in a more powerful voice than ever, exclaimed, "Woe, woe to this city, this temple, and this people!" And then, with a presentment of his own death, added, "Woe, woe to myself!" He had scarcely uttered these words when a stone from one of the Roman engines killed him on the spot.

Such are the prodigies related by Josephus, and excepting the first, he places them in the year immediately preceding the Jewish war. Several of them are recorded also by Tacitus. Nevertheless, it ought to be observed that they are received by Christian writers cautiously and with various degrees of credit. Those, however, who are most skeptical and who resolve them into natural causes, allow the "superintendence of God to awaken his people by some of these means." Whatever the fact, in this respect, it is clear that they correspond to our Lord's prediction of "fearful sights and great signs from heaven" and ought to be deemed a sufficient answer to the objector who demands whether any such appearances are respectably recorded.

Great Persecution

The next prediction of our Lord related to the persecution of His disciples: *"They shall lay their hands on you and persecute you, delivering you up to the synagogues and into prisons, being brought before kings and rulers for my name's sake;"* (Luke 21:12)—*"and they shall deliver you up to councils, and in the synagogues ye shall be beaten;"* (Mark 13:9)—*"and some of You shall they cause to be put to death"* (Luke 21:16). In the very infancy of the Christian Church, these unmerited and unprovoked cruelties began to be inflicted.

Our Lord and his forerunner, John the Baptist, had already been put to death. The apostles Peter and John were first imprisoned, and then, together with the other apostles, were scourged before the Jewish council. Stephen, after confounding the Sanhedrim with his irresistible eloquence, was stoned to death. Herod Agrippa *"stretched forth his hands to vex certain of the church,"* beheaded James the brother of John, and again imprisoned Peter, designing to put him to death also.

Saint Paul pleaded before the Jewish council at Jerusalem and before

Felix the Roman governor, who trembled on the judgment-seat, while the intrepid prisoner "*reasoned of righteousness, temperance, and judgment to come!*" Two years afterward, he was brought before the tribunal of Festus (who had succeeded Felix in the government). King Agrippa the younger was present and, while the governor scoffed, ingenuously acknowledged the force of the apostle's eloquence and, half-convinced, exclaimed, "*Almost thou persuadest me to be a Christian.*" Lastly, he pleaded before the emperor Nero at Rome. He was also brought with Silas before the rulers at Philippi, where both of them were scourged and imprisoned. Paul was likewise imprisoned two years in Judea and afterward twice at Rome, each time for the space of two years. He was scourged by the Jews five times, thrice beaten with rods, and once stoned.

Paul himself, before his conversion, was also an instrument of fulfilling the predictions. Saint Luke relates of him that "*he made havoc of the church, entering into every house, and hating men and women, committed them to prison; when they were put to death he gave his voice against them; he punished them oft in every synagogue, and, persecuted them even into strange cities*"; and to this agree his own declarations (Acts 26:10–11; see Gal. 1:23).

At length, about two years before the Jewish war, the first general persecution commenced at the instigation of the emperor Nero, "who," says Tacitus, "inflicted upon the Christians punishments exquisitely painful." Multitudes suffered a cruel martyrdom amidst derision and insults, and among the rest, were the venerable apostles Saint Peter and Saint Paul.

Our Lord continues—"*And ye shall be hated of all nations for my name's sake*" (Matt. 24:9). The hatred from which the above-recited persecutions sprang was not provoked on the part of the Christians by a resistance to established authority or by any violations of law, but was the unavoidable consequence of their sustaining the name and imitating the character of their master. "It was a war," says Tertullian, "against the very name; to be a Christian was of itself crime enough." And to the same effect is that expression of Pliny in his letter to Trajan: "I asked them whether they were Christians; if they confessed it, I asked them a second and a third time, threatening them with punishment, and those who persevered I commanded to be led away to death." It is added, "*Of all nations.*" Whatever animosity or dissensions might subsist between the Gentiles and the Jews on other points, they were at all times ready to unite and co-operate in the persecution of the humble followers of Him who came to be a light to the former and the glory of the latter.

Cold Love

"And then shall many be offended, and shall betray one another" (Matt. 24:10). Concerning this fact, the following decisive testimony of Tacitus may suffice. Speaking of the persecutions of the Christians under Nero, to which we have just alluded, he adds, "Several were seized, who confessed, and by their discovery a great multitude of others were convicted and barbarously executed."

> **Author's note:** Matthew 24:10–12 may also be in reference to the many false teachings of the first-century church, which caused many believers to step away from the love of Christ into aberrant forms of the faith, such as the Gnostics, Judaizers, and Nicolatians.
>
> As the scholar David Chilton wrote:
>
> We generally think of the apostolic period as a time of tremendously explosive evangelism and Church growth, a "golden age" when astounding miracles took place every day. This common image is substantially correct, but it is flawed by one glaring omission. We tend to neglect the fact that the early Church was the scene of *the most dramatic out-break of heresy in world history.*
>
> But the problem of heresy was not limited to any geographical or cultural area. It was widespread and became an increasing subject of apostolic counsel and pastoral oversight as the age progressed. Some heretics taught that the final Resurrection had already taken place (2 Tim. 2:18), while others claimed that resurrection was impossible (1 Cor. 15:12); some taught strange doctrines of asceticism and angel-worship (Col. 28, 18-23; 1 Tim. 4:1–3), while others advocated all kinds of immorality and rebellion in the name of "liberty" (2 Peter 2:1–3, 10–22; Jude 4, 8, 10–13, 16). Again and again the apostles found themselves issuing stern warnings against tolerating false

teachers and "false apostles" (Rom. 16:17–18; 2 Cor. 11:3–4, 12–15; Phil. 3:18–19; 1 Tim. 1:3–7; 2 Tim. 4:2–5), for these had been the cause of massive departures from the faith, and the extent of apostasy was increasing as the era progressed (1 Tim. 1:19–20, 6:20–21; 2 Tim. 2:16–18, 3:1–9, 13, 4:10, 14–16). One of the last letters of the New Testament, the Book of Hebrews, was written to an entire Christian community on the very brink of wholesale abandonment of Christianity. The Christian Church of the first generation was not only characterized by faith and miracles; it was also characterized by increasing lawlessness, rebellion, and heresy from within the Christian community itself—just as Jesus had foretold in Matthew 24.[18]

Gospel Preached in the Whole World

"And this gospel of the kingdom shall be preached in all the world, for a witness unto all nations, and then shall the end (i.e., of the Jewish dispensation) *come"* (Matt. 24:14). Of the fulfillment of this prediction of the epistles of Saint Paul—addressed to the Christians at Rome, Corinth, Galatia, Ephesus, Philippi, Colosse, Thessalonica—and those of Peter—to such as resided in Pontus, Cappadocia, and Bithynia—are monuments now standing. For neither of these apostles were living when the Jewish war commenced. Saint Paul, too, in his epistle to the Romans, informs them that *"their faith was spoken of throughout the world"* (Rom. 1:8); and in that to the Colossians he observes that the *"gospel had been preached to every creature under heaven"* (Col. 1:23). Clement, who was a fellow-laborer with the apostle, relates of him that "he taught the whole world righteousness, travelling from the East westward to the borders of the ocean." Eusebius says that "the Apostles preached the gospel in all the world, and that some of them passed beyond the bounds of the ocean, and visited the Britannic isles"; so says Theodoret also.

"It appears," says Bishop Newton, "from the writers of the history of the church, that before the destruction of Jerusalem, the gospel was not only preached in the Lesser Asia, and Greece, and Italy, the great theatres of action then in the world, but was likewise propagated as far northward as

Scythia, as far southward as Ethiopia, as far eastward as Parthia and India, as far westward as Spain and Britain." And Tacitus asserts that "the Christian religion, which arose in Judea, spread over many parts of the world, and extended to Rome itself, where the professors of it, as early as the time of Nero, amounted to a vast multitude," insomuch that their numbers excited the jealousy of the government.

Thus completely was fulfilled a prediction contrary to every conclusion that could have been grounded on moral probability and to the accomplishment of which every kind of impediment was incessantly opposed. The reputed son of a carpenter instructs a few simple fishermen in a new dispensation destitute of worldly incentives, but full of self-denials, sacrifices, and sufferings, and he tells them that in about forty years it should spread over the entire world. It spreads accordingly, and in defiance of the bigotry of the Jews and the authority, power, and active opposition of the Gentiles, it is established, within that period, in all the countries into which it penetrates. Can anyone doubt that the prediction and its fulfillment were equally divine?

> **Author's note:** The root word *Oikoumene*, used for "world" in this passage, actually means "inhabited or civilized world," not world as in global planet earth. This is the same Greek word used in Luke 2:1: *"Now in those days a decree went out from Caesar Augustus, that a census be taken of all* ***the inhabited earth****."*
>
> The apostle Paul used this same word later to confirm four times that the gospel had reached the whole civilized world as Jesus predicted (see Rom. 1:8; 10:18; Col 1:5–6,23).
>
> As Philip Doddridge wrote in 1807:
>
> > It appears, from the most credible records, that the *gospel* was preached in Idumea, Syria, and Mesopotamia, by Jude; in Egypt, Marmorica, Mauritania, and other parts of Africa, by Mark, Simon, and Jude; in Ethiopia, by Candace's Eunuch and Mattias; in Pontus, Galatia, and the neighboring parts of Asia, by Peter; in territories of the seven Asiatic

> churches, by John; in Parthia, by Matthew; in Scythia, by Philip and Andrew; in the northern and western parts of Asia, by Bartholomew; in Persia, by Simon and Jude; in Media, Carmania, and several eastern parts, by Thomas; through the vast tract from Jerusalem round about to Illyricum, by Paul, as also in Italy, and probably in Spain, Gaul, and Britain; in most of which places Christian churches were planted, in less than thirty years after the death of Christ, which was *before the destruction of Jerusalem.*[19]

Jesus was saying that the gospel would be preached throughout the Roman Empire before He would come in judgment upon Jerusalem and the Temple. He was right. This has been fulfilled, and it has no further fulfillment in our future. We *are not* waiting for every person to hear the gospel so that the rapture can suddenly take place.[20]

The Beginning of the War

Such, briefly, is the account that history gives of the several events and signs that our Lord said would precede the destruction of the Holy City. No sooner were his predictions regarding the spread of the gospel accomplished than a most unaccountable infatuation seized upon the whole Jewish nation so that they not only provoked, but seemed even to rush into the midst of those unparalleled calamities that, at length, totally overwhelmed them. In an essay of this sort, it is impossible to enter into a minute detail of the origin and progress of these evils, but such particulars as illustrate the fulfillment of the remaining part of the prophecy and justify the strong language used shall be presented to the reader.

From the conquest of their country by Pompey, about 60 BC, the Jews had, on several occasions, manifested a refractory spirit. But after Judas the Gaulonite and Sadduc the Pharisee taught them that submission to the Romans would pave the way to a state of abject slavery, this temper displayed itself with increasing malignity and violence. Rebellious tumults and insurrections became more frequent and alarming, and to these, the mercenary Florus, the Roman governor, contributed a great deal. At length, Eleazer, son of the High Priest, persuaded those who officiated in the Temple to reject the sacrifices of foreigners and to no longer offer up prayers for them. Thus an insult was thrown upon Caesar, his sacrifice was rejected, and the foundation of the Roman war was laid.

The disturbances among the Jews still continuing, Cestius Gallus, president of Syria, marched an army into Judea in order to quell them, and his career was everywhere marked with blood and desolation. As he proceeded, he plundered and burned the beautiful city of Zabulon, Joppa, and all the villages that lay in his way. At Joppa, he killed 8,400 of the inhabitants. He laid waste the district of Narbatene and, sending an army into Galilee, killed there 2,000 of the seditious Jews. He then burned the city of Lydda, and after repulsing the Jews, who made a desperate attempt against him, he encamped at the distance of about one mile from Jerusalem. On the fourth day, he entered its gate and burned three divisions of the city. He may have, by its capture at that time, put an end to the war, but instead of pursuing his advantages, through the treacherous persuasions of his officers, he most unaccountably raised the siege and fled from the city with great haste.

The Jews, however, pursued him as far as Antipatris and, with little loss to themselves, slew nearly 6,000 men of his army. After this disaster had befallen Cestius, the wealthier Jews (says Josephus) forsook Jerusalem as men do a sinking ship. And it is with reason supposed that, on this occasion, many of the Christians, or converted Jews, who dwelled there—remembering the warnings or their divine Master, retired to Pella, a place beyond Jordan situated in a mountainous country (Matt. 16:22). There (according to Eusebius, who resided near the spot) they came from Jerusalem and settled before the war (under Vespasian) began. Other providential opportunities for escaping afterward occurred, of which, it is probable, those who were now left behind availed themselves. It is a striking act, one that cannot be contemplated by the pious mind without devout admiration, that history does not record that even one Christian perished in the siege of Jerusalem. Enduring to the end and faithful to their blessed master, they gave credit to his predictions and escaped the calamity. Thus were fulfilled the words of our Lord, *"He that shall endure unto the end* (i.e., of the scene of this prophecy) *shall be saved"* (Matt. 24:13) from the calamities that would overtake all those who continued obstinate in unbelief.

Time to Flee (Matt. 24:15,21)

Nero, having been informed of the defeat of Cestius, immediately appointed Vespasian, a man of tried valor, to lead the war against the Jews. He, assisted by his son, Titus, soon collected at Ptolemais an army of 60,000 men. From there, in the spring of AD67, he marched into Judea, everywhere spreading the most cruel havoc and devastation—the Roman soldiers, on various occasions, sparing neither infants nor the aged. For fifteen months, Vespasian proceeded in this sanguinary career, during which period he reduced all the strong towns of Galilee and the chief of those in Judea, destroying at least 150,000 of the inhabitants.

Among the terrible calamities, which at this time happened to the Jews, those that befell them at Joppa, which had been rebuilt, deserve particular notice. Their frequent piracies had provoked the vengeance of Vespasian. The Jews fled before his army to their ships, but a tempest immediately arose and pursued those who had set out to sea, and it capsized them. The rest were dashed, vessel against vessel and against the rocks, in the most tremendous manner. In this way, many were drowned, some were crushed by the broken ships, others killed themselves, and those who reached the shore were slain by the merciless Romans. The sea for a long space was stained with blood; 4,200 dead bodies were strewn along the coast, and (dreadful to relate) not an individual survived to report this great calamity at Jerusalem. Such events were foretold by our Lord, when he said, *"There shall be distress of nations, with perplexity; the sea and the waves roaring"* (Luke 21:25).

Vespasian, after proceeding as far as Jericho, returned to Caesarea in order to make preparation for his grand attempt against Jerusalem. While he was thus employed, he received intelligence of the death of Nero. Not knowing what the will of the future emperor might be, he prudently resolved to suspend, for the present, the execution of his design. Thus, the Almighty gave the Jews a second respite, which continued nearly two years. But they did not repent of their crimes; neither were they in the least degree repentant, but rather proceeded to acts of still greater enormity. The flame of civil dissension again burst out and with more dreadful fury.

In the heart of Jerusalem, two factions contended for the sovereignty and raged against each other with ruthless and destructive animosity. A division of one of these factions, having been excluded from the city (*vide* page 26), forcibly entered it during the night. Athirst for blood and inflamed by revenge, they spared neither age, sex, nor infancy, and the morning beheld 8,500 dead bodies lying in the streets of the holy city. They plundered every house, and having found the chief priests, Anaius and Jesus, they not only killed them, but also insulted their bodies by casting them forth unburied. They slaughtered the common people as unfeelingly as if they had been a herd of the vilest beasts. The nobles they first imprisoned and scourged, and when they could not by these means convince them to join their party, they bestowed death upon them as a favor. Of the higher classes, 12,000 perished in this manner. And no one dared to shed a tear or utter a groan openly through fear of a similar fate. Death, indeed, was the penalty of the lightest and heaviest accusations, and none escaped through the lowness of their rank or their poverty. Those who fled were intercepted and slain, and their carcasses lay in heaps on all the public roads. Every symptom of pity seemed utterly extinguished and, with it, all respect for authority, both human and divine.

While Jerusalem was a prey to these ferocious and devouring factions, every part of Judea was scourged and laid waste by bands of robbers and murderers, who plundered the towns. In the case of resistance, they killed the inhabitants, not sparing either women or children. Simon, son of Gioras, the commander of one of these bands of 40,000, with some difficulty entered Jerusalem and gave birth to a third faction. Thus the flame of civil discord blazed out again, with still more destructive fury. The three factions, rendered frantic by drunkenness, rage, and desperation, trampled on heaps of slain people and fought against each other with brutal savageness and madness. Even those who brought sacrifices to the Temple were murdered. The dead bodies of priests and worshippers, both natives and foreigners, were heaped together, and a lake of blood stagnated in the sacred courts.

John Levi of Gischala, who headed one of the factions, burnt storehouses full of provisions, and Simon, his great antagonist, who headed another of them, soon afterward followed his example. Thus they cut the very sinews of their own strength. At this critical and alarming conjuncture, intelligence arrived that the Roman army was approaching the city. The Jews were petrified with astonishment and fear; there was no time for counsel, no hope of pacification, no means of flight: all was wild disorder and perplexity. Nothing was to be heard but *"the confused noise of the warrior,"*—nothing to be seen but *"garments rolled in blood,"*—nothing to be expected from the Romans but signal and exemplary vengeance. A ceaseless cry of combatants was heard day and night, and yet the lamentations of mourners were still more dreadful. The consternation and terror that now prevailed induced many inhabitants to desire that a foreign foe might come, and effect their deliverance. Such was the horrible condition of the place when Titus and his army presented themselves and encamped before Jerusalem.

But, alas—he came not to deliver it from its miseries, but to fulfill the prediction and vindicate the benevolent warning of our Lord: *"When ye see* (he had said to his disciples) *the abomination of desolation, spoken or by the prophet Daniel, standing in the holy place, and Jerusalem surrounded by armies* (or camps) *then let those who are in the midst of Jerusalem depart, and let not those who are in the country enter into her,"* for *"then know that the desolation thereof is nigh"* (Matthew 24:15–16; Luke 21:20,1–11). These armies, we do not hesitate to affirm, were those of the Romans, who now filled the city.

From the time of the Babylonian captivity, idolatry had been held as an abomination by the Jews. This national aversion was manifested even against the images of the Roman gods and emperors, which the Roman armies carried in their standards. We see this, in an earlier time of peace, when Pilate, and afterward Vitellius, at the request of some eminent Jews, avoided marching their forces through Judea because of this very reason. The desolating disposition that now governed the Roman army, the history of the Jewish war, and especially the final demolition of the holy city presents an awful and signal example. Jerusalem was not captured merely, but with its celebrated Temple laid in ruins.

> **Author's note:** By comparing Matthew 24:15–16 with Luke 21:20, we can understand that the abomination that caused the desolation of Jerusalem was the 20,000 Roman soldiers that lay siege to the city. Fortunately, Jesus told His followers that when they saw this, they should flee for the mountains. They did this because they understood what Jesus had said. Both Chrysostom and Augustine wrote agreeing that the abomination that caused the desolation was the Roman Army.

> Chrysostom (born 347 at Antioch, capital of Syria) said, "For this it seems to me that the abomination of desolation means the army by which the holy city of Jerusalem was made desolate."[21]
>
> Saint Augustine (born in 354 in North Africa) said:
>
> > Luke, to show that the same abomination spoken of by Daniel will take place when Jerusalem is captured, recalls these words of the Lord in the same context: When you shall see Jerusalem compassed about with an army, then you know that the desolation thereof is at hand (xxi. 20).[22]

Lest, however, the army of Titus should not be sufficiently designated by this expression, our Lord adds, *"Wherever the carcass is, there the eagles will be gathered together"* (Matt. 24:28 ASV). The Jewish state, indeed, at this time, was fitly compared to a carcass. The scepter of Judah—its civil and political authority, the life of its religion, and the glory of its Temple—were departed. It was, in short, morally and judicially dead. The eagle whose ruling instinct is rapine and murder, fitly represented the fierce and sanguinary temper of the Romans, and perhaps, it might be intended to refer also to the principal image on their ensigns, which, however obnoxious to the Jews, were at length planted in the midst of the holy city and finally on the Temple itself.

> **Author's note:** In other words, the emblem of the eagle was upon the Roman shields and banners; also, Jerusalem was pictured as a dead carcass. As the commentator Barnes wrote:
>
> > The words in this verse are proverbial. Vultures and eagles easily ascertain where dead bodies are, and hasten to devour them. So with the Roman army. Jerusalem is like a dead and putrid corpse. Its life is gone, and it is ready to be devoured. The Roman armies will find it out, as the vultures do a dead carcass, and will come around it to devour it.[23]

The day on which Titus encompassed Jerusalem was the feast of the Passover, and it is worth noting that this was the anniversary of that memorable period in which the Jews crucified their Messiah! At this season, multitudes came up from all the surrounding country, and from distant parts, to keep the festival. How suitable and how kind, then, was the prophetic admonition of our Lord when he said, *"Let not them that are in the countries enter into Jerusalem"* (Luke 21:21).

> **Author's note:** George Peter Holford's book does not address Matthew 24:15–18,20:
>
> > *Then let those who are in Judea flee to the mountains. Let no one on the housetop go down to take anything out of the house. Let no one in the field go back to get their cloak. Pray that your flight will not take place in winter or on the Sabbath.*
>
> I am not sure why he skipped this section, but I will cover it briefly. Here, Jesus was giving very practical advice to His followers about how to stay alive during the AD 70 destruction. We can tell from this passage that Jesus was speaking of a local destruction (flee Judea) and a historical setting (not on a Sabbath). The natural tendency, upon seeing an approaching army, would have been to flee *into* Jerusalem for safety. Jesus told them to fight their natural instinct and flee the city.
>
> > Furthermore, the members of the Jerusalem church, by means of an oracle given by revelation to acceptable persons there, were ordered to leave the City before the war began and settle in a town in Perea called Pella. To Pella those who believed in Christ migrated from Jerusalem; and as if holy men had utterly abandoned the royal metropolis of the Jews and the entire Jewish land, the judgment of God at last overtook them for their abominable crimes against Christ and His apostles, completely blotting out that wicked generation from among men. —Eusebius[24]
> >
> > It is said that *there is reason to believe that not one Christian perished in the destruction of that city,* God having in various ways secured their escape, so that they fled to Pella, where they dwelt when the city was destroyed. —Albert Barnes[25]

> ...it is remarked by several interpreters, and which Josephus takes notice of with surprise, that Cestius Gallus having advanced with his army to Jerusalem, and besieged it, on a sudden without any cause, raised the siege, and withdrew his army, when the city might have been easily taken; by which means a signal was made, and an opportunity given to the Christians, to make their escape: which they accordingly did, and went over to Jordan, as Eusebius says, to a place called Pella; so that when Titus came a few months after, *there was not a Christian in the city...* —John Gill[26]

I find this historical fact alone to be incredible proof that the first-century believers knew that Jesus was speaking to them about AD 70.

Even the translator of Jospehus' works noted:

> There may another very important, and very providential, reason be here assigned for this strange and foolish retreat of Cestius; which, if Josephus had been now Christian, he might probably have taken notice of also; and that is, the affording the Jewish Christians in the city an opportunity to calling to mind the prediction and caution given them by Christ about thirty-three years and half before, that "when they should see the abomination of desolation" [the idolatrous Roman armies, with the images of their idols in their ensigns, ready to lay Jerusalem desolate] "stand where it ought not"; or, "in the holy place"; or, "when they should see Jerusalem encompassed with armies," they should then "flee to the mountains." By complying with which those Jewish Christians fled to the mountains of Perea, and escaped this destruction... Nor was there, perhaps, any one instance of a more unpolitic, but more providential conduct than this retreat of Cestius, visible during this whole siege of Jerusalem; which yet was providentially such a "Great Tribulation, as had not been from the beginning of the world to that time; no, nor ever should be."[27]

Like Lightening (Matt. 24:27)

Nevertheless, the city was at this time crowded with Jewish strangers and foreigners from all parts so that the whole nation may be considered as having been shut up in one prison prior to the execution of the Divine vengeance. According to Josephus, this event took place suddenly, thus, not only fulfilling the predictions of our Lord that these calamities should come like the swift-darting lightning *"that cometh out of the east and shineth even unto the West,"* and *"as a snare on all of them* (the Jews) *who dwelt upon the face of the whole earth"* (Matt. 24:27; Luke 21:35), but justifying, also, his friendly direction that those who fled from the place should use the utmost possible expedition.

Woe to the Pregnant (Matt. 24:19)

On the appearance of the Roman army, the factious Jews united and, rushing furiously out of the city, repulsed the tenth legion, which was with difficulty preserved. This event caused a short suspension of hostilities and, by opening the gates, gave an opportunity to those who were so disposed to make their escape. Before this they could not have attempted an escape without interruption because it would have caused suspicion that they wished to join the Romans.

This success inspired the Jews with confidence, and they resolved to defend their city to the very uttermost, but it did not prevent the renewal of their civil broils. The faction under Eleazer had dispersed and arranged themselves under the two other leaders, **John Levi** and Simon, and afterward ensued a scene of the most dreadful contention, plunder, and conflagration. The middle space of the city was burnt, and the wretched inhabitants were made the prize of the contending parties.

The Romans, at length, gained possession of two of the three walls that defended the city, and fear once more united the factions. This pause to their fury had, however, scarcely begun when famine made its ghastly appearance in the Jewish army. It had for some time been silently approaching, and many of the peaceful and the poor had already perished for want of necessaries. With this new calamity, strange to relate, the madness of the factions again returned, and the city presented a new picture of wretchedness. Impelled by the cravings of hunger, they snatched food out of each other's hands, and many devoured grain unprepared.

Tortures were inflicted for the discovery of a handful of meal; women forced food from their husbands and children from their fathers and even mothers from their infants; while suckling children were wasting away in their arms, they scrupled not to take away the vital drops that sustained them! So justly did our Lord pronounce a woe on *"them that should give suck in those days"* (Matt. 24:19). This dreadful scourge at length drove multitudes of the Jews out of the city into the enemy's camp, where the Romans crucified them in such numbers that, as Josephus relates, space was wanted for the crosses, and crosses for the captives. When it was discovered that some of them had swallowed gold, the Arabs and Syrians, who were incorporated into the Roman army, impelled by avarice, with unexampled cruelty, ripped open two thousand of the deserters in one night.

Titus, touched by these calamities, in person entreated the Jews to surrender, but they answered him with reviling. Exasperated by their obstinacy and insolence, he resolved to surround the city by a circumvallation (a trench of thirty-nine furlongs in circuit and strengthened with thirteen towers), which with astonishing activity was effected by the soldiers in three days. Thus was fulfilled another of our Lord's predictions, for he had said, while addressing this devoted city, *"Thine enemies shall cast a trench about thee, and compass thee round about, and keep thee in on every side"* (Luke 19:43).

As no supplies whatsoever could now enter the walls, the famine rapidly extended itself and, increasing in horror, devoured whole families. The tops of houses and the recesses of the city were covered with the carcasses of women, children, and aged men. The young men appeared like specters in the places of public resort and fell down lifeless in the streets. The dead were too numerous to be interred, and many died while burying others. The public calamity was too great for lamentation. Silence and, as it were, a black and deadly night overspread the city.

But even such a scene could not awe the robbers; they spoiled the tombs and stripped the dead of their grave clothes with an unfeeling and wild laughter. They tried the edges of their swords on the carcasses and even on some that were yet breathing. Simon Goras chose this melancholy and awful period to manifest the deep malignity and cruelty of his nature in the execution of the Priest, Matthias, and his three sons, whom he caused to be condemned as favorers of the Romans. The father, in consideration of his having opened the city gates to Simon, begged that he might be executed previously to his children, but the unfeeling tyrant gave orders that he should be dispatched in the last place, and in his expiring moments, Simon insultingly asked him whether the Romans could then relieve him.

While the city was in this dismal situation, a Jew named Mannæus fled to Titus and informed him that from the beginning of the siege (the 14th of April) to the first of July following, 115,880 dead bodies had been carried through one gate only, which he had guarded. This man had been appointed to pay the public allowance for carrying the bodies out, and was, therefore, obliged to register them. Soon after, several respectable individuals deserted to the Romans and assured Titus that the whole number of the poor who had been cast out at the different gates was not less than 600,000. The report of these calamities excited pity in the Romans and in a particular manner affected Titus, who, while surveying the immense number of dead bodies that were piled raised his hands toward Heaven and, appealing to the Almighty, solemnly protested that he had not been the cause of these deplorable calamities. Indeed, the Jews, by their unexampled wickedness, rebellion, and obstinacy, had brought it down upon their own heads.

After this, Josephus, in the name of Titus, earnestly exhorted **John Levi** and his adherents to surrender, but the insolent rebel returned nothing but reproaches and imprecations, declaring his firm persuasion that Jerusalem, as it was God's own city, could never be taken. Thus he literally fulfilled the declaration of Micah that the Jews, in their extremity, notwithstanding their crimes, would presumptuously *"lean upon the Lord, and say, 'Is not the Lord among us? None evil can come upon us"* (Micah 3:11).

Meanwhile the horrors of famine grew still more melancholy and afflictive. The Jews, for want of food, were at length compelled to eat their belts, their sandals, the skins of their shields, dried grass, and even the manure of oxen. In the depth of this horrible extremity, a Jewess of noble family, urged by the intolerable cravings of hunger, slew her infant child and prepared him for a meal. She had actually eaten one half thereof when the soldiers, allured by the smell of food, threatened her with instant death if she refused to reveal it. Intimidated by this menace, she immediately produced the remains of her son, which petrified them with horror. At the recital of this melancholy and affecting occurrence, the whole city stood aghast and poured forth their congratulations on those whom death had hurried away from such heartrending scenes.

> **Author's note:** This horrific story is an exact fulfillment of the curses spoken to Israel. *"You shall eat the fruit of your own body, the flesh of your sons and your daughters whom the LORD your God has given you, in the siege and desperate straits in which your enemy shall distress you"* (Deut. 28:53 NKJV).

Indeed, humanity at once shudders and sickens at the narration. Nor can any one of the least sensibility reflect upon the pitiable condition to which the female inhabitants of Jerusalem must have been reduced without experiencing the tenderest emotions of sympathy. Nor can he refrain from tears while he reads our Savior's pathetic address to the women who *"bewailed him"* as he was led to Calvary, wherein he evidently refers to these very calamities:

> *"Daughters of Jerusalem, weep not for me, but for yourselves and for your children; for, behold, the days are coming in which they shall say, 'Blessed are the barren, and the wombs that never bare, and the breasts that never gave suck"* (Luke 23:29).

> **Author's note:** Jesus' death was horrible, but He wept for the women and children of Jerusalem. In comparison, He was saying that their deaths would be far worse!

The above melancholy fact was also literally foretold by Moses: *"The tender and delicate women among barbarian,* (said he, addressing Israel) *who would not venture to set the sole of her foot upon the ground for delicateness and tenderness, her eye shall be evil....toward her young one....which she shall bear,"* and *"eat for want of all things, secretly, in the siege and straitness wherewith thine enemy shall distress thee in thy gates"* (Deut. 28:56–57).

And it is important to note—as a circumstance that very greatly enhances the importance of this prophecy—that the history of the world does not record a parallel instance of unnatural barbarity ever occurring during the siege of any other place in any other age or nation. Indeed, Josephus himself declared that, if there had not been many credible witnesses of the fact, he would not have recorded it, "because," as he remarks, "such a shocking violation of nature never having been perpetuated by any Greek or barbarian," the insertion of it might have diminished the credibility of his history.

While famine continued thus to spread its destructive rage through the city, the Romans, after many ineffectual attempts, at length succeeded in demolishing part of the inner wall, possessed themselves of the great tower of Antonia, and advanced toward the Temple, which Titus, in a council of war, had determined to preserve as an ornament to the empire and as a monument of his success. But the Almighty had determined otherwise. Now, in the revolution of ages, had arrived that fatal day (the 10th of August) emphatically called *"a day of vengeance"* (Luke 21:21), on which the Temple had formerly been destroyed by the king of Babylon.

> **Author's note:** In Luke 4:18–19, Jesus read a prophecy from Isaiah 61:1–2:
>
> *The Spirit of the Sovereign LORD is on me, because the LORD has anointed me to proclaim good news to the poor. He has sent me to bind up the brokenhearted, to proclaim freedom for the captives and release from darkness for the prisoners, to proclaim the year of the LORD's favor* ***and the day of vengeance of our God....***
>
> This is the passage as it appears in Isaiah, but when Jesus quoted it, He did not finish the passage. Jesus stopped mid-sentence. The portion in bold, Jesus excluded. Yet in Luke 21:21, Jesus declared *the day of vengeance.* Jesus started His ministry to the Jews in the favor of the Lord, but then after three and a half years, Jesus finished the prophecy by declaring that *the day of vengeance* was now coming.

A Roman soldier, urged, as he declared, by a divine impulse, regardless of the command of Titus, climbed on the shoulders of another and threw a flaming brand into the golden window of the Temple, which instantly set the building on fire. The Jews, anxious above all things to save that sacred edifice in which they superstitiously trusted for security, with a dreadful outcry, rushed in to extinguish the flames. Titus, also hoping to extinguish the conflagration, hastened to the spot in his chariot, attended by his principal officers and legions. But in vain he waved his hand and raised his voice, commanding his soldiers to extinguish the fire; so great was the uproar and confusion that no attention was paid even to him. The Romans, willfully deaf, instead of extinguishing the flames, spread them wider and wider.

Compelled by the fiercest impulses of rancor and revenge against the Jews, they rushed furiously upon them, slaying some with the sword, trampling others under their feet, or crushing them to death against the walls. Many, falling amongst the smoking ruins of the porches and galleries, were suffocated. The unarmed poor and even sick people were slaughtered without mercy. Of these unhappy people, numbers were left weltering in their gore. Multitudes of the dead and dying were heaped round about the altar, to which they had formerly fled for protection, while the steps that led from it into the outer court were literally deluged with their blood.

Finding it impossible to restrain the impetuosity and cruelty of his soldiers, the commander-in-chief proceeded, with some of his superior officers, to take a survey of those parts of the edifice that were still uninjured by the conflagration. It had not, at that time, reached the inner Temple, which Titus entered and viewed with silent admiration. Struck with the magnificence of its architecture and the beauty of its decorations, which even surpassed the report of fame concerning them, and perceiving that the sanctuary had not yet caught fire, he redoubled his efforts to stop the progress of the flames. He condescended even to entreat his soldiers to exert all their strength and activity for this purpose, and he appointed a centurion of the guards to punish them if they again disregarded him. But all was in vain.

The delirious rage of the soldiery knew no bounds. Eager for plunder and for slaughter, they alike ignored the solicitations and menaces of their general. Even while he was thus intent upon the preservation of the sanctuary, one of the soldiers was actually employed in setting fire to the doorposts, which caused the conflagration to become general. Titus and his officers were now compelled to retire, and none remained to check the fury of the soldiers or the flames. The Romans, exasperated to the highest pitch against the Jews, seized every person whom they could find and, without the least regard to sex, age, or quality, first plundered and then slew them. The old and the young, the common people and the priests, those who surrendered and those who resisted, were equally involved in this horrible and indiscriminate carnage.

Meanwhile, the Temple continued burning, until at length, vast as was its size, the flames completely enveloped the whole building. Thus the extent of the fire impressed the distant spectator with an idea that the whole city was now on fire. The tumult and disorder that ensued upon this event, it is impossible (says Josephus) for language to describe. The Roman legions made the most horrid outcries; the rebels, finding themselves exposed to the fury of both fire and sword, screamed dreadfully; while the unhappy people, who were pent up between the enemy and the flames, deplored their situation in the most pitiable complaints. Those on the hill and those in the city seemed mutually to return the groans of each other. Such as were expiring through famine, were revived by this hideous scene and seemed to acquire new spirits to deplore their misfortunes. The lamentations from the city were re-echoed from the adjacent mountains and places beyond Jordan. The flames, which enveloped the Temple, were so violent and impetuous that the lofty hill on which it stood appeared, even from its deep foundations, as one large body of fire.

Author's note: The incineration of Jerusalem is the blazing furnace referenced in Matthew 13:42 about the wheat and tares (more about this in the next chapter). For now, it will suffice to notice the amount of consuming flames in Jerusalem during the destruction.

The blood of the sufferers flowed in proportion to the rage of this destructive element, and the number of the slain exceeded all calculation. The ground could not be seen for the dead bodies, over which the Romans trampled in pursuit of the fugitives, while the crackling noise of the devouring flames, mingled with the clamor of arms, the groans of the dying, and the shrieks of despair, increased the tremendous horror of a scene to which the pages of history can furnish no parallel.

Among the tragic events that at this time occurred, the following is more particularly deserving of notice: A false prophet, pretending to be a divine commission, said that if the people would flee to the Temple, they should behold signs of their speedy deliverance. Accordingly, about six thousand people, chiefly women and children, assembled in a gallery that was yet standing, on the outside of the building. While they waited in anxious expectation of the promised miracle, the Romans, with the most wanton barbarity, set fire to the gallery. Multitudes, rendered frantic by their horrible situation, threw themselves from the gallery onto the ruins below and were killed by the fall. Meanwhile, awful to relate, the rest, without a single exception, perished in the flames. So necessary was our Lord's second premonition not to give credit to *"false prophets"* who should pretend *"to show great signs and wonders."*

The Temple now presented little more than a heap of ruins. The Roman army, as in triumph on the event, came and reared their ensigns against a fragment of the eastern gate, and with sacrifices of thanksgiving, they proclaimed the imperial majesty of Titus with every possible demonstration of joy.

Thus ended the glory and existence of the sacred and venerable Temple, which from its stupendous size, its massy solidity, and its astonishing strength, seemed formed to resist the most violent operations of human force and to stand, like the pyramids, amid the shocks of successive ages until the final dissolution of the globe.

For five days after the destruction of the Temple, the priests who had escaped sat, pining with hunger, on the top of one of its broken walls; at length they came down and humbly asked the pardon of Titus, which, however, he refused to grant them, saying that, "as the Temple, for the sake of which he would have spared them, was destroyed, it was but fit that its priests should perish also"—whereupon he commanded that they should be put to death.

The leaders of the factions, who were now pressed on all sides, begged a conference with Titus, who offered to spare their lives if they would lay down their arms. To this reasonable condition, however, they refused to comply. In response, Titus, exasperated by their obstinacy, resolved that he would hereafter grant no pardon to the insurgents and ordered a proclamation to be made to this effect. The Romans had now full license to ravage and destroy. Early the following morning, they set fire to the castle, the register office, the council chamber, and the palace of the queen

Helena, and then they spread themselves throughout the city, slaughtering wherever they came *and burning the dead bodies that were scattered over every street and on the floors of almost every house.*

In the royal palace, where immense treasures were deposited, the seditious Jews murdered 8,400 of their own people and afterward plundered their property. Prodigious numbers of deserters, also, who had escaped from the tyrants and fled into the enemy's camp, were slain.

The soldiers, however, at length, weary of killing and satiated with the blood that they had spilt, laid down their swords and sought to gratify avarice. For this purpose, they took the Jews, together with their wives and families, and publicly sold them, like cattle in a market. A very multitude were exposed to sale, while the purchasers were few in number. And now were fulfilled the words of Moses: *"And ye shall be sold for bond-men and bond-women, and no man shall buy you"* (Deut. 28:68).

The Romans, having become masters of the lower city, set it on fire. The Jews now fled to the higher, from whence, their pride and insolence yet unabated, they continued to exasperate their enemies and even appeared to view the burning of the town below them with tokens of pleasure. In a short time, however, the walls of the higher city were demolished by the Roman engines, and the Jews, lately so haughty and presumptuous, were now trembling and panic-struck, and they fell on their faces and deplored their own arrogance. Those who were in the towers, which were deemed impregnable to human force, were beyond measure afraid, and they strangely forsook the towers and sought refuge in caverns and subterraneous passages. In these dismal retreats, no less than 2,000 dead bodies were afterward found. Thus, as our Lord had predicted, did these miserable creatures, in effect, say *"to the mountains, 'Fall on us;' and to the rocks, 'Cover us'"* (Luke 23:20).

Since the walls of the city were now completely in the possession of the Romans, they hoisted their colors upon the towers and burst forth into the most triumphant acclamations. After this, all annoyance from the Jews being at an end, the soldiers gave an unbridled license to their fury against the inhabitants. They first plundered and then set fire to the houses. They ranged through the streets with drawn swords in their hands, murdering every Jew whom they met, without distinction, till at length, the bodies of the dead choked up all the alleys and narrow passes while their blood literally flowed down the channels of the city in streams. As it drew toward evening, the soldiers exchanged the sword for the torch, and amidst the darkness of this awful night, they set fire to the remaining divisions of the place.

The vial of divine wrath, which had been so long pouring out upon this devoted city, was now emptying, and Jerusalem, once *"a praise in all the earth"* and the subject of a thousand prophecies, which was deprived of the staff of life, wrapped in flames, and bleeding on every side, finally sunk into utter ruin and desolation. (This memorable siege terminated on the 8th day of September, AD 70. Its duration was nearly five months, the Romans having invested the city on the 14th day of the preceding April.)

Before their final demolition, however, Titus took a survey of the city and its fortifications, and while contemplating their impregnable strength, he could not help ascribing his success to the Almighty himself. "Had not God himself (exclaimed he) aided our operations, and driven the Jews from their fortresses, it would have been absolutely impossible to have taken them; for what could men, and the force of engines, have done against such towers as these?" After this he commanded that the city should be razed to its foundations, excepting only the three lofty towers Hippocos, Phasael, and Mariamne, which he suffered to remain as evidences of its strength and as trophies of his victory. There was left standing, also, a small part of the western wall, as a rampart for a garrison, to keep the surrounding country in subjection.

Titus now gave orders that only those Jews who resisted should be slain, but the soldiers, equally void of pity and remorse, slew even the sick and the aged. The robbers and seditious were all punished with death. The tallest and most beautiful youths, together with several of the Jewish nobles, were reserved by Titus to grace his triumphal entry into Rome. After this selection, all above the age of seventeen were sent in chains into Egypt to be employed there as slaves or distributed throughout the empire to be sacrificed as gladiators in the amphitheaters; those who were under this age were exposed to sale.

During the time that these things were transacted, 11,000 Jews, guarded by one of the generals, named Fronto, were literally starved to death. This melancholy occurrence happened partly through the scarcity of provisions and partly through their own obstinacy and the negligence of the Romans.

Of the Jews destroyed during the siege, Josephus reckons not less than one million and one hundred thousand, to which must be added above

237,000 who perished in other places and innumerable multitudes who were swept away by famine and pestilence and of which no calculation could be made. Not less than 2,000 laid violent hands upon themselves. Of the captives, the whole was about 97,000. Of the two great leaders of the Jews, who had both been made prisoners, **John Levi** was doomed to a dungeon for life, while Simon, together with **John Levi**, in triumph at Rome was scourged, and Simon was put to death as a malefactor.

> **Author's note:** *"If those days had not been cut short, no one would survive, but for the sake of the elect those days will be shortened"* (Matt. 24:22). We can see from the number above that if the slaughter had not been cut short, the Jews could have been completely annihilated.

In executing the command ofTitus regarding the demolition ofJerusalem, the Roman soldiers not only threw down the buildings, but even dug up their foundations. They so completely leveled the whole circuit of the city that a stranger would scarcely have known that it had ever been inhabited by human beings. Thus was this great city, which only five months before had been crowded with nearly two million people, who gloried in its impregnable strength, entirely depopulated and leveled to the ground. Thus also was our Lord's prediction that her enemies should *"lay her even with the ground,"* and *"should not leave in her one stone upon another"* (Luke 19:44) most strikingly and fully accomplished!

This fact is confirmed by Eusebius, who asserts that he himself saw the city lying in ruins, and Josephus introduces Eleazer as exclaiming, "Where is our great city, which, it was believed, God inhabited? It is altogether rooted and torn up from its foundations, and the only monument of it that remains, is the camp of its destroyers pitched amidst its relics!"

Concerning the Temple, our Lord foretold particularly that, notwithstanding their wonderful dimensions, there should *"not be left one stone upon another that should not be thrown down;"* (Matt. 24:2). Accordingly, it is recorded, in the Talmud and by Maimonides that Terentius Rufus, captain of the army ofTitus, absolutely ploughed up the foundations of the Temple with a ploughshare. Now, also, was literally fulfilled that prophecy of Micah—*"Therefore shall Zion, for your sakes* (i.e., for your wickedness,) *be ploughed as a field, and Jerusalem shall become heaps, and the mountain of the Lord's house as the high places of the forest"* (Micah 3:12).

> **Author's note:** "Today's Western Wall (also called the Wailing Wall) in Jerusalem was never a part of the Temple that existed in Jesus' day. It was a part of the parapet (protective fort-like wall) that King Herod had built around the Temple."[28]

Thus awfully complete and beyond example were the calamities which befell the Jewish nation and especially the city of Jerusalem. With what truth, then, did our Lord declare that there should *"be great tribulation, such as was not since the beginning of the world, no, nor ever shall be!"* (Matt. 24:21).

> **Author's note:** There is no such thing as two fulfillments to a given prophecy. That idea, although popular, is not biblical or sensible. If a prophecy is given, it has one fulfillment. To say it has two fulfillments just means that one interpretation was incorrect. Not only is double fulfillment not sensible, but also Jesus went out of His way to declare that Matthew 24 would only be fulfilled once (see Matt. 24:21). This removes the possibility of double fulfillment.
>
> Jesus pointed out that this tribulation would be the worst that had ever happened and the worst that ever would happen, implying that time would continue after this event, not that this event would be at the end of time. Many have taught that this prophecy of Jesus would happen at the end of time, but that is inconsistent with Jesus saying that it this event would occur in the middle of the timeline, not at the end of human history!
>
> How should one quantify "the worst thing to ever happen"? I suppose we have two options, literal and hyperbolic. If I were to answer with the literal, I would say that the destruction of the Jewish state, the Temple, and the priesthood; the death of 1.1 million Jews; and the destruction of the genealogical records, which ensures that the priesthood system can *never* be restored, would easily be the worst thing to ever happen to Israel.
>
> If I were to take a hyperbolic approach, I would agree with DeMar's comments:

> One reason offered for the belief that the great tribulation is still a future event is the seemingly unqualified statement in Matthew 24:21 concerning a "great tribulation, such as has not occurred since the beginning of the world until now, nor ever shall." This language is nearly identical to Ezekiel 5:9: "And because of all your abominations, I will do among you what I have not done, and the like of which I will never do again." Ezekiel 5:9 refers to the destruction of Jerusalem in the sixth century B.C. by the Babylonians, and yet Bible commentators who hold out for a yet future great tribulation state that "never again would God execute a judgment like this." But God did execute a greater judgment in the destruction of Jerusalem in A.D. 70, and dispensationalists claim that there will be yet an even greater tribulation sometime in the near future. The language of Ezekiel 5:9 and Matthew 24:21 is obviously proverbial and hyperbolic.[29]

Such was the prediction, and the language in which Josephus declares its fulfillment is an exact counterpart to it: "If the misfortunes," says he, "of all nations, from the beginning of the world, were compared with those which befell the Jews, they would appear far less in comparison." And again he says, "No other city ever suffered such things, as no other generation, from the beginning of the world, was ever more fruitful in wickedness." These were, indeed, *"the days of vengeance,"* that all things that are written (especially by Moses, Joel, and Daniel) might be fulfilled (Luke 21:2).

Nor were the calamities of this ill-fated nation even now ended. There were still other places to subdue, and our Lord had thus predicted, *"wheresoever the carcass is, there will the eagles be gathered together"* (Matt. 24:28). After the destruction of Jerusalem, 1,700 Jews who surrendered at Macherus were slain, and of fugitives, not less than 3,000 were killed in the wood of Jardes. Titus, having marched his army to Caesarea, there with great splendor celebrated the birthday of his brother, Domitian. And according to the barbarous manner of those times, he punished many Jews in honor of it. The number who were burned and who fell by fighting with wild beasts and in mutual combats exceeded 2,500.

At the siege of Massada, Eleazer, the Jewish commander, instigated the garrison to burn their stores and to destroy first the women and children and then themselves. Dreadful as it is to relate, this horrid design was executed. They were in number 960. Ten were chosen to perform the bloody work: The rest sat on the ground and, embracing their wives and children, stretched out their necks to the sword. One was afterward appointed to destroy the remaining nine and then himself. The survivor, when he had looked round to see that all were slain, set fire to the place and plugged his sword into his own bosom. Nevertheless, two women and five children successfully concealed themselves and witnessed the whole transaction. When the Romans advanced to the attack in the morning, one of the women gave them a distinct account of this melancholy affair and struck them with amazement at the contempt of death that had been displayed by the Jews.

After this event, if we exclude the transitory insurrection of the Sicarii under Jonathan, all opposition on the part of the Jews everywhere ceased. It was the submission of impotence and despair. The peace that ensued was the effect of the direst necessity. The rich territory of Judea was converted into a desolate waste. Everywhere ruin and desolation presented itself to the solitary passenger, and a melancholy and death-like silence reigned over the whole region. The mournful and desolate condition of Judea, at this time, is exactly described by the prophet Isaiah, in the following of his prophecies: *"The cities were without inhabitant, and the houses without a man, and the land was utterly desolate, and the LORD had removed men far away, and there was a great forsaking in the midst of the land"* (Isa. 6:11–12).

The catastrophe which has now been reviewed cannot but be deemed one of the most extraordinary that has happened since the foundation of the world. As it has pleased the Almighty to make it the subject of a very large proportion of the prophecies, both of the Jewish and Christian Scriptures, so he has ordained that the particular events which accomplished them should be recorded with very remarkable precision and by a man most singularly preserved, qualified, and circumstanced for this purpose.

But with respect to this latter point, he shall speak for himself: "At first," says Josephus, "I fought against the Romans, but was afterwards forced to be present in the Roman camp. At the time I surrendered, Vespasian and Titus kept me in bonds, but obliged me to attend them continually. Afterwards I was set at liberty, and accompanied Titus when he came from Alexandria to the siege of Jerusalem. During this time nothing was done that escaped my knowledge. What happened in the Roman camp I saw, and wrote down carefully. As to the information the deserters brought out of the city, I was the only man that understood it. Afterwards I got leisure at Rome; and when all my materials were prepared, I procured the help of one to assist me in writing Greek. Thus I composed the history of those transactions, and I appealed both to Titus and Vespasian for the truth of it; to which also Julius Archelaus, Herod, and King Agrippa, bore their testimony."

All remark here is needless, but it should not be forgotten that Josephus was a Jew, obstinately attached to his religion, and that, although he has circumstantially related every remarkable event of that period, he seems studiously to have avoided such as had any reference to Jesus Christ, whose history he sums up in about twelve written lines. No one, therefore, can reasonably entertain a suspicion that the service he has rendered to Christianity, by his narrative of the transactions of the Jewish war, was at all the effect of design. The fidelity of Josephus as an historian is, indeed, universally admitted, and Scaliger even affirms that, not only in the affairs of the Jews, but in those of foreign nations also, he deserves more credit than all the Greek and Roman writers put together.

Nor is the peculiar character of Titus, the chief commander in this war, unworthy of our particular regard. Vespasian, his father, had risen out of obscurity and was elected emperor, contrary to his avowed inclination, about the commencement of the conflict. Thus the chief command devolved upon Titus, the most unlikely man throughout the Roman armies to become a scourge to Jerusalem. He was eminently distinguished for his great tenderness and humanity, which he displayed in a variety of instances during the siege. He repeatedly made pacific overtures to the Jews and deeply lamented the infatuation that rejected them. In short, he did everything that a military commander could do to spare them and to preserve their city and Temple, but without effect. Thus was the will of God accomplished by Titus, although contrary to the wish of Titus, and God's predicted interposition to punish his rebellious and apostate people, in this way, was rendered more conspicuously evident.

The history of the Jews, subsequently to the time of Josephus, still further corroborates the truth of our Savior's prophecies concerning that oppressed and persecuted people. Into this inquiry, however, the limits of the present essay will not allow us to enter particularly. Our Lord foretold, generally, that they should *"fall by the edge of the sword, and be led away captive into all nations; and that Jerusalem should be trodden down of the Gentiles, until the times of the Gentiles should be fulfilled"* (Luke 21:24), and these predictions may be regarded as a faithful epitome of the circumstances of the Jews and also of their city, from the period in which it was delivered down even to our own times.

The Remainder of Matthew 24

For whatever reason, George Peter Holford's book does not address the rest of Matthew 24 (verses 29–51). I will finish out this chapter by addressing the remaining verses.

Signs in the Sky

> *Immediately after the distress of those days: "the sun will be darkened, and the moon will not give its light; the stars will fall from the sky, and the heavenly bodies will be shaken"* (Matthew 24:29).

To the first-century Jewish listeners, this was a figure of speech from the Old Testament. This apocalyptic language meant the destruction of a government or a city.

As John Forster writes:

> In ancient Hieroglyphic writings the sun, moon, and stars represented empires and states, with their sovereigns and nobility. The eclipse of these luminaries was said to denote temporary national disasters, or an entire overthrow of any state. This is still an Eastern mode of writing, and there are some classical examples of it. The Prophets frequently employ it, so that their style seems to be a speaking hieroglyphic. Thus Isaiah describes the destruction of Babylon, and Ezekiel that of Egypt.[30]

Similarly, DeMar writes:

> Where in the Scripture do we find nations compared to heavenly bodies? As with all Bible study, it is best to start at the beginning. The first chapter of Genesis gives us a clue as to why the Bible compares the sun, moon, and stars to rulers and their kingdoms: The sun ("greater light") and the moon ("lesser light") are said to "govern the day" and "night" (Gen. 1:16). Can we find examples of the sun and moon being used as symbols of government? In a dream Joseph saw "the sun and moon and eleven stars...bowing down" to him (37:9). The sun, moon, and stars represented Joseph's father, mother, and brothers. Joseph, being only "seventeen years old" (37:2), was under the government of his father, mother, and older brothers. In reality, they ruled over Joseph. Upon hearing about Joseph's dream, Jacob asked him, "What is this dream that you have had? *Shall I and your mother and your brothers actually come to bow ourselves down before you to the ground?"* (37:10). Joseph's father and brothers immediately understood the significance of the images in his dream. They were not looking for the sun, moon, and stars to bow down before Joseph.[31]

There are multiple times in the Old Testament where cities received prophecies of their destruction that were described in the same terms, such as:

> ***Egypt:*** *When I snuff you out, I will cover the heavens and darken their stars; I will cover the sun with a cloud, and the moon will not give its light. All the shining lights in the heavens I will darken over you; I will bring darkness over your land, declares the Sovereign LORD* (Ezekiel 32:7-8).

> ***Edom:*** *All the stars in the sky will be dissolved and the heavens rolled up like a scroll; all the starry host will fall like withered leaves from the vine, like shriveled figs from the fig tree. My sword has drunk its fill in the heavens; see, it descends in judgment on Edom, the people I have totally destroyed* (Isaiah 34:4-5).

> ***Babylon:*** *The stars of heaven and their constellations will not show their light. The rising sun will be darkened and the moon will not give its light* (Isaiah 13:10).

> *The LORD is slow to anger but great in power; the LORD will not leave the guilty unpunished. His way is in the whirlwind and the storm, and clouds are the dust of his feet* (Nahum 1:3).

> *"In that day," declares the Sovereign LORD, "I will make the sun go down at noon and darken the earth in broad daylight* (Amos 8:9).

Also, Habakkuk 3, which is about Babylon coming to destroy Israel, has much of the same sort of imagery. It is typical in biblical language to represent the people of Israel as stars (see Gen. 22:17; 26:4; Deut. 1:10). So, in Matthew 24:29, Jesus' hearers would have known that He was speaking in Old Testament pictorial language about the destruction of Jerusalem, not the end of the world.

Coming on the Clouds

> *Then will appear the sign of the Son of Man in heaven. And then all the peoples of the earth* [the tribes of the land] *will mourn when they see the Son of Man coming on the clouds of heaven, with power and great glory* (Matthew 24:30).

First, we must recognize that this passage does not refer to a global event. Where it says "earth," the root word is *ge*, which means "land," as in the land of Israel.[32] This passage does not use the word *kosmos*, which would refer to the whole planet earth. That is why many translations use the phrase *"tribes of the land"* (inserted above) or, at the very least, include it in the footnotes.

Second, the phrase *"coming on clouds of heaven,"* would have triggered in the first-century Jewish listener the Old Testament "cloud-comings" of God in judgment upon ancient historical people and nations (see Ps. 18:7–15; 104:3; Isa. 19:1; Joel 2:1–2; Zeph. 1:4,15). I will discuss the "cloud-comings" more in the next chapter, but for now it is simply important to realize that when Jesus talks about the coming of the Son of Man, He is referring to a coming of judgment, not to His final return.

Third, the "sign of the son of man in heaven" is likely a reference to the sign we read about earlier from Josephus—the sword that hung in the sky for a year over Jerusalem before AD 70.

Gathering the Elect

> *And he will send his angels with a loud trumpet call, and they will gather his elect from the four winds, from one end of the heavens to the other* (Matthew 24:31).

David Chilton writes of this passage:

> Finally, Jesus announced, the result of Jerusalem's destruction will be Christ's sending forth of His "angels" to gather the elect. Isn't this the rapture? No. The word *angels* simply means *messengers* (cf. James 2:25), regardless of whether their origin is heavenly or earthly; it is the *context* which determines whether these are heavenly creatures being spoken of. The word often means *preachers of the Gospel* (see Matthew 11:10; Luke 7:24; 9:52; Revelation 1-3). In context, there is every reason to assume that Jesus is speaking of the worldwide evangelism and conversion of the nations, which will follow upon the destruction of Israel.[33]

After the destruction of the Temple and the Jewish religious system, God began to gather people into His Kingdom from the four corners of the earth. A great explanation of this is found in *Victorious Eschatology.*

> To many people, this can speak only of the second coming of Christ at the end of history. But that is not what Jesus said it meant. Only three verses after this, He states, "this generation will not pass away until all these things take place." Jesus said that this verse was descriptive of one of the things that would happen within the span of one generation.
>
> How can we understand this? As Jesus sat down on His throne, all authority was given to Him in heaven and earth. Everything

> changed the moment Jesus came into His kingdom. The blowing of a trumpet meant to the Jews that a royal decree was going out. And what was that decree? It was time to release angels of God to go and gather His people from every nation. At the same time, the disciples of Jesus were commissioned to go and preach the gospel, making disciples of every nation. No longer was the Jewish nation the only people allowed within a covenant relationship with God [this occurred in Acts 10]. Jesus had become the Good Shepherd who was gathering His sheep from across the world.[34]

Also, we should not immediately think *rapture* when we see the word *gather.* Contextually, Jesus had spoken of gathering previously as the bringing together of Jews and Gentiles, which He did by His Atonement:

> *He did not say this on his own, but as high priest that year he prophesied that Jesus would die for the Jewish nation, and not only for that nation but also for the scattered children of God, to bring them together and make them one* (John 11:51–52).

A final thought on the gathering together comes from DeMar:

> These messengers in Matthew 24:31 call together God's people "from the four winds," a reference to the four corners of the earth (Zech. 2:6; 13:29), and from one end of the sky to the other. This is a reference to the entire horizon of the world (Psalm 22:27; Deut. 4:32; Matt. 28:18-20). We should not be pressed to interpret "four winds" in a scientific fashion. "Four winds" suggests a square world, as does "four corners of the earth" or "land of Israel" (Isa. 11:12; Ezek. 7:2; Rev. 7:1; 20:8). The Bible, speaking in theological terms, depicts the earth as a house. Heaven is described in a similar fashion (John 14:2). None of this language suggests that the earth is flat or a cube, something that a wooden literalism would demand. The Bible alludes to the earth's circularity in Isaiah 40:22: "'It is he that sits upon the circle of the earth'—'circle' being the translation of the

> Hebrew khug, sphere." By using this metaphor of the four winds, Jesus is telling us that the elect are gathered from everywhere, not limited to the land, or house (Matt. 15:24), of Israel (8:11).[35]

The Fig Tree

> *Now learn this lesson from the fig tree: As soon as its twigs get tender and its leaves come out, you know that summer is near. Even so, when you see all these things, you know that it is near, right at the door* (Matthew 24:32-33).

This is a simple parable; in the same way that there are signs that summer is near, there would be obvious signs that the destruction of Jerusalem was upon them. The most obvious are the first eight signs. There is no deeper meaning about Israel being restored as a nation in this verse. Because Adam covered himself with fig leaves, the fig is typically a negative symbol. Jesus also had previously cursed the fig tree (see Mark 11:12–14).

Also, we can see from the parallel passage in Luke that Jesus' point was not about the type of tree being a representation but that trees blossoming in the springtime are parabolic of how obvious these signs of the destruction would be. Notice the generalization of *trees.*

> *He told them this parable: "Look at the fig tree and all the trees. When they sprout leaves, you can see for yourselves and know that summer is near. Even so, when you see these things happening, you know that the Kingdom of God is near"* (Luke 21:29–31).

Surprisingly, John Walvoord, a dispensationalist, agrees that the fig tree does not represent Israel:

> Actually, while the fig tree could be an apt illustration of Israel, it is not so used in the Bible. In Jeremiah 24:1–8, good and bad figs illustrate Israel in the captivity, and there is also mention of figs in 29:17. The reference to the fig tree in Judges 9:10–11 is obviously not Israel. Neither the reference in Matthew 21:18–20 nor that in Mark 11:12–14 with its interpretation in 11:20–26, gives any indication that it is referring to Israel, any more than

the mountain referred to in the passage. Accordingly, while this interpretation is held by many, there is no clear scriptural warrant.

A better interpretation is that Christ was using a natural illustration. Because the fig tree brings forth new leaves late in the spring, the budding of the leaves is evidence that summer is near. In a similar way, when those living in the great tribulation see the signs predicted, this will know that the second coming of Christ is near. The signs in this passage, accordingly, are not the revival of Israel, but the great tribulation.[36]

This Generation

Truly I tell you, this generation will certainly not pass away until all these things have happened. Heaven and earth will pass away, but my words will never pass away (Matthew 24:34-35).

To the Jewish people, a generation is forty years. This is visible in the fact that a "generation" died in the wilderness during the forty-year journey (see Deut. 29:5). Therefore, Jesus was saying that this prophecy would happen before forty years had gone by. Jesus said this in AD 30, and the entirety of His Matthew 24 prophecy was fulfilled in AD 70.

Some have tried to make the word *generation* into *race*, as in, "the Jewish race will not pass away until all these things have come to pass." David Chilton responds to this idea excellently:

> *Not one* of these references [to the word *generation* in the New Testament] is speaking of the entire Jewish race over thousands of years; *all use the word in its normal sense of the sum total of those living at the sum total of those living at the same time.* It always refers to *contemporaries.* (In fact, those who say it means "race" tend to acknowledge this fact, but explain that the word suddenly *changes* its meaning when Jesus uses it in Matthew 24:34! We can smile at such transparent error, but we should also remember that this is very serious. We are dealing with the Word of the living God.)[37]

Also, I am regularly asked, *How could God have poured out such judgment and wrath upon that generation?* Perhaps a survey of what God said about that evil generation would help. Here are twelve statements I have paraphrased from my own study of the New Testament.

1. ***This generation*** never responded correctly to God (see Matt. 11:16–19; Luke 7:31–34).
2. When ***this generation*** came to demand a sign, Jesus wouldn't s ubmit to their demands (see Mark 8:11–12).
3. ***This generation*** was called wicked, adulterous, sinful, unbelieving, perverse, warped, and crooked (see Luke 9:41; 11:29; Mark 8:38; 9:19; Matt. 17:17; Phil. 2:15).
4. The Queen of Sheba would have condemned ***this generation*** (see Matt. 12:42; Luke 11:31).
5. Even the men of Nineveh would have condemned ***this generation*** (see Matt. 12:41; Luke 11:32).
6. As Jonah was a sign of judgment to Nineveh, so Jesus was a sign of judgment upon ***this generation*** (see Luke 11:30).
7. Jesus would suffer many things and be rejected by ***this generation*** (see Luke 17:25).
8. ***This generation*** would not pass away until all the curses of Matthew 23 would come upon ***this generation*** (see Matt 23:34,36).
9. ***This generation*** wouldn't pass away until the destruction of Jerusalem had occurred (see Mark 13:30; Luke 21:32; Matt. 24:34).
10. All the sin and bloodshed of the Old Testament would be charged against ***this generation*** (see Luke 11:49–51).
11. After Jesus swept Jerusalem clean spiritually, Jerusalem became seven times worse in that wicked ***generation*** leading up to the AD 70 destruction (see Matt. 12:43–45).
12. Peter pled with his audience to save themselves from the corruptness of ***this generation*** (see Acts 2:40).

These were dark days indeed, darker than we might imagine. This is why Jesus made a comparison between that generation and the generation alive during the days of Noah. The Bible tells us that, because of the evil of that generation, God actually regretted making humanity (see Gen. 6:6).

No One Knows the Hour

In that context, Jesus made this declaration about the coming destruction:

> *But about that day or hour no one knows, not even the angels in heaven, nor the Son, but only the Father. As it was in the days of Noah, so it will be at the coming of the Son of Man. For in the days before the flood, people were eating and drinking, marrying and giving in marriage, up to the day Noah entered the ark; and they knew nothing about what would happen until the flood came and took them all away. That is how it will be at the coming of the Son of Man* (Matthew 24:36-39).

There was no clearer picture of utter destruction than Noah's flood to the Jewish mind. In the days of the flood, Noah declared a coming destruction, yet people carried on with normal life and ignored his warnings. They ignored him right to the last moment, when they were then destroyed. So it was in AD 70, when Jesus in His *coming* destroyed Jerusalem like the flood. As we discussed earlier, *coming*, as used throughout Matthew 24, indicates God coming in judgment, not the final return of Christ (more on this in the next chapter).

Gary DeMar has compiled excellent information regarding Matthew 24:36 from the famous commentaries of John Gill, Adam Clarke, and John Lightfoot.

> John Gill writes: *But of that day and hour knoweth no man, &c.*] Which is to be understood, not of the second coming of Christ, the end of the world, and the last judgment; but of the coming of the son of man, to take vengeance on the Jews, and of their destruction; for the words manifestly regard the date of the several things going on before, which only can be applied to that catastrophe, and dreadful desolation.

Gill assumes that the previous context of the chapter governs the meaning of "that day." As was pointed out above, Matthew 24:29 is a familiar Old Testament description of the "passing away of heaven and earth," that is, the end of a social, religious, and political system.

Adam Clarke offers a similar interpretation: "Verse 36. *But of that day and hour*] [The Greek word] *Ora* is translated *season* by many eminent critics, and is used in this sense by both sacred and profane authors. As the *day* was not known, in which Jerusalem should be invested by the Romans, therefore our Lord advised his disciples to pray that it might not be on a *Sabbath*; and as the *season* was not known, therefore they were to pray that is might not be in the *winter*; ver. 20. See on Mark xiii 32.

John Lightfoot's comments show that the only possible reference was to the destruction of Jerusalem in A.D. 70: "That the discourse is of the day of the destruction of Jerusalem is so evident, both by the disciples' question, and by the whole thread of Christ's discourse, that it is a wonder any should understand these words of the *day and hour* of the last judgment.[38]

One Taken, One Left

Two men will be in the field; one will be taken and the other left. Two women will be grinding with a hand mill; one will be taken and the other left (Matthew 24:40-41).

As I discussed in the previous chapter on the rapture, these verses are in reference to the arbitrary way in which the Romans would seize upon and kill the Jews in AD 70.

Keep Watch

Therefore ***keep watch****, because you do not know on what day your Lord will come. But understand this: If the owner of the house had known at what time*

> *of night the thief was coming, he would have kept watch and would not have let his house be broken into. So you also must* ***be ready****, because the Son of Man will come at an hour when* ***you do not expect him****.*
>
> *Who then is the faithful and wise servant, whom the master has put in charge of the servants in his household to give them their food at the proper time? It will be good for that servant whose master finds him doing so when he returns. Truly I tell you, he will put him in charge of all his possessions. But suppose that servant is wicked and says to himself,* ***"My master is staying away a long time,"*** *and he then begins to beat his fellow servants and to eat and drink with drunkards. The master of that servant will come on a day when he* ***does not expect him*** *and at an hour he is not aware of. He will cut him to pieces and assign him a place with the hypocrites, where there will be weeping and gnashing of teeth* (Matthew 24:42-51).

Verses 42–51 are a connected admonition to keep watch, be ready, and be expectant. It would have been a temptation for the Christians, over the course of forty years of waiting, to become complacent and even unbelieving that Jesus would be coming in judgment upon Jerusalem. In fact, we find in Second Peter 3:4 that there were even people mocking Jesus prophecy saying, *"Where is this 'coming' he promised? Ever since our ancestors died, everything goes on as it has since the beginning of creation."* Notice even in this remark that *coming* is in quotations because this was not in reference to Jesus' final return, but was the Hebrew figure of speech regarding the judgment of God upon a city.

The servant in the story thought that the master (Jesus) was going to be gone a long time, but he was completely wrong and was caught by surprise. The fact is that Jesus has been gone a long time, but this parable illustrates how people during the period of time between AD 30 and AD 70 thought that Jesus' coming to bring judgment was a long way off, and they were caught by surprise.

In Summary

I know that for many of you, this has probably been completely new information. If you need to confirm the accuracy of what you just read, it is a matter of public record. By reading the works of the historians—Josephus, Eusebius, and Tacitus—as well as looking up a few Greek root words in *Vine's Expository Dictionary,* you can confirm everything contained in this chapter.

Also, I recognize that what you just read was incredibly graphic and heart-wrenching. As I mentioned at the beginning of this chapter, the first time I read Holford's work, I had tears streaming down my face while on an airplane. Although graphic, this portion of history is important to understand as a Christian.

David Chilton has written an excellent summary of this period:

> Josephus has left us an eyewitness record of much of the horror of those years, and especially of the final days in Jerusalem. It was a time when "the day-time was spent in the shedding of blood, and the night in fear"; when it was "common to see cities filled with dead bodies"; when Jews panicked and began indiscriminately killing each other; when fathers tearfully slaughtered their entire families, in order to prevent them from receiving worse treatment from the Romans; when, in the midst of terrible famine, mothers killed, roasted, and ate their own children (cf. Deuteronomy 28:53); when the whole land "was all over filled with fire and blood"; when the lakes and seas turned red, dead bodies floating everywhere, littering the shores, bloating in the sun, rotting and splitting apart; when the Roman soldiers captured people attempting to escape and then crucified them—at the rate of 500 per day.[39]

CHAPTER POINTS

- In Matthew 24, Jesus prophesied the Great Tribulation, which happened in AD 70 during the destruction of Jerusalem.
- The events of AD 70 happened within the timeframe that Jesus gave—a generation, or forty years.
- Jesus gave eight signs that would precede the Great Tribulation, and all were fulfilled prior to AD 70.
- There is no future Great Tribulation. Jesus said that nothing so terrible had ever happened before or would ever happen again.

DISCUSSION QUESTIONS

1. Did you consider skipping this chapter? Why or why not?

2. Did you know so many major church leaders throughout history believed Matthew 24 already happened at AD 70?

3. Have you ever heard of the events of AD 70? How did learning about AD 70 make you feel?

4. Have you ever considered Matthew 24 as a fulfilled prophecy before? Why or why not?

5. What parts of this chapter were the most memorable or stunning? What did you find convincing and why? What parts are you still questioning and why?

THE END OF THE WORLD

In Matthew 24, we found that the disciples asked Jesus three questions: *"Tell us,"* they said, *"when will this happen, and what will be the sign of your coming and of the end of the age?"* (Matt. 24:3).

As we saw in the previous chapter, in Matthew 24 Jesus prophesied exactly what would take place in the destruction of Jerusalem and the Temple in AD 70. But did Jesus answer the other two questions: "What is the sign of your coming and of the end of the age?" Before we can understand the answers Jesus gave, we have to be sure that we understand all three questions.

Question #1: "When will this happen?"

This question is clearly in reference to what Jesus had *just* been saying about the destruction of the Temple and Jerusalem being left desolate. Since we have already focused on this in the previous chapter, I will focus more on the second and third questions.

Question #2: "What is the sign of your coming?"

The automatic, almost knee-jerk reaction is to think that the disciples were asking about Jesus' second coming. But if we step back and think for a moment, we will remember that the disciples had no idea that Jesus was about to die and be resurrected. It is unrealistic to think they were asking

Jesus about His second coming, which would be thousands of years away. They were still in shock about Jesus chewing out the Pharisees; they weren't suddenly asking Jesus about His second coming, but about something else very similar and closely related to the first question.

After Jesus answered their first question in great detail, He responded about the sign of His "coming":

> *And then the sign of the son of man will appear in the sky, and then all the tribes of the earth* [literally, "tribes of the land"] *will mourn, and they will see* ***the son of man coming on the clouds of the sky*** *with power and great glory* (Matthew 24:30 NASB).

Keeping in mind that the disciples were not asking about Jesus' second coming, thousands of years later, here is a much more sensible understanding of what they were truly asking. The Bible scholar David Chilton says regarding this passage:

> In order to understand the meaning of Jesus' expressions in this passage, we need to understand the Old Testament much more than most people do today. Jesus was speaking to an audience that was intimately familiar with the most obscure details of Old Testament literature. They had heard the Old Testament read and expounded countless time throughout their lives, and had memorized lengthy passages. Biblical imagery and forms of expression had formed their culture, environment, and vocabulary from earliest infancy, and this had been true for generations. The fact is that when Jesus spoke to His disciples about the fall of Jerusalem, He used prophetic vocabulary. There was a "language" of prophecy, instantly recognizable to those familiar with the Old Testament.[1]

Knowing the Jewish culture, Jesus answered that they would see "the SON OF MAN COMING ON THE CLOUDS OF THE SKY with power and great glory" (Matt. 24:30). Throughout the Old Testament, when God was going to bring destruction upon a city or a nation, it was said that He would "come on clouds in the sky." In the Jewish culture, the phrase *"sign of your coming"* had little to do with location and arrival. It was understood to mean, "to come in judgment upon a city or nation," as we will see in the following verses.

Each of the following passages was fulfilled by the destruction of an Old Testament city or nation:

> *He parted the heavens and came down;* ***dark clouds*** *were under his feet. He mounted the cherubim and flew; he soared on the wings of the wind. He made darkness his covering, his canopy around him—**the dark rain clouds of the sky. Out of the brightness of his presence clouds advanced,** with hailstones and bolts of lightning* (Psalm 18:9-12).

> *The LORD wraps himself in light as with a garment; he stretches out the heavens like a tent and lays the beams of his upper chambers on their waters.* ***He makes the clouds his chariot*** *and rides on the wings of the wind* (Psalm 104:2-3).

> *A prophecy against Egypt: See, the LORD rides* ***on a swift cloud and is coming*** *to Egypt. The idols of Egypt tremble before him, and the hearts of the Egyptians melt with fear* (Isaiah 19:1).

> *Blow the trumpet in Zion; sound the alarm on my holy hill. Let all who live in the land tremble, for the day of the LORD is coming. It is close at hand—a day of darkness and gloom,* ***a day of clouds*** *and blackness. Like dawn spreading across the mountains a large and mighty army comes, such as never was in ancient times nor ever will be in ages to come* (Joel 2:1-2).

> *The great day of the LORD is near—near and coming quickly. The cry on the day of the LORD is bitter; the Mighty Warrior shouts his battle cry. That day will be a day of wrath—a day of distress and anguish, a day of trouble and ruin, a day of darkness and gloom,* ***a day of clouds*** *and blackness* (Zephaniah 1:14-15).

> *The LORD is slow to anger but great in power; the LORD will not leave the guilty unpunished. His way is in the whirlwind and the storm, and* ***clouds are the dust of his feet*** (Nahum 1:3).

Now that we have some of the Hebraic cultural context, we can understand that: 1) the disciples were asking about when Jesus would "come" in judgment upon Jerusalem, and 2) Jesus responded with many signs that would lead up to verse 30, where He would finally "come on clouds" and bring judgment.

Question #3: "What about the end of the age?"

As a modern reader, it is easy to jump to the conclusion that the disciples were now asking about the end of the world. Yet, there is no sensible explanation for why they would suddenly be over the shock of Jesus rebuking the Pharisees and declaring the destruction of the Temple. It just doesn't make logical sense, in context, that they would be suddenly switching topics mid-sentence to ask about something completely unrelated. Therefore, it only fits that the disciples were still asking questions about their immediate thoughts. When they asked about the "end of the age," they were *not* asking about the *end of the world.*

This is easily confirmed by looking at the original languages. In Greek, the word for "world" is *kosmos*, whereas the word for "age" is *aion*. The disciples asked Jesus about the end of the *aion*. They did not ask about the end of the *kosmos*.

So if they were not asking about the end of the world, what were they asking Jesus about? It is clear from the context that Jesus was going to come and bring destruction to Jerusalem and the Temple; therefore, if the Temple was destroyed, it would mean the end of sacrifice. No Temple would mean no more sacrifice, which would mean no more priesthood and rituals. This would be the end of an age or, as we might say it, *the end of an era*. The disciples were asking when *the end of the Age of Moses*, which Jesus had just prophesied, would happen.

The Jewish people recognized two ages—the one in which they then lived (under the Law) and the future age of the Messiah. "A common Jewish conception was that the appearing of the Messiah would close 'this age,' and introduce 'the coming age'—these phrases often occurring in the Talmud."[2]

Another commentator wrote:

> Time was divided by the Jews into two great periods, the age of the law and the age of the Messiah. The conclusion of the one was the beginning of the other, the opening of that kingdom which the Jews believed the Messiah was to establish, which was to put an end to their sufferings, and to render them the greatest people upon the earth. The apostles, full of this hope, said to our Lord, immediately before his ascension, "Lord, wilt thou at this time restore the kingdom to Israel?" [Acts 1:6]. Our Lord used the phrase of his coming to denote his taking vengeance upon the Jews by destroying their city and sanctuary.[3]

Throughout the New Testament, there is much written about the Age of Moses, which was about to come to an end, but there is very little said about the end of the whole world. Realizing that the Israelites had lived as the chosen people with exclusive access to God for approximately 4,000 years, we can understand that this was to be the single largest event to ever occur in national history. Also, it is interesting to note that Jesus was the only prophet prophesying that He was going to come on the clouds to destroy Jerusalem and that the Age of Moses was about to end. By comparison, all the false prophets were declaring that they had come to save Israel from the Roman rule.

Because many have taught that Jesus was talking about the end of the world, the understanding of many other verses has also been distorted. By realizing that the disciples were asking about the end of the Age of Moses, we can clearly understand many verses that are scattered throughout the New Testament. These verses are about the end of the Age of Moses and the destruction in AD 70; they are not about the end of the world. For example:

> ...*You* [the twelve] *will not have gone through the cities of Israel before the Son of Man comes* (Matthew 10:23).

> ...*You* [the high priest] *will see the Son of Man coming on the clouds of heaven* (Matthew 26:64).

> *Now it is high time to awake out of sleep...the night is far spent, the day is at hand...* (Romans 13:11-12).

> ...*The form of this world is passing away* (1 Corinthians 7:31 NASB).

> *On* [us]...*the ends of the ages have come* (1 Corinthians 10:11 NASB).

> ...*The Lord is at hand* (Philippians 4:5 NKJV).

> ...*The coming of the Lord is at hand.... Behold, the Judge is standing at the door* (James 5:8-9 NKJV).

> *The end of all things is at hand ...* (1 Peter 4:7 NKJV).

> ...*It is the last hour...we know that it is the last hour* (1 John 2:18 NKJV).

It is true that Jesus will return in bodily form to resurrect the dead and bring final judgment. Yet, most of the "end of the age" language used in the New Testament was in reference to the biggest thing ever in Jewish history—which was about to happen. The first-century Jews were not focused on the end of the planet; that is a modern obsession that had almost no relevance to them.

The End of the Age

To prove this, let's look at more passages that discuss the end of the age and, from them, glean the truth of what this phrase meant to first-century Christians.

Jesus' famous words in Matthew 28 are one of the most well-known passages about the end of the age: "teaching them to observe all things that I have commanded you; and lo, I am with you always, even to the end of the age" (Matt. 28:20 NKJV). In this reference to the "end of the age," Jesus was *not saying* that He would only be with them until AD 70. He specified that He would be with them *always*. But the disciples of the first century wouldn't have been focused on whether Jesus would be with His followers 2,000 years later. They would have been more focused on whether He would be *with them* when the end of the age came because Jesus' description in Matthew 24 of the way in which the end of the age would come was quite terrifying.

Another interesting and relevant quote from Jesus is found in Matthew 12.

> *Anyone who speaks a word against the Son of Man will be forgiven, but anyone who speaks against the Holy Spirit will not be forgiven, either in this age or in the age to come* (Matthew 12:32).

This verse is fascinating because Jesus was speaking during the Age of Moses, saying that blaspheming the Holy Spirit would not be forgiven in the Age of Moses or in the coming age—the Kingdom Age in which we are currently living.

Jesus also told a parable about the end of the age that many have wrongly interpreted to be about the end of the world.

> *Jesus told them another parable: "The kingdom of heaven is like a man who sowed good seed in his field. But while everyone was sleeping, his enemy came and sowed weeds among the wheat, and went away. When the wheat sprouted and formed heads, then the weeds also appeared. The owner's servants came to him and said, 'Sir, didn't you sow good seed in your field? Where then did the weeds come from?' 'An enemy did this,' he replied. The servants asked him, 'Do you want us to go and pull them up?' 'No,' he answered, 'because while you are pulling the weeds, you may uproot the wheat with them. Let both grow together until the harvest. At that time I will tell the harvesters: First collect the weeds and tie them in bundles to be burned; then gather the wheat and bring it into my barn"* (Matthew 13:24-30).

After Jesus shared this parable, His disciples were confused and asked Him to explain it to them. Now that we have the context, let's examine Jesus' explanation of the parable.

> *Then he left the crowd and went into the house. His disciples came to him and said, "Explain to us the parable of the weeds in the field." He answered, "The one who sowed the good seed is the Son of Man. The field is the world, and the good seed stands for the people of the kingdom. The weeds are the people of the evil one, and the enemy who sows them is the devil.* ***The harvest is the end of the age,*** *and the harvesters are angels. As the weeds are pulled up and burned in the fire, so it will be at* ***the end of the age.***

> *The Son of Man will send out his angels, and they will weed out of his kingdom everything that causes sin and all who do evil. They will throw them into **the blazing furnace,** where there will be **weeping and gnashing of teeth"*** (Matthew 13:36-42).

It is clear from the original manuscripts that the end of the age (*aion*) is in reference to the end of the Age of Moses, not the end of the planet earth. Yet, with a surface reading of this passage, it is easy to come to the conclusion that it is about the final judgment.

If we look closer, though, we can see that the phrase *blazing furnace* is not a reference to any of the normal terms that refer to eternal punishment, such as:

- Gehenna
- Sheol
- Hades
- The Lake of Fire

None of the Greek wording in this passage points to the final judgment. This is not about hell and the final judgment.

Jesus describes the blazing furnace as a place where there will be weeping and gnashing of teeth. If this parable was about hell and the final judgment, Jesus would have used His more normal descriptions, which include everlasting punishment (such as in Matt. 18:8; 25:46; Jude 7; 2 Thess. 1:9). Rather, here Jesus simply describes the emotional pain involved. This creates a clear demarcation between the blazing furnace and the places of eternal punishment mentioned above. They are not the same.

It is more sensible to understand this passage in its historical context. During the AD 70 destruction, Jerusalem literally became as a great "blazing furnace" that incinerated the bodies of thousands upon thousands of both the living and the dead. Jerusalem was consumed with the sounds of weeping and the painful gnashing of teeth in anguish—as Holford's book, quoted in the last chapter, so vividly described.

Clearly, if you were to put yourself in the mind of a first-century Christian living in Israel, you would understand that you only have forty years to spread the gospel before Jesus comes on clouds to destroy Jerusalem and you would have to flee to the mountains. You would use language in your letters speaking of it being *the last hour* and *the latter times,* and you would say things like, *He is standing at the door,* and *the Lord is at hand and the day is about to come.* We must choose to consciously stop taking what the New Testament authors meant for those living between AD 30 and AD 70 and applying it to our future.

Many false doctrines have been created by not reading the Bible according to its historical and cultural context. Two clear examples that we will look at next are the wrong expectations of an apostasy of the Church and coming false teachers.

Apostasy

One major false teaching that currently exists is the concept of a future "fallen apostate church." Some have even tried to force Church history into seven time periods and line them up with the seven churches in Revelation 2 and 3. These individuals say that the modern Church is the church of Laodicea, which Jesus threatened to vomit out of His mouth. Not only is this concept deeply incorrect, but it also contradicts everything Jesus said about His Kingdom growing (see Matt. 13:31–33).

Here are some of the verses that are used to substantiate this teaching.

> *Let no man deceive you by any means: for that day shall not come, except there come* ***a falling away first,*** *and that man of sin be revealed, the son of perdition* (2 Thessalonians 2:3 KJV).

This verse has been used extensively in the last fifty years to claim that the majority of the Church is not actually walking with God. Those who teach this say that the true Church is merely a remnant of those who claim to be the Church. But it is an error to drag the Old Testament remnant idea into the New Testament, where it does not belong (I will discuss this more in a later chapter). So this verse should not be used to substantiate that false doctrine. Also, it is important to note that this verse is about a rebellious person called the man of sin, not about the Church falling apart. This verse is better understood in the NIV translation:

Don't let anyone deceive you in any way, for that day will not come until ***the rebellion occurs*** *and the man of lawlessness is revealed, the man doomed to destruction* (2 Thessalonians 2:3).

The rebellion occurred in the first century under John Levi, as we saw in the previous chapter. We are not looking for a future "falling away" to fulfill this passage. (For easy reference, his name, **John Levi**, has been put in bold in The Great Tribulation chapter.)

False Teachers

Similar to the idea of the apostate Church is the belief that there will be many false teachers before the return of Christ. This has created a great excuse for finger-pointing in the Body of Christ and empowers a suspicious and fearful attitude toward others. As you may guess, however, the verses that are used to support this teaching were, in fact, referring to the time leading up to AD 70, not to our own day. For example:

For the time will come when people will not put up with sound doctrine. Instead, to suit their own desires, they will gather around them a great number of teachers to say what their itching ears want to hear. They will turn their ears away from the truth and turn aside to myths (2 Timothy 4:3-4).

The "sound doctrine" would have been that judgment was coming to Jerusalem, but the "itching ears" wanted to hear from false prophets and teachers that declared God's protection from destruction. This provided a stage for a major rise in false prophets and teachers between AD 30 and AD 70. Now look at this verse:

Now the Spirit expressly says that ***in latter times*** *some will depart from the faith, giving heed to deceiving spirits and doctrines of demons* (1 Timothy 4:1 NKJV).

These latter times referred to by Paul were not 2,000 years later. This was in reference to the false teachers and false prophets of the first century (the same is true of Second Timothy 3). We must choose to interpret Scripture correctly and not pull verses out of their intended context to fit our personal agenda.

Here is another passage that many have misunderstood:

> *"The days are coming," declares the Sovereign LORD, "when I will send a famine through the land—not a famine of food or a thirst for water, but a famine of hearing the words of the LORD"* (Amos 8:11).

This is not a New Testament prophecy. This was fulfilled by the 400 years between the end of the Old Testament and the start of the New Testament, where there is no recorded spoken word from God.

Now look at these two passages, the first from the apostle Paul and the second from Jesus:

> *I know that **after I leave,*** [not 2,000 years later] *savage wolves will come in among you and will not spare the flock. Even from your own number men will arise and distort the truth in order to draw away disciples after them. So be on your guard! Remember that for three years I never stopped warning each of you night and day with tears* (Acts 20:29-31).

> *And will not God bring about justice for his chosen ones, who cry out to him day and night? **Will he keep putting them off?** I tell you, **he will see that they get justice, and quickly.** However, when the Son of Man **comes,** will he find faith on the earth?* (Luke 18:7-8)

Will He keep putting them off? No, Jesus will not. He will see that they get justice quickly. Remember that the word *comes* is a reference to the first-century destruction of Jerusalem, not to events 2,000 years later. This was perfectly fulfilled; they got justice and quickly!

CHAPTER POINTS

- There is no separation in the three questions that the disciples asked Jesus.
- There is no separation in the answers that Jesus gave His disciples.
- When the New Testament mentions the end of the age, it is referring to the end of the Age of Moses, not the end of the world.
- The idea of the seven churches of Revelation corresponding with seven periods in Church history has no foundation.
- The Kingdom of God is growing, and we are not looking for a future "falling away" of the Church.
- The passages that speak of false teachers, teachings, and prophets were all fulfilled in the first century. These have no *prophetic* significance for the modern day, although they have *practical* significance. We still need to use discernment regarding teaching and judge the fruit, but we are not looking for a future apostasy.

DISCUSSION QUESTIONS

1. What are the three questions of Matthew 24:3?
2. Would the disciples be asking about the end of the world and the rapture in this passage? Why or why not?
3. Define the meanings of *aion* and *kosmos.*
4. Explain the important difference of translation between *end of the world* and *end of the age* in Matthew 24:3.
5. What does *end of the age* mean? When was the end of the age?
6. Since the last days of the Mosaic Age ended in AD 70, what *age* do we live in now?

chapter five

MELTING ELEMENTS

For almost two decades, I believed that one day in the future the whole earth would be consumed by fire when Jesus returned. Considering that God had promised Noah that He wouldn't use water to destroy the earth (see Gen. 9:11), I figured He would be able to destroy the earth with fire and still keep His promise to Noah. This was my understanding of Second Peter 3:5–7:

> *But they deliberately forget that long ago by God's word the heavens came into being and the earth was formed out of water and by water. By these waters also the world of that time was deluged and destroyed. By the same word the present heavens and earth* [Ge] *are reserved for fire, being kept for the day of judgment and destruction of the ungodly.*

Like many others, I had never looked very closely at the context of this passage and had simply arrived at my conclusion: Peter was describing God's crafty way around His promise to Noah by destroying earth without using water. Now that I have studied this passage, it is humorous to look back at what I used to think. It makes me wonder sometimes how wrong I might still be in other areas I haven't studied yet.

Awaiting His Coming

Here I would like to show you the context of Second Peter 3, starting with verse one.

> *Dear friends, this is now my second letter to you. I have written both of them as reminders to stimulate you to wholesome thinking. I want you to recall the words spoken in the past by the holy prophets and the command given by our Lord and Savior through your apostles* (2 Peter 3:1-2).

In this letter, Peter is going to remind his readers about some specific words and commands given from (1) the Old Testament, (2) Jesus, and (3) the apostles. He hasn't told us yet what He is referring to, but he will in the next verses.

> *Above all, you must understand that in the last days scoffers will come, scoffing and following their own evil desires. They will say, "**Where is this 'coming' he promised?** Ever since our ancestors died, everything goes on as it has since the beginning of creation"* (2 Peter 3:3-4).

Peter has now clarified that he is referring to Jesus' promise that He would "come," which as we learned previously, is a reference to the destruction of Jerusalem. The historical context of Peter's writing is between AD 30 and AD 70. At that time, the Jews were bringing tremendous persecution upon the Christians. The Christians were clinging to the hope of Jesus' words in Matthew 24 that judgment was about to come upon Jerusalem and the religious system. As we see in the above passage, the Christians were being mocked for believing that Jesus was actually coming to bring judgment upon the Temple.

> *But they deliberately forget that long ago by God's word the heavens came into being and the earth was formed out of water and by water. By these waters also the world of that time was deluged and destroyed. By the same word the present heavens and earth* [Ge] *are reserved for fire, being kept for the day of judgment and destruction of the ungodly* (2 Peter 3:5-7).

Peter is now responding to the mocker's statements by showing how God has judged before and affirming that God will judge again.

> *But do not forget this one thing, dear friends: With the Lord a day is like a thousand years, and a thousand years are like a day* (2 Peter 3:8).

If there is one passage that is abused more than almost any other, it is 2 Peter

3:8. Countless people have used this passage to make prophetic mathematics work in their wild end-time theories. Yet Peter is simply quoting from Psalm 90:4; he was not proposing a formula by which to figure out the end of the world. *"For a thousand years in your sight are like a day that has just gone by, or like a watch in the night"* (Psalm 90:4).

Peter was *not* saying that to God time is nebulous or relative. Peter was quoting from a psalm that speaks of how time is of little value or importance to an infinite eternal God. Time is real to God, but not in the same way as it is for us.

> *The Lord is not slow in keeping his promise, as some understand slowness.* ***Instead he is patient with you, not wanting anyone to perish, but everyone to come to repentance*** (2 Peter 3:9).

In Matthew 24:34, Jesus said His words would come to pass *within* a generation. Here is a simple equation for the timeframe of his prophecy: AD 30 + forty-year generation = AD 70. Jesus could have come back in AD 50, midway through the prophesied generation, but He chose to wait until the last moment of His forty-year prophecy so that people would have more time to repent.

> *But the day of the Lord will come like a thief. The heavens will disappear with a roar;* ***the elements will be destroyed*** *by fire…* (2 Peter 3:10).

The phrase *the elements will be destroyed* is tremendously significant in understanding this whole chapter. Since it appears again in the passage, I will address this phrase further in a moment.

> *…and the* ***earth…*** (2 Peter 3:10).

The word for "earth" used here in the Greek is *ge*, not *kosmos*. *Ge* is the word for "land," whereas *kosmos* is the word for "the whole world." This is not about the destruction of the planet earth (*kosmos*), but it is about the destruction of the land of Israel (*ge*).

> *…and* ***everything done in it*** *will be laid bare* (2 Peter 3:10).

Since the root word ge is used, this verse is clearly saying, *"everything done in it* [in the land] *will be laid bare."* This is exactly what took place at the AD 70 destruction. The sacrifices were stopped, the priesthood was killed, the Temple was destroyed, and the buildings were leveled to the ground. Jerusalem was laid bare.

> ***Since everything will be destroyed in this way,*** *what kind of people ought you to be? You ought to live holy and godly lives as you look forward to the day of God and speed its coming...* (2 Peter 3:11-12).

The question Peter poses to his readers is: "Considering that this great wrath is about to be poured out upon the religious system, how should one live?" Peter encourages his readers to live godly lives as they await and hasten the arrival of the Day of the Lord. This is not an isolated reference; throughout the New Testament, we read that the first-century believers were eagerly awaiting the *coming* of the Lord (see 1 Cor. 1:6–8; Phil. 3:20; 1 Thess. 1:9–10).

One element of waiting for Jesus' coming was *hastening it,* and Jesus instructed His disciples concerning how they were to hasten His arrival. He told them that if they petitioned God for justice, God would certainly hear their prayers and avenge them quickly by means of the coming of the Son of Man.

> *And will not God bring about justice for his chosen ones, who cry out to him day and night? Will he keep putting them off? I tell you, he will see that they get justice, and quickly. However, when the Son of Man comes, will he find faith on the earth?"* (Luke 18:7-8)

The first-century Church under persecution cried out to God *day and night.* This was a part of the hastening process.

The Elements

Peter continued his letter, saying:

> *...That day will bring about the destruction of the heavens by fire, and* ***the elements*** *will melt in the heat* (2 Peter 3:12).

The Greek word Peter used for "elements" is *stoicheion*. This word appears only five other times in the New Testament (see Gal. 4:3, 9; Col. 2:8, 20; Heb. 5:12), and in each occurrence, it refers to the basic principles of the Mosaic Law.

In Galatians, Paul referred twice to these elements. First, he stated that the Jews had been under the elements of the world until the fullness of time had come; then, he asked his readers why they would want to return to these elements.

> *So also, when we were underage, we were in slavery under the elemental spiritual forces of the world* (Galatians 4:3).

> *But now after you have known God, or rather are known by God, how is it that you turn again to the weak and beggarly* ***elements,*** *to which you desire again to be in bondage?* (Galatians 4:9 NKJV)

In context, these elements concerned rituals and observances of feast days (see Gal. 4:9-10). Thus, Paul was trying to keep his readers from coming under the principles of the Law again (see Gal. 5:1).

In Colossians, Paul also referred twice to these elements, warning his readers not to let anyone hold them captive to the elements of the world, for by accepting Christ, they had died to these elements; therefore, they did not need to submit to such things (see Col. 2:8,20–22).

> *See to it that no one takes you captive through hollow and deceptive philosophy, which depends on human tradition and the* ***elemental*** *spiritual forces of this world rather than on Christ* (Colossians 2:8).

> *Since you died with Christ to the* ***elemental*** *spiritual forces of this world, why, as though you still belonged to the world, do you submit to its rules: "Do not handle! Do not taste! Do not touch!"?* ***These rules,*** *which have to do with things that are* ***all destined to perish*** *with use, are based on merely human commands and teachings* (Colossians 2:20-22).

As the context of this letter makes clear, Paul was encouraging his readers not to let anyone judge them for failing to observe feast days, festivals, and

Sabbaths because those things merely foreshadowed the person and work of Christ (see Col. 2:16). So again, we find that the elements of the world referred to the principles of Judaism—and Paul went on to remind his readers that these rules were destined to perish!

The writer of Hebrews also commented on these elements saying:

> *By this time you ought to be teachers, you need someone to teach you the* ***elementary*** [stoicheion] ***truths*** [logion] *of God's word all over again. You need milk, not solid food* (Hebrews 5:12).

The Greek word the writer used for "truths" is *logion*, a word used elsewhere in the New Testament to refer to the Old Covenant (see Acts 7:38; Rom. 3:2). In context, the author was expressing regret that he had to teach his Jewish readers how the basics of the Law foreshadowed the work of Christ in order to implore them to leave those principles for the sake of a new and better covenant (see Heb. 5:12–14; 6:1; 7:22; 10:1). The apostle Peter was not talking about the destruction of the elements as in the elements of the periodic table. He was writing of the destruction of the elements of Judaism.

New Heaven and New Earth

In the next verse of Second Peter 3, Peter makes an important shift:

> *But in keeping with his promise we are looking forward to a new heaven and a new earth, where righteousness dwells* (2 Peter 3:13).

As you will remember, Peter started this chapter by saying, "I want you to recall the words spoken in the past by *the holy prophets* and the command given by our *Lord and Savior* through your *apostles*" (2 Pet. 3:2). This is important because, in verses 3–12, Peter has been speaking of the prophecy from Jesus in Matthew 24.

Up until this point, Peter has not yet quoted from the ***holy prophets*** of old. In verse 13, Peter makes a departure from the words of the apostles (Paul and the destruction of the Jewish elements) and from the words of Jesus (about the destruction of the land). And Peter begins to quote from the *holy prophets* of old:

> *For, behold, I create new heavens, and a new earth: and the former shall not be remembered, nor come into mind* (Isaiah 65:17 NASB).

> *"For as the new heavens and the new earth which I will make shall remain before Me," says the LORD...* (Isaiah 66:22 NKJV).

Like Peter and the holy prophets, we also are looking forward to the new heavens and the new earth (just as John also saw it in Revelation 21:1).

Peter then continues:

> *So then, dear friends, since you are looking forward to this, make every effort to be found spotless, blameless and at peace with him. Bear in mind that our Lord's patience means salvation,* ***just as our dear brother Paul also wrote you*** *with the wisdom that God gave him. He writes the same way* ***in all his letters, speaking in them of these matters.*** *His letters contain some things that are hard to understand, which ignorant and unstable people distort, as they do the other Scriptures, to their own destruction* (2 Peter 3:14-16).

As Peter concluded his prophecy concerning the burning of the elements of the world, he declared that he was writing of the same things of which Paul wrote. As we have seen, when Paul wrote concerning the elements of the world, he was referring to the basic principles of the Old Covenant. Thus, our understanding that Peter was speaking of the passing of *the elements of Judaism* is further confirmed.

Confirming Voices

Although what I have presented in this chapter may seem deeply unfamiliar to many readers, it is by no means an obscure interpretation. In his book, *Last Days Madness*, Gary DeMar also connects the "End of the Age" (from Matt. 24:3) to the end of the Mosaic Covenant in AD 70. He demonstrates this from Second Peter 3 especially. DeMar brings out the following information from the famous commentators John Owen and John Lightfoot:

> John Owen (1616–1683) maintained that the "passing of heaven and earth" in 2 Peter 3:5–7 had reference, "not to the last and final

judgment of the world, but to that utter desolation and destruction that was to be made of the Judaical church and state" in A.D. 70. John Brown (1784–1858), commenting on Matthew 5:18, follows the same methodology.

> "Heaven and earth passing away," understood literally, is the dissolution of the present system of the universe; and the period when that is to take place, is called the "end of the world." But a person at all familiar with the phraseology of the Old Testament Scriptures, knows that the dissolution of the Mosaic economy, and the establishment of the Christian, is often spoken of as the removing of the old earth and heavens, and the creation of a new earth and new heavens."
>
> After surveying how this language is used throughout the Bible and in Jewish literature, John Lightfoot applies the "passing away of heaven and earth" to the "destruction of Jerusalem and the whole Jewish state...as if the whole frame of this world were to be dissolved."[4]

I believe DeMar has hit the nail on the head and drives home one of the major points of the New Testament, the removal of the Old Covenant and its world.

Maimonides also observes that:

> The Arabs likewise [as the Hebrew prophets] say of a person who has met with a serious accident, "His heavens, together with his earth, have been covered"; and when they speak of the approach of a nation's prosperity, they say, "The light of the sun and moon has increased," A new heaven and a new earth has been created," or they use similar phrases.[5]

Moreover, Josephus records how the Temple (tabernacle) was a representation of the universe—the heavens and earth:

> ...for if any one do but consider the fabric of the tabernacle, and take a view of the garments of the high priest, and of those vessels which we make use of in our sacred ministration, he will find that our legislator was a divine man, and that we are unjustly reproached by others; for if any one do without prejudice, and with judgment, look upon these

things, he will find they were everyone made in way of imitation and representation of the universe. When Moses distinguished the tabernacle into three parts, and allowed two of them to the priests, as a place accessible and common, he denoted the land and the seas, these being of general access to all; but he set apart the third division for God, because heaven is inaccessible to men. And when he ordered twelve loaves to be set on the table, he denoted the year, as distinguished into so many months. By branching out the candlestick into seventy parts, he secretly intimated the Decani, or seventy divisions of the planets; and as to the seven lamps upon the candlesticks, they referred to the course of the planets, of which that is the number. The veils, too, which were composed of four things, they declared the four elements; for the fine linen was proper to signify the earth, because the flax grows out of the earth; the purple signified the seas, because that color is dyed by the blood of a seas shell-fish; the blue is fit to signify the air; and the scarlet will naturally be an indication of fire. Now the vestment of the high priest being made of linen, signified the earth; the blue denoted the sky, being like lightning in its pomegranates, and in the noise of the bells resembling thunder. And for the ephod, it showed that God had made the universe of four elements; and as for the gold interwoven, I suppose it related to the splendor by which all things are enlightened. He also appointed the breastplate to be placed in the middle of the ephod, to resemble the earth, for that has the very middle place of the world. And the girdle which encompassed the high priest round, signified the ocean, for that goes round about and includes the universe. Each of the sardonyxes declares to us the sun and moon; those, I mean, that were in the nature of buttons on the high priest's shoulders. And for the twelve stones, whether we understand by them the months, or whether we understand the like number of the signs of that circle which the Greeks call the Zodiac, we shall not be mistaken in their meaning. And for the mitre, which was of a blue color, it seems to me to mean heaven; for how otherwise could the name of God be inscribed upon it? That it was also illustrated with a crown, and that of gold also, is because of that splendor with which God is pleased. Let this explication suffice at present, since the course of my narration will often, and on many occasions, afford me the opportunity of enlarging upon the virtue of our legislator.[6]

Since we have seen that the heavens, earth, and elements were references to the Mosaic Age and its passing away, we will benefit from examining one last passage of Scripture, "the shaking of the heavens and earth" in Hebrews 12:

> *See to it that you do not refuse him who speaks. If they did not escape when they refused him who warned them on earth, how much less will we, if we turn away from him who warns us from heaven? At that time his voice shook the earth, but now he has promised, "Once more I will shake not only the earth but also the heavens."* ***The words "once more" indicate the removing of what can be shaken—that is, created things—so that what cannot be shaken may remain.*** *Therefore,* ***since we are receiving a kingdom*** *that cannot be shaken, let us be thankful, and so worship God acceptably with reverence and awe* (Hebrews 12:25–28).

The one last "shaking" in Hebrews 12:25–28 is specifically referring to the removal of the physical, natural Temple age of the first century. It was about to be shaken, and only the invisible Kingdom of God would remain once the shaking of AD 70 was finished. Disappointingly, many preachers reference Hebrews 12 when major catastrophes occur, such as earthquakes, economic downturns, wars, and terrorist attacks. They refer to Hebrews 12 out of its natural context because they do not understand its context. The writer of Hebrews was referring to AD 70 and nothing else. It was about moving from physical worship (see Heb. 12:18–21) to a spiritual form of worship (see Heb. 12:22–24).

Concerning this shaking of the earth and the heavens, Russell wrote:

> What, then, is the great catastrophe symbolically represented as the shaking of the earth and heavens? No doubt it is the over-throw and abolition of the Mosaic dispensation, or the old covenant; the destruction of the Jewish church and state, together with all the institutions and ordinances connected therewith. There were "heavenly things" belonging to that dispensation: the laws, and statutes, and ordinances, which were divine in their origin, and might be properly called the "*spiritualia*" of Judaism-these were the *heavens*, which were to be shaken and removed. There were the heavens, which were to be shaken and removed. There were also "earthly things": the literal Jerusalem, the material temple, the land of Canaan-these were the *earth*,

> which was in like manner to be shaken and removed. The symbols are, in fact, equivalent to those employed by our Lord when predicting the doom of Israel. "Immediately after the tribulation of those days shall the sun be darkened, and the moon shall not give her light, and the powers of *the heavens shall be shaken."* (Mt 24:29) Both passages refer to the same catastrophe and employ very similar figures; besides which we have the authority of our Lord for fixing the event and the period of which He speaks within the limits of the generation then in existence; that is to say, the references can only be to the judgment of the Jewish nation and the abrogation of the Mosaic economy at the Parousia.[7]

Regarding the transition from the Old Covenant world to the New Covenant world, consider C.H. Spurgeon's words:

> Did you ever regret the absence of the burnt-offering, or the red heifer, or any one of the sacrifices and rites of the Jews? Did you ever pine for the feast of tabernacles, or the dedication? No, because, though these were like the old heavens and earth to the Jewish believers, they have passed away, and we now live under new heavens and a new earth, so far as the dispensation of the divine teaching is concerned. The substance is come, and the shadow has gone: and we do not remember it.[8]

In Conclusion

We can learn two important points from this passage in Second Peter. First, we see that Peter was not speaking about the whole world being destroyed by fire. The word *elements* was, rather, a reference to the Mosaic Law. The Law was passing away. Second, by doing our research, we discover that *not one* verse in the New Testament predicts the destruction of the *kosmos*, of planet earth. When the New Testament speaks of the destruction of the world, it uses the root word *ge*, which means "land," not globe. There is not one verse that predicts the destruction of the globe!

CHAPTER POINTS

- In Second Peter 3, Peter reminds his readers of the words of Jesus in Matthew, Paul's teachings, and Old Testament prophecy—specifically in relation to the promised destruction of Jerusalem.
- Jesus came in judgment on Jerusalem at the end of the prophesied generation (forty years) to give people as much time as possible to repent.
- The word translated "earth" here is *ge*, meaning "land," not the planet earth. This prophecy is about the destruction of the land of Israel, not the whole world.
- Jesus said the early believers could "hasten" His coming by petitioning Him for justice.
- The phrase "the elements" refers to the Jewish Law, not to the periodic table elements, which is confirmed by many other New Testament passages.
- At the end of this passage, Peter refers to the prophets' words about the new heaven and new earth—something that we are yet looking forward to.

DISCUSSION QUESTIONS

1. Have each person summarize how they previously understood Second Peter 3 before they read this chapter.

2. What is the meaning and usage of the word *stoicheion* (elements)?

3. Regarding the heavens, earth, and elements passing away, could this be about the destruction of the Old Covenant system? Why or why not?

4. Where did Second Peter 3 fit into your thinking before? Where does it fit now?

THE ANTICHRIST

In my life, I have watched the meteoric rise of credit cards, cell phones, and the Internet. I have heard the preachers, authors, and bomb shelter–builders tell me that modern technology is paving the way for the antichrist to rule the world with his "mark of the beast" like in no other age. From radio frequency chips implanted under the skin to national identification numbers, there are a lot of concerns in the air.

In fact, I have heard these concerns for a long, long time. For a few years leading up to Y2K, I listened to my local Calvary Chapel radio station every day. Many of my friends' parents stocked their basements with food and other supplies in preparation for the "grid" going down. I always thought that the best currency to stock up on for the coming apocalypse would be toilet paper, but nobody took my theory seriously. Now, over a decade later, my friend's parents still have 55-gallon drums of wheat in their basement, which are finally expiring.

The idea that society is heading toward complete corruption and a one-world leader has been around a long time, and many dictators have tried to make this a reality. Yet it begs the question, what does the Bible say about this "antichrist?"

The idea of the antichrist, as it is commonly taught, comes primarily from a compilation of four different passages of Scripture. Therefore, in this chapter, I will examine these four passages of Scripture, and my intention is to show you that there is no future *one-world ruler* prophesied in the Bible.

Passage #1: 1 and 2 John

To begin, we must realize that the term *antichrist* does not appear in the Book of Revelation at all. A simple search of a *Strong's Concordance* will reveal that the term *antichrist* is only used in four passages in the Bible, three times in First John and once in Second John.

To understand the term *antichrist*, we must first understand the context of John's writings.[1] During the time of the first-century Church, there was a cult system called Gnosticism. They taught that the spirit was good and the physical/emotional realms were evil, therefore Jesus could not have come to earth in an actual physical body.[2] They taught that Jesus came to earth only as an ethereal spirit being. This teaching is heretical because it negates the truth of Jesus shedding His human blood for the remission of sin. The Gnostics gained so many followers in the early Church (about a third of the first-century Church) that John wrote his first epistle in response to their heresy.

> *That which was from the beginning,* ***which we have heard, which we have seen with our eyes, which we have looked at and our hands have touched****—this we proclaim concerning the Word of life. The life appeared; we have seen it and testify to it, and we proclaim to you the eternal life, which was with the Father and has appeared to us. We proclaim to you what we* ***have seen and heard,*** *so that you also may have fellowship with us. And our fellowship is with the Father and with his Son, Jesus Christ* (1 John 1:1-3).

John was writing to prove, as an eyewitness, that Jesus was not an ethereal ghost, but a real physical person. John was the disciple who leaned his head upon Jesus' chest, and he knew that Jesus was not merely a spirit. He even remarked in John 1:14, *"The Word* ***became flesh*** *and made his dwelling among us.* ***We have seen*** *his glory, the glory of the one and only Son, who came from the Father, full of grace and truth."* The apostle's writings were very focused on those who had fallen into the first-century Gnostic thinking. John went on, in his epistle, to say that those who claimed Jesus didn't have a physical body were actually *antichrist*.

> *Dear friends, do not believe every spirit, but test the spirits to see whether they are from God, because many false prophets have gone out into the world. This is how you can recognize the Spirit of God: Every spirit that* ***acknowledges that Jesus Christ has come in the flesh*** *is from God,* ***but every spirit that does not acknowledge*** *Jesus is not from God.* ***This is the spirit of the antichrist,*** *which you have heard is coming and even now is already in the world* (1 John 4:1-3).

> *Many deceivers,* ***who do not acknowledge Jesus Christ as coming in the flesh,*** *have gone out into the world.* ***Any such person is the deceiver and the antichrist*** (2 John 1:7).

Any person who denies that Jesus came in the flesh, which is what the Gnostics of the first century were doing, is operating in the spirit of antichrist. The antichrist isn't a person; it is a belief system, specifically, Gnosticism.

John further mentions the antichrist spirit as something that the early believers had already heard of:

> *Dear children, this is the last hour; and as you have heard that antichrist is coming...* (1 John 2:18 NASB).

First, it is important to note that certain Bible translations have inserted a word that is not in the Greek manuscripts; this has led to much confusion. These translations capitalize the word *antichrist* in First John 2:18. The reason for the capitalization is because the translators inserted *the* word the before the word *antichrist,* thus making *antichrist* into a proper noun, which requires capitalization.

The early Church had heard that antichrist (false teaching) was coming, but they had not heard that the Antichrist (a one-world ruler) was coming. The insertion of *the* and the capitalization of *Antichrist* was added 1,500 years later by the translators. As I noted in Chapter 1, Martin Luther and the Protestants wanted to be able to point the condemning finger at the Catholic Church, and by making antichrist into a proper noun, they could easily identify her as being such.

With that understanding, we can discern the true meaning of John's letter. John said, *"As you have heard that antichrist is coming...."* The important question is, when had the readers of John's letter heard this message of an impending antichrist? Considering that the term *antichrist* refers to Gnosticism (false teachers), it makes sense that John would be referencing what Jesus warned in Matthew 24—the coming of false teachers. The Gnosticism that John addressed in First and Second John was the false teaching that Jesus predicted.

The verse continues, *"...even now many antichrists have come..."* (1 John 2:18). In other words, many false teachings had already come: Gnosticism, the Nicolatian heresy, and the Judiazers' heresy (see Rev. 2:6,9,15; 3:9). John finishes this verse with, *"This is how we know it is the last hour"* (1 John 2:18). This again shows that John was referring to Jesus' prediction in Matthew 24 that one sign of the coming destruction of Jerusalem would be false teachers. So the appearance of Gnostic heresy was a sign of it being *the last hour* before the destruction of Jerusalem.

John continued:

> *They went out from us, but they did not really belong to us. For if they had belonged to us, they would have remained with us; but their going showed that none of them belonged to us* (1 John 2:19).

The apostle John, writing before the AD 70 destruction, pointed to the fact that many had left the true Church and that this was proof that they were in the last hours of Jesus' prophecy from Matthew 24 being fulfilled.

> *But you have an anointing from the Holy One, and all of you know the truth. I do not write to you because you do not know the truth, but because you do know it and because no lie comes from the truth. Who is the liar? It is* ***whoever denies that Jesus is the Christ. Such a person is the antichrist****—denying the Father and the Son. No one who denies the Son has the Father; whoever acknowledges the Son has the Father also* (1 John 2:20-23).

John writes that those *who deny that Jesus is the Christ* are antichrist, which is a much broader definition than one individual being a future one-world ruler. Clearly, we can see that John was writing about Gnosticism in the first-century Church. He never refers to a future one-world ruler possessed by satan himself. *Antichrist* does not refer to a one-world government ruler, but to ancient Gnosticism.

Let's look at our next passage.

Passage #2: Daniel 9:24-27

Many modern end-times teachers use Daniel 9 to glean much of their information about the evil one-world government ruler that they believe is in our future. Yet there is *no mention* of an antichrist figure in Daniel 9. The commentaries written before the 1830s agree that this passage is about Jesus, not the antichrist. As the famous commentator Matthew Henry says of Daniel 9, "We have here the answer that was immediately sent to Daniel's prayer, and it is a very memorable one, as it contains *the most illustrious prediction of Christ and gospel-grace that is extant in all the Old Testament.*"[3]

But for the sake of conjecture, supposing that we believe that Daniel 9 is about a satan-possessed antichrist figure, let's look at what would need to happen in the future, according to Daniel 9. The requirements involved for this system to work are as follows:

- The Temple in Jerusalem must be rebuilt on the same exact spot as the current Dome of the Rock, which is currently a Muslim mosque.
- A functional priesthood must be reinstated.
- Animal sacrifice must be reinstituted in this rebuilt Temple.
- The prophecies regarding the "Anointed one" in Daniel 9 have to be drastically changed in order to fit the antichrist (instead of Christ).
- The antichrist must make a covenant with the whole world for three and a half years.
- The antichrist will enter the Temple and sit down as God and end animal sacrifice.

It is clear from a simple reading of Daniel 9:24–27 and a basic understanding of history that this passage has been fulfilled by Christ. There is no antichrist in Daniel 9. I will address this passage in greater detail in a coming chapter.

Passage #3: 2 Thessalonians 2:1-8

> *Concerning* ***the coming of our Lord Jesus Christ and our being gathered to him,*** *we ask you, brothers and sisters, not to become easily unsettled or alarmed by the teaching allegedly from us—whether by a prophecy or by word of mouth or by letter—***asserting that the day of the Lord has already come*** (2 Thessalonians 2:1-2).

In an earlier chapter, we have seen that the phrase, *"the coming of our Lord Jesus Christ,"* is in reference to the destruction of Jerusalem. Also, we saw that the *"gathering"* mentioned here is a reference to the Christians fleeing Judea to the mountains and being gathered and protected by the Lord during the destruction of Jerusalem. From these starting points, next we will see that the Thessalonians apparently thought that the *coming* had already happened.

The fact that the Thessalonians could think such a thing proves that they were expecting a local event to occur in Jerusalem, not a global apocalypse. This letter to the Thessalonians was written in approximately AD 50, and Thessalonica is hundreds of miles from Jerusalem. We can see from this letter that they were under the impression that the *coming* of Christ had already happened, which means they thought Jerusalem had been destroyed. In response to this, Paul writes this:

> *Don't let anyone deceive you in any way, for that day will not come until* ***the rebellion occurs*** *and the man of lawlessness is revealed, the man doomed to destruction* (2 Thessalonians 2:3).

The apostle Paul told the Thessalonians that the destruction of Jerusalem would not come until the rebellion had occurred and the leader of the rebellion, the "man of lawlessness," was revealed. He then told them what types of things this rebel leader would do.

> *He will oppose and will exalt himself over everything that is called God or is worshiped, so that he sets himself up in God's temple, proclaiming himself to be God* (2 Thessalonians 2:4).

This is a clear indicator of who could and could not be the "man of sin." For example, this would have to be a person who would have physically been able to stand in the Temple and proclaim himself God. This would require a person who was living before AD 70, when the Temple was destroyed, because at no time since AD 70 has there been a Temple for the man of sin to stand in. Also, there is no New Testament verse, *not even one,* that predicts a rebuilt Jewish Temple. So the Temple had to be standing for the man of lawlessness to stand in it.

When we read in Chapter 3 about the destruction of Jerusalem, we met a few characters involved in that story. The main rebel *who caused* the destruction of Jerusalem was John Levi of Gischala. I believe that he clearly fits the description of the man of lawlessness in this passage.

The Jewish historian Josephus wrote of how John Levi was a selfish, unscrupulous man with persuasive powers who convinced many that he was sent by God to liberate them. Further, John Levi took over the Temple, set himself up in the Temple as the Jewish savior (as God), looted the vessels of the Temple for their gold, and caused the daily animal sacrifices to cease. He also plundered the people, even burning their storehouses of food and causing the great famine that starved tens of thousands to death, and he enlisted aid from the Idumeans, who killed 8,500 of the Jews, including the priests. (Second Thessalonians 2:9 speaks of counterfeit signs, the main one being that John Levi declared that he was God and would deliver the people from the Romans. He commanded the storehouses of food to be burned in faith that God would miraculously deliver them from their enemies. Instead they starved to death.)

Even when the Roman General Titus pleaded that John Levi leave the Temple, so that it wouldn't be destroyed in battle, John flatly refused. John Levi caused the Temple to be destroyed; without him, the Temple might have been spared, considering that it was one of the wonders of the ancient world.[4]

Paul goes on to explain more about the man of lawlessness:

> *Don't you remember that when I was with you I used to tell you these things?* ***And now you know what is holding him back*** [Ananus], *so that he may be revealed at the proper time. For the secret power of lawlessness is already at work; but* ***the one who now holds it back*** [Ananus] *will continue to do so till he is taken out of the way* (2 Thessalonians 2:5-7).

John was not only a rebel leader, but also a false messiah. He claimed godhood by taking over the Temple, and the only person who stood in his way was the Jewish Chief Priest, Ananus. Ananus had tremendous diplomatic skills and had been able to negotiate peace treaties with Rome many times before. Ananus was literally able to *restrain* the full-scale rebellion that John Levi was aiming to accomplish.[5] That is why Paul referred to the one who restrained, who must be taken out of the way.

Even Josephus noted that once Ananus (the one who restrains) was killed, then the destruction of Jerusalem began:

> I should not mistake if I said that the death of Ananus was *the beginning of the destruction of the city,* and that from this very day may be dated the overthrow of her wall, and the ruin of her affairs.[6]

As Josephus recorded, this happened exactly as the apostle Paul laid out for the Thessalonians:

> *And then the lawless one will be revealed, whom the Lord Jesus will overthrow with the breath of his mouth and* ***destroy by the splendor of his coming*** (2 Thessalonians 2:8).

When the "coming of the Lord" occurred with the destruction of Jerusalem, John Levi was finally dealt with. He was the cause of the rebellion, which led to the attack by the Romans. John was a deceiver who declared *"lying signs and wonders"* (2 Thess 2:9–12) and caused the people to burn all the storehouses of food, claiming he was God and would provide for them! Then he set up his militia in the Temple, murdered all the priests, and caused not only all of Jerusalem to be destroyed, but even the Temple, which the Romans didn't want to harm. John Levi was so evil it boggles the mind!

A Final Thought

When we think about this passage from the perspective of its original recipients, it does not make sense that Paul would have written a mysterious passage that would be of no value to his original readers and would have no value until 2,000 years in the future.

The "secret power of iniquity" was already in operation in the first century; this culminated in the AD 70 judgment of iniquity (see 2 Thess. 2:7). The "secret power of iniquity" hasn't been in operation for 2,000 years waiting for *our* future. Instead, Paul was clearly talking about an evil person in the first century and another person who was restraining this evil. John Levi and Ananus fulfill this passage.

Passage #4: The Beast of Revelation 13 and 17

Revelation 13 speaks of the Beast, which the majority of Church history has taught represents the Roman Empire of the first century. As F.W. Farrar wrote in 1882:

> Every Jewish reader, of course, saw that the Beast was a symbol of Nero. And both Jews and Christians regarded Nero as also having close affinities with the serpent or dragon....All the earliest Christian writers on the Apocalypse, from Irenaeus down to Victorinus of Pettau and Commodian in the fourth, and Andreas in the Fifth, and St. Beatus in the eighth century, connect Nero, or some Roman Emperor, with the Apocalyptic Beast.[7]

Revelation 17 speaks of another beast, which Church history has taught also represents the Roman Emperor Nero. I agree that these are both excellent and sensible explanations.

Revelation 17:10—The Emperor Nero

> *They are also seven kings.* ***Five have fallen, one is, the other has not yet come;*** *but when he does come, he must remain for only a little while* (Revelation 17:10).

This passage, which is speaking of the line of rulers in Rome, tells us exactly how many rulers had already come, which one was currently in power, and that the next one would only last a short while. Take a look at how that perfectly fits with Nero and the Roman Empire of the first century. The rule of the first seven Roman Emperor's are as follows:

Julius Caesar (49–44 BC)
Augustus (27 BC–AD 14)
Tiberius (AD 14–37)
Caligula (AD 37–41)
Claudius (AD 41–54)
"Five have fallen..."
Nero (AD 54–68)
"One is..."
Galba (June AD 68–January AD 69, a six month ruler-ship)
"the other has not yet come; but when he does come, he must remain for only a little while."

Of the first seven kings of the Roman Empire, five had come (Julius Caesar, Augustus, Tiberius, Gaius, and Claudius), one was now in power (Nero), and one had not yet come (Galba), but would only remain a little time (six months). The vast majority throughout Church history have understood that the beast in Revelation 17 is a reference to Nero.

Revelation 13:1-4—The Roman Empire

...And I saw a beast coming out of the sea. It had...seven heads....One of the heads of the beast seemed to have had a fatal wound, but the fatal wound had been healed. The whole world was filled with wonder and followed the beast. People worshiped the dragon because he had given authority to the beast, and they also worshiped the beast and asked, "Who is like the beast? Who can wage war against it?" (Revelation 13:1-4).

We have just seen from Revelation 17 that Nero fits the timeline as the sixth of the seven heads and that Galba is *the one to come that shall only remain a little while.* I would propose that Rome was metaphorically wounded and faltering as an empire because of Nero. Nero was not only a psychopath who burned down one third of Rome and pinned the blame on the Christians and persecuted them brutally, but also, when Nero killed himself (in AD 68), the political climate of Rome changed dramatically. One of the major changes was that Nero was officially the last of the Julio-Claudian line of emperors; thus the line ended, and it would have seemed, symbolically, as if the head of the empire had been wounded to death.

Nero's sudden death caused an event that has been historically called the "Year of the Four Emperors." Because of tumult caused by his suicide, three short-lived emperors followed Nero. Many thought that the Roman Empire was about to die.[8]

Here is the timeline of AD 69, the *"Year of the Four Emperors":*

Nero (AD 54–68)
Galba (AD 68–69)
Otho (AD 69)
Vitellius (AD 69)
Vespasian (AD 69–80)

Can you imagine if the United States had four presidents in office in a one-year period? This was a very painful year for Rome, and many thought the beast of the Roman Empire had been wounded unto death. In fact, this was the most tumultuous time in Roman history since Mark Antony's death in 30 BC, nearly 100 years earlier.

Yet, by what appeared to be a miraculous turn around, the Empire was revived under Vespasian and Titus. When they came into power, they established the Flavian dynasty of Caesars. Instead of the beast dying, it resurrected under Vespasian, and he ruled for a solid ten years.

Often this subject of the beast is connected in people's minds with the infamous "mark of the beast" found in Revelation 13:16–17. This "mark of the beast" has been the cause of much fear, so I will address it here, even though I am not covering the entire Book of Revelation (for more on Revelation, read my forthcoming book, *Revelation Simplified*, and see the recommended reading list in Appendix 5.) Regarding the "mark of the beast," it is important to note that in the ancient culture of Rome, the public market was the main source of trade and retail. For people to enter the public market, they had to pass through the main gate. It was required of all who entered the main gate to pay homage to the idol of the Emperor. Once homage was paid, ashes were placed on the hand or on the forehead of the individual, and then they were allowed to pass through the gates and buy and sell merchandise.[9] This was taking the mark. The parallels between this and the "mark of the beast" are stunning, and they further confirm the reality that the beast was Nero and the Roman Empire.

The prestigious N.T. Wright writes regarding this:

> What's more, worshipping or nor worshipping was quickly becoming the dividing line between people who were acceptable in the community and people who weren't. Not long after this time, some local officials introduced a formal requirement that unless you had offered the required sacrifices you weren't allowed in the market. There were various kinds of marks and visible signs, which were used to set people apart either as 'able to trade' or as 'not able to trade'. From quite early on the Christians were faced with a stark alternative: stay true to the lamb and risk losing your livelihood, the ability to sell or buy; capitulate to the monster, sacrifice to Caesar at the behest of the local officials, and then everything will be all right-except your integrity as one of the lamb's followers.[10]

Another author adds:

> The Christians of the first century were under the military authority of Rome, a nation which openly proclaimed its rulers, the Caesars, to be divine. All those under the jurisdiction of Rome were required by law to publicly proclaim their allegiance to Caesar by burning a pinch of incense and declaring, "Caesar is Lord." Upon compliance with this law, the people were given a papyrus document called a "libellus," which they were required to present when either stopped by the Roman police or attempting to engage in commerce in the Roman marketplace, increasing the difficulty of "buying or selling" without this mark. This is the essence of Scripture's warnings to the

early Christians against taking upon themselves the "mark of the beast."[11]

Many ancient sources spoke of Nero as a beast, as R.C. Sproul shows in his book, *The Last Days According to Jesus*:

> [Kenneth] Gentry gives a synopsis of Nero's violence-studded life, including the murders of his own family members, the castration of a boy Nero "married," and the brutal murder of his pregnant wife by kicking her to death. Bizarre behavior was noted by the historian Suetonius, who wrote that Nero even "devised a kind of game, in which, covered with the skin of some wild animal, he was let loose from a cage and attacked the private parts of men and women, who were bound to stakes."
>
> Nero began his reign as emperor in A.D. 54. His imperial persecution of the Christian community was launched in A.D. 64, the same year as the famous fire (which burned 1/3 of Rome) that many believe was set by Nero himself. It is often assumed that the persecution of Christians, whom Nero blamed for the fire, was a diversionary tactic to shift blame for his own actions to others. Nero committed suicide in A.D. 68, when he was but 31 years of age.
>
> Since the beast's appearance is one of the "things, which must shortly take place" (Rev. 1:1), Nero is at least a *prima facie* candidate for the role of the beast. As described by ancient historians, Nero is a singularly cruel and unrestrained man of evil. Many ancient writers cite the bestial character of Nero, and Gentry summarizes these references:
>
>> Tacitus...spoke of Nero's "cruel nature" that "put to death so many innocent men." Roman naturalist Pliny the Elder... described Nero as "the destroyer of the human race" and "the poison of the world." Roman satirist Juvenal...speaks of "Nero's cruel and bloody tyranny." ...Apollonius of Tyana...specifically

> mentions that Nero was called a "beast": "In my travels, which have been wider than ever man yet accomplished, I have seen many many wild beasts of Arabia and India; but this beast, that is commonly called a Tyrant, I know not how many heads it has, nor if it be crooked of claw, and armed with horrible fangs... And of wild beasts you cannot say that they were ever known to eat their own mother, but Nero has gorged himself on this diet."[12]

The beast is not a coming antichrist or the man of lawlessness. The beast was Nero and the Roman Empire. It is amazing how perfectly the visions of John fit with what has taken place in the past!

CHAPTER POINTS

- The antichrist is not and never was a person; it is a spiritual system of false teaching, specifically Gnosticism.
- Jesus is the perfect and sensible fulfillment of Daniel 9; there is no antichrist in this passage.
- The man of lawlessness was a first-century individual; the restrainer was another first-century individual—specifically John Levi and the High Priest Ananus.
- The beast of Revelation is the Roman Empire, especially under Nero Caesar.
- There is nothing in the Bible that points to a future one-world government ruler such as has been popularized in the last century.

DISCUSSION QUESTIONS

1. What fruit have you seen from the one-world ruler teaching in the Church?
2. What four passages are used to create the composite known as the antichrist?
3. Who is Daniel 9:24–27 speaking of?
4. What did Matthew Henry say about Daniel 9?
5. What was John writing about in First and Second John when he mentioned the spirit of antichrist?
6. Who was John Levi, and what did he do?
7. Who was the beast?

chapter seven

THE PERSECUTION MINDSET

Now that we've addressed several major end-time misconceptions, I want to look at something I call the persecution mindset. In a nutshell, it is defined like this: Many western Christians believe that Christianity in countries with persecution is better than Christianity in countries with no physical persecution. Some even see the lack of persecution as evidence of the Church being anemic!

Typically, one of the first thoughts to come to mind when pondering persecution is the ever-popular quote from Tertullian, "The blood of the martyrs is the seed of the church." I appreciate Glenn Penner's take on it:

> Some have mistakenly believed that these words can be found in the New Testament. They're not. In fact, the phrase, itself, is a paraphrase of a statement made by an early church leader called Tertullian in 197 A.D. in a book he entitled The Apology. In it, Tertullian writes to the Roman governor of his province, refuting various false charges being made against Christians and the Christian faith, arguing that the followers of Christ were loyal subjects of the empire, and thus, should not be persecuted. At any rate, Tertullian observes, the persecution was failing to destroy Christianity. He writes, "kill us, torture us, condemn us, grind us to dust; your injustice is the proof that we are innocent. Therefore God suffers (allows) that we thus suffer. When you recently condemned a Christian woman to the leno (pimp, i.e.,

> accused her of being a prostitute) rather than to the leo (lion), you made confession that a taint on our purity is considered among us something more terrible than any punishment and any death. Nor does your cruelty, however exquisite, avail you; it is rather a temptation to us. The oftener we are mown down by you, the more in number we grow; the blood of Christians is seed."
>
> As is true with many popular statements, this phrase has been taken at face value for so long that to challenge it is, in the minds of some, paramount to challenging the very words of Scripture. The notion that persecution always causes church growth is so widespread that it is considered irrefutable by some. An accompanying assumption is that persecution typically causes the Church to be purified, and believers to walk more closely with God. Thus, persecution is often seen to have a benefit for the Church.[1]

People who think according to the persecution mindset will say (or believe) things like, "If only America had some persecution; then our churches would have 'better' Christians." However, as we can see from Penner's explanation, this was not Tertullian's intention whatsoever. He was describing the reality that persecution could not kill the Church, not naming persecution as the force behind Church growth and holiness.

Many Bible verses speak of the early Church's experience of persecution, but we must be careful to read these verses in their historical context. We must not apply the historical reality that they faced to all generations, for all time. Following are some of the passages that speak of persecution:

> *Blessed are those who have been persecuted for the sake of righteousness, for theirs is the kingdom of heaven. Blessed are you when men cast insults at you, and persecute you, and say all kinds of evil against you falsely, on account of Me. Rejoice, and be glad, for your reward in heaven is great, for so they persecuted the prophets who were before you* (Matthew 5:10–12).

Love your enemies and pray for those who persecute you (Matthew 5:43).

And I say to you, My friends, do not be afraid of those who kill the body, and after that have no more that they can do (Luke 12:4).

If the world hates you, keep in mind that it hated me first. If you belonged to the world, it would love you as its own. As it is, you do not belong to the world, but I have chosen you out of the world. That is why the world hates you. Remember what I told you: "A servant is not greater than his master." If they persecuted me, they will persecute you also. If they obeyed my teaching, they will obey yours also. They will treat you this way because of my name, for they do not know the one who sent me. If I had not come and spoken to them, they would not be guilty of sin; but now they have no excuse for their sin. Whoever hates me hates my Father as well. If I had not done among them the works no one else did, they would not be guilty of sin. As it is, they have seen, and yet they have hated both me and my Father. But this is to fulfill what is written in their Law: "They hated me without reason" (John 15:18–25).

These things I have spoken to you, that in Me you may have peace. In the world you will have tribulation; but be of good cheer, I have overcome the world (John 16:33).

And when they had called for the apostles and beaten them, they commanded that they should not speak in the name of Jesus, and let them go. So they departed from the presence of the council, rejoicing that they were counted worthy to suffer shame for His name (Acts 5:40–41).

We must go through many hardships to enter the kingdom of God (Acts 14:22).

You, however, know all about my teaching, my way of life, my purpose, faith, patience, love, endurance, persecutions, sufferings—what kinds of things happened to me in Antioch, Iconium and Lystra, the persecutions I endured. Yet the Lord rescued me from all of them. In fact, everyone who wants to live a godly life in Christ Jesus will be persecuted, while evildoers and impostors

> *will go from bad to worse, deceiving and being deceived* (2 Timothy 3:10–13).

This passage could easily be misinterpreted as applying to *all Christians* for *all time*. However, the context is clearly the "last days" of Jerusalem (AD 30–70), as Second Timothy 3:1, nine verses earlier, makes obvious.

> *Consider it pure joy, my brothers, whenever you face trials of many kinds* (James 1:2).

> *In all this you greatly rejoice, though now for a little while you may have had to suffer grief in all kinds of trials* (1 Peter 1:6).

> *Dear friends, do not be surprised at the fiery ordeal that has come on you to test you, as though something strange were happening to you* (1 Peter 4:12).

When considered in their historical context and with the understanding that most of the "end-times" events prophesied in the Bible happened in AD 70, we can see that these verses were written regarding only the earliest period of Church history (AD 30–70). During that time, Christians faced horrible persecution under the evil Temple leaders. Men like Saul (who later became Paul) persecuted the Church from house to house and dragged people from their homes (see Acts 7:54–8:3).

While persecution certainly did not end with the destruction of Jerusalem at AD 70, we should not take from these verses a universal expectation of persecution for all time. Such an idea is an assumption that removes these verses completely from their context.

Here are four things we *do* learn from these passages:

1. We recognize the valor of the early Church to stand up as a witness for Christ, even to the point of death.
2. We learn that we must love all people, even those who would be enemies. The early Church did not become hateful toward their persecutors but continued to love.
3. We learn that we should be willing to follow the early Church's example and suffer persecution if the need arises.

4. We see that, as the context indicates, *they* were going through fiery trials, but we are not told to expect every Christian to face persecution everyday of their lives for all time. That is a modern fallacy.

The New Testament was written regarding first-century realities. It does *not* teach an expectation that *all Christians* are to suffer persecution for *all time*. Even Jesus wasn't persecuted as much as some with the persecution mindset say that Christians should be. This leads us to the question, *If Jesus is our model, then who should be persecuting us?*

Jesus was beloved of sinners, and even the government leaders found no fault in Him (see Matt. 27:23–24). At first, only the religious leaders hated and persecuted Jesus. Even the early Church suffered persecution primarily at the hands of the Jewish religious leaders until AD 64, when Nero burned one third of Rome and began to vigorously persecute Christianity.

Proof Texting

The proof text of the persecution mindset is found in Jesus' command to pick up our cross and follow Him. I addressed this misunderstood passage in my earlier work, *Eyes of Honor*:

> Many have been taught that *self* must be daily crucified and that *the self* is evil and must be denied. Although Jesus did say to deny *self*, the definition of *self* has been very convoluted. When Jesus referred to *self*, He was not talking about the soul. Also, He was not talking about the *self* as synonymous with *the flesh*. We know this because Jesus said to deny *self*, whereas the only answer for *the flesh* is crucifixion in Christ (see Gal. 2:20).
>
> The best way to understand *self* is to define it as a person's *reputation*. Let's look again at what Jesus said regarding denying *self* with our new definition:
>
> *Then he called the crowd to him along with his disciples and said, "If anyone would come after me, he must* ***deny himself*** *and take up his*

cross and follow me. For whoever wants to save ***his life*** *will lose it, but whoever loses* ***his life*** *for me and for the gospel will save it"* (Mark 8:34–35).

Then he said to them all: "If anyone would come after me, he must ***deny himself*** *and take up his cross daily and follow me. For whoever wants to save* ***his life*** *will lose it, but whoever loses* ***his life*** *for me will save it"* (Luke 9:23–24).

Then Jesus said to his disciples, "Whoever wants to be my disciple must ***deny themselves*** *and take up their cross and follow me. For whoever wants to save* ***their life*** *will lose it, but whoever loses* ***their life*** *for me will find it"* (Matthew 16:24–25).

It is clear in these passages that Jesus is talking to the non-believers and telling them how to become His followers. "Deny yourself" is something Jesus told those who were considering becoming His followers. He told them what it would cost them. The cost would be that they would lay down their lives and the control of their lives. This point is even clearer in Luke 14:

Large crowds were traveling with Jesus, and turning to them he said: "If anyone comes to Me and does not hate father and mother, wife and children, brothers and sisters—yes, even their own life—such a person cannot be My disciple. And whoever does not carry their cross and follow Me cannot be My disciple.

"Suppose one of you wants to build a tower. Won't you first sit down and estimate the cost to see if you have enough money to complete it? For if you lay the foundation and are not able to finish it, everyone who sees it will ridicule you, saying, 'This person began to build and wasn't able to finish.'

"Or suppose a king is about to go to war against another king. Won't he first sit down and consider whether he is able with ten thousand men to

> *oppose the one coming against him with twenty thousand? If he is not able, he will send a delegation while the other is still a long way off and will ask for terms of peace. In the same way, those of you who do not give up everything you have cannot be My disciples* (Luke 14:25–33).

> Jesus spoke very plainly in these verses instructing His potential followers not to expect life to be easy. The first-century understanding of "taking up the cross" meant being willing to lay down one's reputation and be branded by society as a criminal. Jesus died a criminal's death on a criminal's cross, and His followers had to count the cost of laying down their reputations to become rejects of society.[2]

Clearly, these passages are not, as some have interpreted, about embracing persecution in our daily lives.

On Earth as in Heaven

So many have held up persecution as a saintly quality in the Christian's life, but let's think about it in light of the growth of the Kingdom of God. If our prayers are effective and if Jesus is answering them, then this world will become *"on earth as it is in heaven"* (Matt. 6:10), which would certainly include a lack of persecution. We can pretty safely assume no Christians are being persecuted in Heaven. Logically, if the Lord's Prayer is being progressively answered, the outcome should be that earth becomes more and more like Heaven. Thus, the more the Kingdom expands on this earth and the saints mature into their calling as ambassadors of that Kingdom, the less persecution Christians should face.

Where God's will is in full effect, persecution does not exist. It wasn't present in the Garden of Eden, and it isn't present in Heaven, either. Between that historical point and our future goal, many Christians have experienced persecution. That does not make it holy. Rather, while we live in the interim timeline between the Garden of Eden and the Garden City of Revelation 22, we are to pray Heaven into the earth. And thankfully, the outcome of this expansion of the Kingdom of God will include a squelching of all persecution.

CHAPTER POINTS

- The New Testament verses about persecution applied to specific people and circumstances historically, and they are not to be read as statements that apply to all people for all time.
- In their historical context, these verses tell us about the intense persecution Christians faced leading up to the AD 70 destruction of Jerusalem.
- Though persecution has always existed, we should not expect it, call it evidence of the radical Christian life, or believe it is the "seed bed" of Christianity.
- Much of the persecution that Jesus and the early Church experienced happened at the hands of the religious leaders.
- When Jesus said to "deny yourself," He was talking to potential converts (not believers), telling them about the cost of being His followers and the scorn it would bring upon them in that day.
- Heaven is a persecution-free zone, and naturally, persecution will decrease as the Church brings the culture of Heaven down to earth.

DISCUSSION QUESTIONS

1. Have you encountered the persecution mindset? What does it sound like?

2. Had you ever considered that the persecution Jesus spoke of was for His followers in the first century?

3. If Jesus is our example of being persecuted, who are we to be persecuted by: sinners or religious leaders?

4. What is a clearer word for "denying self"?

5. If we are to pray Heaven into the earth, how much persecution of Christians is happening in Heaven? How does this question affect your perspective of the future?

chapter eight

THE ISRAEL OF GOD

During the Presidential race between George W. Bush and Al Gore, I realized something interesting. Although I could have based my vote on a variety of issues, I had decided to vote for Bush because he seemed more pro-Israel. This was more of an unconscious decision until a friend challenged me as to why I was voting for Bush. I happened to blurt out, "Because God blesses those that bless Israel" (see Gen. 12:3). My older and wiser friend asked if I understood that verse in its proper context. I thought I did (being young and arrogant), so I said yes, but his query left a question mark in my mind for years to come. The echo of that question has helped me look beyond the hype and return to examine the Word.

Christians agree that the Bible reveals who God is and what He is like. In the New Testament, we can see that the Old Testament foreshadowed Jesus Christ. The whole point of the Old Testament is to direct us to the person of Jesus Christ. Yet even Jesus' own disciples didn't understand this until He explained it to them. On the road to Emmaus, after His resurrection, we find Jesus revealing this to them.

As the two disciples walked, they encountered Jesus, but they did not know it was Him. They were discussing the events surrounding His death, and when He asked them about their conversation, they said they were talking about what had happened to Jesus, who *"was a prophet powerful in word and deed before God and all the people"* (Luke 24:19). They went on to explain the events of Jesus' crucifixion, the encounter with angels who said He was alive, and the discovery of the empty tomb. However, they clearly were missing the revelation inherent in these events. After listening to their report, Jesus actually rebuked them:

> *Then Jesus said to them, "You foolish people!* ***You find it so hard to believe all that the prophets wrote in the Scriptures. Wasn't it clearly predicted*** *that the Messiah would have to suffer all these things before entering his glory?"* ***Then Jesus took them through the writings of Moses and all the prophets, explaining from all the Scriptures the things concerning himself*** (Luke 24:25-27 NLT).

The Old Testament was intended to point humankind to God, specifically the person of Jesus. The apostles understood this better as time went by. When we read the letters of the New Testament, we observe the writers referring to the Old Testament as foreshadowing Christ.

> *Therefore do not let anyone judge you by what you eat or drink, or with regard to a religious festival, a New Moon celebration or a Sabbath day.* ***These are a shadow*** *of the things that were to come;* the ***reality, however, is found in Christ*** (Colossians 2:16-17).

> ***Just as*** *Moses lifted up the snake in the desert, so the Son of Man must be lifted up* (John 3:14).

> *They serve at a sanctuary that is* ***a copy and shadow*** *of what is in heaven. This is why Moses was warned when he was about to build the tabernacle: "See to it that you make everything according to the pattern shown you on the mountain"* (Hebrews 8:5).

> *It was necessary, then, for the* ***copies*** *of the heavenly things to be purified with these sacrifices, but the heavenly things themselves with better sacrifices than these. For Christ did not enter a sanctuary made with human hands that was only* ***a copy of the true one;*** *he entered heaven itself, now to appear for us in God's presence* (Hebrews 9:23-24).

Examples of Shadows

In fact, the life of Jesus contains some amazing parallels to the Old Testament nation of Israel. Let's look at some of the most significant ones. In Genesis, there is a man named Jacob (see Gen. 32:27–28) who has a son named Joseph (see Gen. 37:3). This Joseph has a dream (see Gen. 37:6) that takes him down into Egypt (see Gen 37:28). And the Israelite nation grows while in bondage. God then calls Israel His Son (see Exod. 4:22) and leads him out of Egypt (see Hos. 11:1). After that, Israel was baptized (see 1 Cor. 10:1–2) and wandered in the desert for forty years (see Exod. 16:35).

The New Testament also begins with a man named Jacob (see Matt. 1:16) who has a son named Joseph (see Matt. 1:16). This Joseph has a dream (see Matt. 1:20) that also takes him down into Egypt (see Matt. 2:13–14). Jesus is born into this Joseph's house. God then calls Jesus His Son (see Matt. 3:17) and leads him out of Egypt (see Matt. 2:15). After that, Jesus was baptized (see Matt. 3:13–15) and wandered in the desert for forty days (see Matt. 4:1–2).

The parallels don't end there. In fact, much of Jesus' three and a half years of ministry was reenacting the story of Israel in His own life as the True Israel.

Let's continue by noticing the strange comment that Jesus made at His baptism about *"fulfilling all righteousness"* (Matt. 3:13–15). This comment finally makes sense when we see that Jesus was fulfilling all the Old Testament shadows that pointed to Him. He understood that He needed to be baptized in order to fulfill everything that was in His shadow. As Israel had to wander in the desert for forty years, so Jesus spent forty days in the wilderness to fulfill the shadow.

Even in the wilderness temptation, we see that Jesus refuted the devil using only quotes from the Book of Deuteronomy—the book that chronicles the time when Israel walked in the wilderness for forty years (see Matt. 4:4,7,10).

In Exodus 24, Moses gave the Law the first time from Mount Sinai. In Matthew 5–7, Jesus took the Law and interpreted it properly to the people in the Sermon on the Mount.

In Exodus, Moses said to the twelve tribes, *"This is the blood of the covenant that the LORD has made with you in accordance with all these words"* (Exod. 24:8). In Matthew, Jesus said to the twelve apostles, *"This is my blood of the covenant, which is poured out for many for the forgiveness of sins"* (Matt. 26:28).

Israel was God's Vine: *"You transplanted a vine from Egypt; you drove out the nations and planted it"* (Ps. 80:8). Then Jesus became God's Vine: *"I am the true vine, and my Father is the gardener"* (John 15:1).

Israel was considered the seed of Abraham *"But you, Israel, my servant, Jacob, whom I have chosen, you descendants of Abraham my friend"* (Isa. 41:8). In the New Testament, the Seed of Abraham is Jesus.

The promises were spoken to Abraham and to his seed. Scripture does not say *"and to seeds,"* meaning many people, but *"and to your seed,"* meaning one person, who is Christ" (see Gal 3:16).

In the Old Testament, God took one man (Jacob) and brought a nation out of him (Israel). In the New Testament, God took Jesus and brought a *holy* nation out of Him (see 1 Pet. 2:9).

In Hebrews, we learn that the Old Testament places of worship were a shadow modeled after Heaven (see Heb. 8:5; 9:23–24).

Jesus fulfilled all the things written about His life. As Jesus said on the cross, *"It is finished"* (John 19:30) so *"that all things which are written may be fulfilled"* (Luke 21:22). He accomplished much more than I have written here; this is just a sampling of all the shadows that led to Him.

God's Promises

In the Old Testament, God made three big promises, and each of them He has fulfilled. There exists a lot of confusion around these promises, so let's look closer.

1. The Promises to Abraham—God promised four things to Abraham:

Promise #1: He would make Abraham's name great.

I will make you into a great nation, and I will bless you; I will make your name great, and you will be a blessing (Genesis 12:2).

Fulfillment: God has made Abraham's name great. Christianity, Judaism, and Islam all honor and value Abraham.

Promise #2: Abraham would have numerous physical descendants.

I will make your offspring like the dust of the earth, so that if anyone could count the dust, then your offspring could be counted (Genesis 13:16).

FULFILLMENT: The Old Testament tells us of this promise being fulfilled in First Kings:

Your servant is here among the people you have chosen, a great people, too numerous to count or number (1 Kings 3:8).

The people of Judah and Israel were as numerous as the sand on the seashore; they ate, they drank, and they were happy (1 Kings 4:20).

Promise #3: All the families of the world would be blessed through Abraham.

I will bless those who bless you, and whoever curses you I will curse; and all peoples on earth will be blessed through you (Genesis 12:3).

And through your offspring all nations on earth will be blessed, because you have obeyed me (Genesis 22:18).

FULFILLMENT: Through Christ, the Seed of Abraham, all the families of the earth have been blessed.

Scripture foresaw that God would justify the Gentiles by faith, and announced the gospel in advance to Abraham: "All nations will be blessed through you." So those who rely on faith are blessed along with Abraham, the man of faith (Galatians 3:8-9).

Promise #4: Abraham would be the father of a multitude of nations.

As for me, this is my covenant with you: You will be the father of many nations. No longer will you be called Abram; your name will be Abraham, for I have made you a father of many nations (Genesis 17:4-5).

FULFILLMENT: Also through Christ, Abraham has become the father of a multitude of nations. *"If you belong to Christ, then you are Abraham's seed, and heirs according to the promise"* (Gal. 3:29).

2. The Covenant with Moses

The Mosaic Covenant was a conditional covenant that either brought God's direct blessing for obedience or God's direct cursing for disobedience upon the nation of Israel. Part of the Mosaic Covenant was the Ten Commandments found in Exodus 20, but also included the rest of the Law, which contained 613 commands. A good overview of how God related this conditional covenant is found in Deuteronomy 11, specifically verses 26–28:

> *See, I am setting before you today a blessing and a curse—the blessing if you obey the commands of the LORD your God that I am giving you today; the curse if you disobey the commands of the LORD your God and turn from the way that I command you today by following other gods, which you have not known* (Deuteronomy 11:26-28).

After Deuteronomy, where the Law is given, the history books of the Old Testament (Joshua through Esther) detail how Israel rarely succeeded at obeying the Law and mostly how Israel failed miserably at obeying the Law.

Hebrews 7–10 speaks in great detail about how the entire covenant with Moses was insufficient and merely a physical shadow of the spiritual fulfillment in Christ. Jesus fulfilled the Mosaic Covenant as our "great high priest" (see Heb. 2:17; 3:1; 4:14; 10:21). He instituted what the writer of Hebrews consistently calls the "better covenant" (see Heb. 7:22; 8:6; 12:24).

3. The Promise to David

In Second Samuel 7, we find that God promised King David a lasting kingdom because he would have a descendant who would sit upon his throne and rule forever. In Luke 1:32–33, an angel declared to Mary that Jesus was the one to fulfill God's promise to David.

He will be great and will be called the Son of the Most High. The Lord God will give him the throne of his father David, and he will reign over Jacob's descendants forever; his kingdom will never end (Luke 1:32-33).

Then on Pentecost, Peter pointed to the fact that Jesus had fulfilled this promise to David and now sits on the promised eternal throne.

Fellow Israelites, I can tell you confidently that the patriarch David died and was buried, and his tomb is here to this day. ***But he was a prophet*** *and knew that God had promised him on oath that he would place one of his descendants on his throne. Seeing what was to come,* ***he spoke of the resurrection of the Messiah,*** *that he was not abandoned to the realm of the dead, nor did his body see decay. God has raised this Jesus to life, and we are all witnesses of it. Exalted to the right hand of God, he has received from the Father the promised Holy Spirit and has poured out what you now see and hear. For David did not ascend to heaven, and yet he said, "The Lord said to my Lord: Sit at my right hand until I make your enemies a footstool for your feet." Therefore let all Israel be assured of this: God has made this Jesus, whom you crucified,* ***both Lord and Messiah*** (Acts 2:29-36).

The Land Promises

God also made promises regarding a nation that would come from Abraham's lineage and specific boundaries of land they would inhabit. The geographical boundaries of the Abrahamic Covenant are laid out on more than one occasion in the Book of Genesis.

The LORD appeared to Abram and said, "To your offspring I will give this land." So he built an altar there to the LORD, who had appeared to him (Genesis 12:7).

On that day the LORD made a covenant with Abram and said, "To your descendants I have given this land, ***from the river of Egypt [the Nile] to the great river, the River Euphrates****"* (Genesis 15:18 NASB).

There are many confused teachers who claim that Israel never received the fulfillment of the land promise, yet the Bible says they did. God completely fulfilled the land promises.

> ***So the LORD gave Israel all the land he had sworn to give the ancestors, and they took possession of it and settled there.*** *The LORD gave them rest on every side, just as he had sworn to their ancestors. Not one of their enemies withstood them; the LORD gave all their enemies into their hands.* **Not one of all the LORD's good promises to Israel failed; every one was fulfilled** (Joshua 21:43-45).

> *And Solomon ruled over all the kingdoms from the Euphrates River to the land of the Philistines, as far as the border of Egypt. These countries brought tribute and were Solomon's subjects all his life* (1 Kings 4:21).

> *He ruled over all the kings from the Euphrates River to the land of the Philistines, as far as the border of Egypt* (2 Chronicles 9:26).

> *Praise be to the LORD, who has given rest to his people Israel just as he promised.* **Not one word has failed of all the good promises** *[land included] he gave through his servant Moses* (1 Kings 8:56).

> *You are the LORD God, who chose Abram and brought him out of Ur of the Chaldeans and named him Abraham. You found his heart faithful to you, and* **you made a covenant** *with him to give to his descendants the land of the Canaanites, Hittites, Amorites, Perizzites, Jebusites and Girgashites.* **You have kept your promise** *because you are righteous.... Their children went in* **and took possession of the land.** *You subdued before them the Canaanites, who lived in the land; you gave the Canaanites into their hands, along with their kings and the peoples of the land, to deal with them as they pleased* (Nehemiah 9:7-8,24).

> *Jerusalem has had powerful kings* **ruling over the whole of Trans-Euphrates,** *and taxes, tribute and duty were paid to them* (Ezra 4:20).

From these passages, we clearly see that Israel did, in fact, receive the full land inheritance that was promised to them and that, for a period of time, they possessed it completely.

A Conditional Promise

However, it is important to note that the land was not given to them unconditionally: The fact that God's promise of the land to Israel was not unconditional is clearly demonstrated in God's words to Solomon in the following passage:

> *As for you,* ***if you*** *walk before me faithfully as David your father did, and do all I command, and observe my decrees and laws, I will establish your royal throne, as I covenanted with David your father when I said, "You shall never fail to have a successor to rule over Israel."* ***But if you*** *turn away and forsake the decrees and commands I have given you and go off to serve other gods and worship them,* ***then I will uproot Israel from my land, which I have given them, and will reject this temple I have consecrated for my Name. I will make it a byword and an object of ridicule among all peoples*** (2 Chronicles 7:17-20).

The land was never promised to Abraham and his descendants for an everlasting possession *apart from their obedience.* God is not under any obligation to keep Israel in the land, nor to bring them back to the land at any time in the future, apart from their willingness to abide by His commandments and follow Him.

It's also significant to note the conditional aspects of even the Abrahamic covenant:

> ***But if*** *they will confess their sins and the sins of their ancestors—their unfaithfulness and their hostility toward me, which made me hostile toward them so that I sent them into the land of their enemies—then when their uncircumcised hearts are humbled and they pay for their sin, I will remember my covenant with Jacob and my covenant with Isaac and my covenant with Abraham, and I will remember the land* (Leviticus 26:40-42).

> *If you pay attention to these laws and are careful to follow them, then the LORD your God will keep his covenant of love with you, as he swore to your ancestors* (Deuteronomy 7:12).

Although Genesis 17:8 says the land was given as an everlasting possession, yet we must read it in the context of a verse that comes only five verses later, where God says that circumcision is also an everlasting covenant (see Gen. 17:13). We know from the New Testament that circumcision has been changed from physical circumcision to circumcision of the heart (see 1 Cor. 7:19). So it is imperative that we leave room for God to correct our understanding.

God even went so far as to say that He would vomit them from out of the land for their disobedience:

> *Do not defile yourselves in any of these ways, because this is how the nations that I am going to drive out before you became defiled. Even the land was defiled; so I punished it for its sin, and the land vomited out its inhabitants. But you must keep my decrees and my laws. The native-born and the foreigners residing among you must not do any of these detestable things, for all these things were done by the people who lived in the land before you, and the land became defiled.* ***And if you defile the land, it will vomit you out as it vomited out the nations that were before you*** (Leviticus 18:24-28).

> *Keep all my decrees and laws and follow them, so that the land where I am bringing you to live may not vomit you out* (Leviticus 20:22).

In the Old Testament, God gave Israel all the land He had promised them. This has been fulfilled; we are not waiting for a future fulfillment. He also put conditions on their ability to retain the land, and they failed to keep those conditions. God didn't abandon or break the covenant; they did.

In the Old Testament, God made covenant with sinful humanity, and they constantly failed to hold up their end of the deal. Knowing humanity's frailty and inability, God created a new plan. He put on flesh and became a man. This enabled God the Father to make a New Covenant with Jesus as a man; therefore, God would be on both sides of this deal, and it would be perfectly upheld. Being inside Jesus, we get to rest in all the benefits of His perfect righteousness.

The New Covenant and the Israel of God

God made the New Covenant with the same people whom He made the Old Covenant with—*those who would walk with God by faith.* All who have faith in Christ are the children of Abraham. As Paul wrote, "So also Abraham 'believed God, and it was credited to him as righteousness.' Understand, then, that ***those who have faith are children of Abraham***" (Gal. 3:6-7).

We can see from this verse that, although many Jews would claim to be children of Abraham because of bloodline, God only regards those with faith as the children of Abraham. The apostle Paul wrote about this at length. Let's back up and see where this idea began in the New Testament:

> *In those days John the Baptist came, preaching in the wilderness of Judea and saying, "Repent, for the kingdom of heaven has come near." ...But when he saw many of the Pharisees and Sadducees coming to where he was baptizing, he said to them: "You brood of vipers! Who warned you to flee from the coming wrath? Produce fruit in keeping with repentance. And* ***do not think you can say to yourselves, 'We have Abraham as our father.'*** *I tell you that out of these stones God can raise up children for Abraham.* ***The ax is already at the root of the trees, and every tree that does not produce good fruit will be cut down and thrown into the fire*** (Matthew 3:1-2,7-10).

John the Baptist declared that they should not trust in their lineage for safety. Even at the beginning of the New Testament, John was already prophesying the threat of coming destruction. Later, Jesus also echoed this declaration:

> *"Abraham is our father," they answered.* ***"If you were Abraham's children,"*** *said Jesus,* ***"then you would do what Abraham did*** [walk by faith]. *As it is, you are looking for a way to kill me, a man who has told you the truth that I heard from God. Abraham did not do such things. You are doing the works of your own father." "We are not illegitimate children," they protested. "The only Father we have is God himself. "Jesus said to them, "If God were your Father, you would love me, for I have come here from God. I*

have not come on my own; God sent me. Why is my language not clear to you? Because you are unable to hear what I say. ***You belong to your father, the devil, and you want to carry out your father's desires.*** *He was a murderer from the beginning, not holding to the truth, for there is no truth in him. When he lies, he speaks his native language, for he is a liar and the father of lies. Yet because I tell the truth, you do not believe me! Can any of you prove me guilty of sin? If I am telling the truth, why don't you believe me? Whoever belongs to God hears what God says. The reason you do not hear is that* ***you do not belong to God"*** (John 8:39-47).

Jesus went even farther than John. Rather than just telling the Jews that their lineage doesn't matter, Jesus went so far as to say their father was the devil! Jesus said they didn't even belong to God. According to the Word, being a Jew is not simply a racial reality. It is not a matter of simply obeying the Law, either. It is a state of the heart, a heart of faith that is walking with God.

We know from Genesis 17:3 that circumcision was the sign that set apart those in covenant with God. In Romans 2 and in Philippians 3, Paul showed that in the New Testament God only honors His covenant with those who have been circumcised in their hearts, not merely in the flesh.

Now you, if you call yourself a Jew; if you rely on the law and boast in God.... Circumcision has value if you observe the law, but if you break the law, you have become as though you had not been circumcised. So then, if those who are not circumcised keep the law's requirements, will they not be regarded as though they were circumcised? The one who is not circumcised physically and yet obeys the law will condemn you who, even though you have the written code and circumcision, are a lawbreaker. A person ***is not a Jew who is one only outwardly,*** *nor is circumcision merely outward and physical. No,* ***a person is a Jew who is one inwardly;*** *and circumcision is circumcision of the heart, by the Spirit, not by the written code. Such a person's praise is not from other people, but from God* (Romans 2:17,25-29).

For ***it is we who are the circumcision,*** *we who serve God* ***by his Spirit,*** *who boast in Christ Jesus, and who put* ***no confidence in the flesh****—though I myself have reasons for such confidence. If someone else thinks they have reasons to put confidence in the flesh, I have more: circumcised*

> *on the eighth day, of the people of Israel, of the tribe of Benjamin, a Hebrew of Hebrews; in regard to the law, a Pharisee; as for zeal, persecuting the church; as for righteousness based on the law, faultless. But whatever were gains to me I now consider loss for the sake of Christ. What is more, I consider everything a loss because of the surpassing worth of knowing Christ Jesus my Lord, for whose sake* ***I have lost all things. I consider them garbage,*** *that I may gain Christ and be found in him, not having a righteousness of my own that comes from the law, but* ***that which is through faith in Christ—the righteousness that comes from God on the basis of faith.*** *I want to know Christ—yes, to know the power of his resurrection and participation in his sufferings, becoming like him in his death, and so, somehow, attaining to the resurrection from the dead* (Philippians 3:3-11).

I don't know if you realize the importance of what you just read, but according to Paul, God does not honor covenant with those who follow the Law, *but don't walk by faith.* God only honors covenant with those who are walking with Him by faith. Only circumcision of the heart matters to God.

In fact, Paul continues in Romans and states that even the idea of Israel being God's people is faith-based.

> *I have great sorrow and unceasing anguish in my heart. For I could wish that I myself were cursed and cut off from Christ for the sake of my people, those of my own race,* ***the people of Israel*** [Israel of the flesh]. *Theirs is the adoption to sonship; theirs the divine glory, the covenants, the receiving of the law, the temple worship and the promises. Theirs are the patriarchs, and from them is traced the human ancestry of the Messiah, who is God over all, forever praised! Amen. It is not as though God's word had failed.* ***For not all who are descended from Israel are Israel. Nor*** *because they* ***are his descendants*** *are they* ***all Abraham's children.*** *On the contrary, "It is through Isaac that your offspring will be reckoned." In other words,* ***it is not the children by physical descent who are God's children, but it is the children of the promise who are regarded as Abraham's offspring*** (Romans 9:2-8).

Verse 6 refers to the promises of God and says that God's promises did not fail. Even though the nation of Israel failed to walk with God, His promises did not fail because He only made those promises to those who walk by faith. God never broke His covenant nor did He transfer it.

God has only made covenant with those who choose to walk with Him by faith. That is why, in the Old Testament, people of other countries could become a part of Israel if they would be circumcised, which was to take on covenant with God.

It is unbiblical to think that God is in covenant with unbelievers, whether Jew or Gentile. God only makes covenant on the condition that the other party is walking in faith. He will not be unequally yoked. *God is only in covenant with those of faith—whether Jew or Gentile—both in the Old and New Testaments.*

One last passage that reiterates what I am sharing is in Galatians 4. Here Paul uses the two sons of Abraham to draw a contrast between those who receive Jesus by faith and those who trust in the Law and works.

> *For it is written that Abraham had two sons, one by the slave woman and the other by the free woman. His son by the slave woman was born* ***according to the flesh,*** *but his son by the free woman was born as the result of a* ***divine promise.*** *These things are being taken figuratively:* ***The women represent two covenants.*** *One covenant is from Mount Sinai and bears children who are to be slaves: This is Hagar. Now Hagar stands for Mount Sinai in Arabia and corresponds to the present city of Jerusalem, because she is in slavery with her children. But the Jerusalem that is above is free, and she is our mother. For it is written: "Be glad, barren woman, you who never bore a child; shout for joy and cry aloud, you who were never in labor; because more are the children of the desolate woman than of her who has a husband." Now you, brothers and sisters, like Isaac, are children of promise. At that time the son* ***born according to the flesh*** *persecuted the son* ***born by the power of the Spirit.*** *It is the same now. But what does Scripture say?* ***"Get rid of the slave woman and her son, for the slave woman's son will never share in the inheritance with the free woman's son."*** *Therefore, brothers and sisters, we are not children of the slave woman, but of the free woman* (Galatians 4:22-31).

Paul says to get rid of the slave woman and her son. God is only honoring those born by the power of the Spirit (by faith). There is no sharing of inheritance; only those born of the Spirit, by faith, will receive an inheritance.

"And as many as walk according to this rule, peace and mercy be upon them, and upon the Israel of God" (Gal. 6:16 NASB). Paul wraps up his letter by declaring peace and mercy upon those who walk in faith, and he gives them a new name. Rather than calling them the Israel of the flesh, he refers to those who walk by faith as the *Israel of God.*

All Israel Will Be Saved

There is a lot of confusion surrounding the verse that says, *"...all Israel will be saved..."* (Rom. 11:26). Because of this verse, many people think we are waiting for a coming Jewish revival. That is not what this verse is saying. Typically this verse is quoted alone and without an understanding of the context. In fact, even the first half of the verse is rarely quoted. Here is the first half: *"And in this way, all Israel will be saved...."* This is a concluding statement. In other words, it comes at the end of a long series of thoughts and is meant to wrap up those thoughts with, *"**And in this way,** all Israel will be saved...."* For this reason, we must back up to the beginning of this series of thoughts to grasp the context of this concluding statement.

> *I ask then: Did God reject his people? By no means! I am an Israelite myself, a descendant of Abraham, from the tribe of Benjamin. God did not reject his people, whom he foreknew. Don't you know what Scripture says in the passage about Elijah—how he appealed to God against Israel: "Lord, they have killed your prophets and torn down your altars; I am the only one left, and they are trying to kill me"? And what was God's answer to him? "I have reserved for myself seven thousand who have not bowed the knee to Baal." So too, at the present time there is a remnant chosen by grace. And if by grace, then it cannot be based on works; if it were, grace would no longer be grace* (Romans 11:1-6).

In the Old Testament and in the New Testament, there has always been a remnant of the Jews who have followed God, even when the vast majority has turned away; God has always had a remnant of faithful ones (the *ekklesia* or *called out ones*).

> *What then? What the people of Israel sought so earnestly they did not obtain. The elect among them did, but the others were hardened, as it is written: "God*

> *gave them a spirit of stupor, eyes that could not see and ears that could not hear, to this very day." And David says: "May their table become a snare and a trap, a stumbling block and a retribution for them. May their eyes be darkened so they cannot see, and their backs be bent forever"* (Romans 11:7-10).

In response to those who didn't pursue God by faith, He blinded their eyes and hardened them into their decision.

> *Again I ask: Did they stumble so as to fall beyond recovery? Not at all! Rather, because of their transgression, salvation has come to the Gentiles to make Israel envious. But if their transgression means riches for the world, and their loss means riches for the Gentiles, how much greater riches will their full inclusion bring! I am talking to you Gentiles. Inasmuch as I am the apostle to the Gentiles, I take pride in my ministry in the hope that I may somehow arouse my own people to envy and save some of them. For if their rejection brought reconciliation to the world, what will their acceptance be but life from the dead? If the part of the dough offered as firstfruits is holy, then the whole batch is holy; if the root is holy, so are the branches. If some of the branches have been broken off, and you, though a wild olive shoot, have been grafted in among the others and now share in the nourishing sap from the olive root, do not consider yourself to be superior to those other branches. If you do, consider this: You do not support the root, but the root supports you. You will say then, "Branches were broken off so that I could be grafted in." Granted. But they were broken off because of unbelief, and you stand by faith. Do not be arrogant, but tremble. For if God did not spare the natural branches, he will not spare you either* (Romans 11:11-21).

The Jews are the natural branch, and the Gentiles are the wild branch. As we saw earlier, being of Jewish lineage, yet not walking in faith, amounts to nothing before God. As seen in Romans 11:20, *"They were broken off because of unbelief, but you stand by faith."* We have been grafted into the Israel of God, the true Israel, the Israel that knows God by faith, the Israel that God has always made and kept His covenants with. This is what we are grafted into by grace through faith.

> *Consider therefore the kindness and sternness of God: sternness to those who fell, but kindness to you, provided that you continue in his kindness. Otherwise, you also will be cut off. And if they do not persist in unbelief, they will be grafted in, for God is able to graft them in again. After all, if you were cut out of an olive tree that is wild by nature, and contrary to nature were grafted into a cultivated olive tree, how much more readily will these, the natural branches, be grafted into their own olive tree* (Romans 11:22-24).

God is stern toward those walking in unbelief, whereas He is kind to those walking in faith. If Jews will turn from trusting in dead works and will, instead, walk with God by faith in the Messiah, then they will be grafted back into the Israel of God and be His people again. Jews may be of national Israel, but if they are not of faith, then they are under the sternness of God. If an individual Jew or Gentile is walking in faith, then that person is pleasing to God and walks under His kindness.

> *I do not want you to be ignorant of this mystery, brothers and sisters, so that you may not be conceited: Israel has experienced a hardening in part until the full number of the Gentiles has come in, and* ***in this way all Israel will be saved.*** *As it is written: "The deliverer will come from Zion; he will turn godlessness away from Jacob"* (Romans 11:25-26).

As we saw earlier, God has taken those who rejected Him and hardened them into their decision. This allows for the Gentiles to come in and join the Israel of God by walking in faith. The remnant portion of Jews who follow God by faith and the Gentiles who are following by faith together make up what is called the Israel of God (see Gal 6:16). God has always made His covenants and related with His true Israel, those who walk with Him by faith.

Who Is Israel?

In the past, there remained a majority of Jews who bore the name Israel while not walking with God. For example, "*...Not all who are descended from Israel are Israel*" (Rom. 9:6). True Israel has always been defined as those who are walking by faith, while at the same time there have been many others under the name Israel who shared the bloodline but weren't really Israel according to God.

Now that God has given His Son, He clearly delineates that only those who put their faith in Jesus are a part of the Israel of God. Therefore it says, *"And in this way, all Israel will be saved..."* (Rom. 11:26). In what way? What Paul is saying is that all Israel—the true Israel of God—the Israel that currently exists in God's mind is made up of Jews and Gentiles who have put faith in Jesus. Therefore, in that way, everyone who is a part of Israel will be saved. This is the new line of demarcation, rather than the Old Testament division between the unbelieving Jews and the remnant of faith. From now forward, "all Israel" is made up of those who are saved through faith in Jesus!

Frequently Asked Questions

Q: Did the Church replace Israel?

A: No. I am not saying that God has replaced Israel with the Church. I am showing that the Bible teaches that God has always only made covenant with those who follow Him by faith. In the Old Testament, this was always a smaller portion of the larger whole of Israel. The remnant that followed God by faith was called the *ekklesia*, which means *called out ones*.

In the New Testament, the Greek root word for "Church" is *ekklesia*. There is actually no distinction between Israel and the Church. The *ekklesia* under the Old Covenant is added to by the *ekklesia* in the New Covenant. The *ekklesia* of the Old Covenant are joined by the grafting in of the Gentile *ekklesia* of the New Covenant. There is a perfect continuation. There is no replacement.

This is well stated by Brian L. Martin:

> Again, we wish to note that we view this position as "fulfilled theology" rather than "replacement theology." We do not believe that Israel was "wiped off the table" and that God started over with the New Covenant. Rather, just as a butterfly cannot come into existence without the caterpillar metamorphosing, so the New Covenant could not come into being apart from the Old. Was the caterpillar "replaced"? No, it became the butterfly. Likewise, the Old Covenant had always pointed to the New; that was always God's ultimate goal. When the New Covenant emerged from the Old, what remained physically was just a cocoon, that which had effected the transformation. The old system of types and shadows, like the cocoon, was no longer needed.[1]

Q: Can we be sure that "all Israel" isn't simply referring to all of the natural Jews eventually getting saved?

A: The apostle Paul is very clear that the entire nation of Israel is not the same as "all Israel" in Romans 11:26 (see Rom. 2:28–29; 9:6–8). Here are four additional points that support this:

- In Romans 10:1, it was Paul's *longing* that his brethren would be saved, not a guarantee.
- Paul said that, though the Jews were as sand on the seashore, only a remnant would be saved (see Rom. 9:27).
- Paul used *if* statements regarding Israelites being re-grafted (see Rom. 11:23); he was not expressing a guarantee of re-grafting.
- According to God, there is neither Jew nor Gentile; we are all the same (see Gal 3:26–29).

Q: Isn't there an end-time promise that the Jewish people will declare: "Blessed is he who comes in the name of the Lord?" Are we waiting for this to be fulfilled?

A: Yes, Jesus prophesied that Jerusalem wouldn't see Him again until they declared, *"Blessed is He who comes in the name of the Lord."*

> *Jerusalem, Jerusalem, you who kill the prophets and stone those sent to you, how often I have longed to gather your children together, as a hen gathers her chicks under her wings, and you were not willing. Look, your house is left to you desolate. I tell you, you will not see me again until you say,* ***"Blessed is he who comes in the name of the Lord"*** (Luke 13:34-35).

But in Luke 13, Jesus was not prophesying a Jewish revival 2,000 years in the future. Jesus was actually declaring that Jerusalem would not see Him again until Palm Sunday, which was fulfilled in Luke 19.

> *When he came near the place where the road goes down the Mount of Olives, the whole crowd of disciples began joyfully to praise God in loud voices for all the miracles they had seen:* ***"Blessed is the king who comes in the name of the Lord!"*** *"Peace in heaven and glory in the highest!" Some of the Pharisees in the crowd said to Jesus, "Teacher, rebuke your disciples!" "I tell you," he replied, "if they keep quiet, the stones will cry out"* (Luke 19:37-40).

Q: Has God rejected Israel?

A: No, God has not rejected Israel, as Romans 11:1,11 clearly states. What God extends, He never takes back (see Rom. 11:29). But Israel chose to reject God (see Rom. 9:30–32; 11:15).

Q: Is Israel to be restored as a nation?

A: There is *not even one* New Testament promise or prophecy regarding Israel being restored as a nation. Every promise and prophecy of the New Testament speaks of judgment and condemnation for the nation of Israel. Every time a preacher tries to claim the restoration of Israel, the preacher has to pull verses from the Old Testament out of context. In the Old Testament, there were promises to restore Israel after their exile to Babylon. Yet every one of these Old Testament prophecies has been fulfilled. Many have twisted Scripture out of context to create this teaching.

Q: Is the Temple to be rebuilt?

A: There is *not even one* New Testament promise or prophecy regarding a rebuilt Temple. Every promise and prophecy of the New Testament speaks of judgment and the destruction of the Temple. Again, every time preachers try to claim the restoration of the Temple, they have to pull verses from the Old Testament out of context. In the Old Testament, there were promises to rebuild the Temple, such as were fulfilled in the Books of Ezra and Nehemiah. Yet every one of these prophecies has been fulfilled.[2]

Q: So is the 1948 restoration of the Nation of Israel prophetic in any way?

A: I will quote from Gary DeMar on this one:

> There is not a single verse in the New Testament that supports the claim that there is prophetic significance in Israel's restoration as a nation. Beyond A.D. 70, Israel as a nation plays no prophetic role. The New Testament only addresses Israel's near destruction never its distant restoration. There is no mention of a temple being rebuilt or Jews returning to their land as was predicted in the Old Testament. The Jews did return to their land as prophesied (Jer. 29:14), "when seventy years have been completed for Babylon" (29:10; cf. Dan. 9:2).

The temple was eventually rebuilt as predicted (Ezra 5:16; John 2:20). These prophecies have been fulfilled. Isaiah 11:11 does mention Israel returning to their land after the Babylonian captivity. The first time was "the day that they came up out of the land of Egypt" (11:16). (William Hendriksen, *Israel in Prophecy,* Grand Rapids, MI, Zondervan, 1970, pg 53-54.) There is no mention of a third time. If the Old Testament is the pattern, then we should expect to see specific New Testament prophecies regarding the future reestablishment of Israel as a nation and the rebuilding of the temple [but we do not!].[3]

Q: Doesn't He have an everlasting covenant?

A: God has always and only made His covenants with those who will walk with Him by faith. Therefore, He is continuing to keep all of His covenants to the Israel of faith, which is made up of both Jews and Gentiles. Only those who have accepted Jesus as the Messiah are a part of the Israel of faith.

Q: Aren't the Israelites God's chosen people?

A: Chosen for what? In the Bible, we find that a few have been chosen to carry Christ.

- Abraham's family line was *chosen to carry the seed* (Christ) and bring Him into the earth (see Gal. 3:16).
- Mary, the mother of Jesus, was *chosen to carry the seed* and bring Him into the earth directly (see Luke 1:26–38).
- The Church has been *chosen to carry the seed* of God (Christ) and bring Him into the earth (see 1 Pet. 2:9).

Abraham was *chosen* and fulfilled his assignment; Mary was *chosen* and fulfilled her assignment; now the Church (made of Jews and Gentiles) is currently the *chosen* and is fulfilling her assignment.

Q: Do I need to pray for Israel?

A: Psalm 2:8 says, *"Ask of me and I will give you the nations as an inheritance."* I believe that we should pray for all the nations of the world, as well as our families, spiritual leaders, and government leaders. Since the true Israel of God is those who walk by faith, there is no reason to pray for the nation of Israel more than any other nation. I believe that many Christians' racism is visible in the way that they favor Israel in prayer over and against the Muslims of the same region. Those Muslims desperately need prayer, too.

Q: I have heard that lots of Jews are moving to Israel and that this is a prophetic sign; what do you think?

A: *Victorious Eschatology* says:

> It is true that approximately 800,000 Jews have emigrated from Russia to Israel in recent years; however, a large percentage of them have used Israel as a transfer station to gain entrance into the USA. Jews have been migrating in from other locations as well, but the Israeli Daily, Yediot Ahronot, reported on April 4, 2007 that there is actually a net exodus of people from the country. The truth is that there are more Jews in the USA today than in Israel, and the largest population gathered in any one location is in New York City. The idea that Jews are now returning en masse to Israel is simply a myth.[4]

Q: When will Zechariah 12:10 be fulfilled?

And I will pour out on the house of David and the inhabitants of Jerusalem a spirit of grace and supplication. ***They will look on me, the one they have pierced,*** *and they will mourn for him as one mourns for an only child, and grieve bitterly for him as one grieves for a firstborn son.*

A: The Bible tells us it was fulfilled in John 19:36-37:

These things happened so that the scripture would be fulfilled: *"Not one of his bones will be broken," and, as another scripture says,* ***"They will look on the one they have pierced."***

And also Acts 2:36-37 says:

"Therefore let all Israel be assured of this: God has made this Jesus, whom you crucified, both Lord and Messiah." When the people heard this, they were ***cut***

to the heart [grieved] *and said to Peter and the other apostles, "Brothers, what shall we do?"*

In Summary

I am aware that, for many Christians, I have just written a chapter on the king of the sacred cows. The shift in thinking that this chapter presents will be very large for some, but I would ask you to simply ponder and review what I have presented here. A hurried judgment is not necessary.

CHAPTER POINTS

- The Old Testament is a shadow pointing to Christ.
- The Abrahamic covenant is fulfilled.
- The Mosaic Covenant is fulfilled.
- The Davidic Covenant is fulfilled.
- The Land Promise was fulfilled within the Old Testament.
- God only has covenant with the Israel of Faith.
- We are not waiting for Israel to say, "Blessed is He who comes in the name of the Lord."
- There is no promise to restore Israel as a nation.
- There is no promise to rebuild the Jewish Temple.

DISCUSSION QUESTIONS

1. What are some of the ways Old Testament Israel served as a type and shadow pointing to Jesus?

2. Which three Old Testament characters did God make and fulfill His promises to in this chapter?

3. Was God faithful to fulfill His land promises to Israel?

4. Did God put "if" conditions upon His promises?

5. In terms of covenant, does God value faith or family bloodline?

6. Read aloud and discuss as a group what Romans 9:2–8 means.

7. Read aloud and discuss as a group what Galatians 4:22–31 means.

8. Who is "all Israel" in Romans 11:26?

9. Is there biblical reason to believe the Temple will be rebuilt in Jerusalem?

chapter nine

THE KINGDOM TRANSITION

As a husband, the idea of my wife committing adultery is one of the most hurtful thoughts I can imagine. But what if she were to commit adultery a dozen times? What about a few dozen times? This would be a completely devastating and heart-rending experience. Yet, this is exactly what happened to God. In Jeremiah 31:31–33, we see the heartbreak that God experienced:

> *"The days are coming," declares the LORD, "when* ***I will make a new covenant*** *with the people of Israel and with the people of Judah.* ***It will not be like the covenant I made with their ancestors*** *when I took them by the hand to lead them out of Egypt, because* ***they broke my covenant, though I was a husband to them,****" declares the LORD* (Jeremiah 31:31-32).

All throughout their history, the Israelites failed to keep their covenant with God, and they played the whore with idols and false gods. As God saw they were completely unable to keep up their side of the covenant, He determined He would make a new covenant. Since humanity couldn't hold up their side of the covenant, this new covenant would be made between God the Father and Jesus. This transition is predicted throughout the Old Testament. For example:

> *The scepter* ***will not depart*** *from Judah, nor the ruler's staff from between his feet,* ***until he whom it belongs shall come*** *and the obedience of the nations shall be his* (Genesis 49:10).

Daniel's Prophecy

In Daniel chapter 9, there is a prophecy that declares five specific things: the timing of the Messiah's arrival, His death, the end of the Old Covenant, the confirming of the New Covenant, and the coming destruction of Jerusalem.

> *Seventy "sevens" are decreed for your people and your holy city to: finish transgression, to put an end to sin, to atone for wickedness, to bring in everlasting righteousness, to seal up vision and prophecy and to anoint the Most Holy Place* (Daniel 9:24).

There are six activities prophesied in this passage. Jesus fulfilled all six in His first coming.

- To finish the transgression: By crucifying Christ, the Jews filled up the measure of their transgression; thus it was finished and judgment was due upon that generation.
- To make an end of sins: Christ offered one sacrifice for sins forever (see Heb. 10:12) and purged our sins (see Heb. 1:3).
- To make reconciliation for iniquity: Prior to Christ's atoning sacrifice, we were enemies of God; now we have been reconciled to Him (see Rom. 5:8–11).
- To bring in everlasting righteousness: The everlasting New Covenant provides a righteousness apart from the Law of the Old Covenant, by which no flesh was justified (made righteous) (see Rom. 3:19–26).
- To seal up vision and prophecy: Not a fulfilling, but a sealing up. This was part of the punishment upon national Israel, that both vision and prophet—eye and ear—were closed up so that "seeing they would not see, and hearing they would not hear" (Isa. 6:10; Acts 28:17–28; cf. Mic. 3:1–7).

- To anoint the Most Holy: This is the pouring out of the Holy Spirit upon the Church at Pentecost, anointing the temple of the living God (see 2 Cor. 6:16), the Most Holy.[1]

Simply put, God spoke to Israel, giving them 490 years of grace for them to straighten up and change their ways. Scholars typically agree that prophetic numerology shows that the "seventy sevens" of this page equals 490 years (see Gen. 29:27; Lev. 25:8; Num. 14:34; Ezek. 4:4–6).

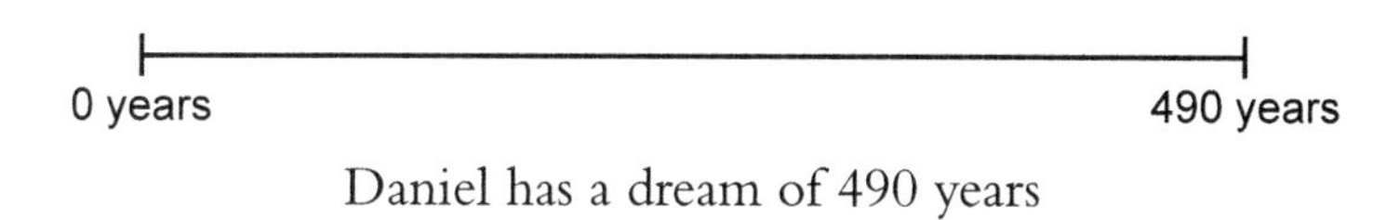

Daniel has a dream of 490 years

In the next verse, God also stated that He would not start the clock right away, but that the 490 years would start when the king said to rebuild Jerusalem. He also announced in this passage exactly when His Son, the Messiah, would come to Israel.

> *Know and understand this: From the time the word goes out to restore and rebuild Jerusalem until the Anointed One the ruler, comes, there will be seven "sevens," and sixty-two "sevens"* [483 years]. *It will be rebuilt with streets and a trench, but in times of trouble* (Daniel 9:25).

The edict to restore Jerusalem was declared in 457 BC under Artaxerxes, the king of Persia (see Ezra 7:12–26).

Edict to restore Jerusalem

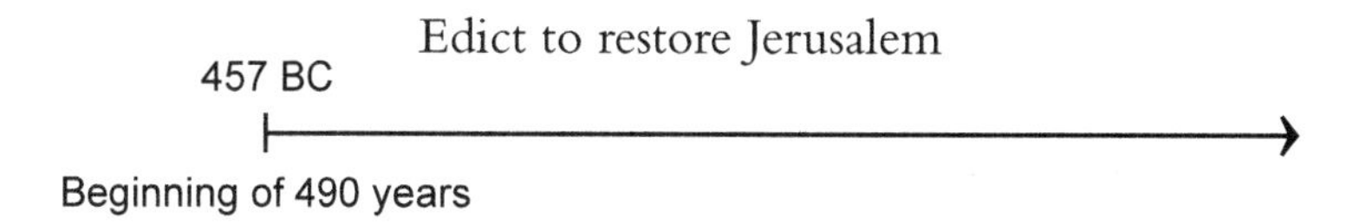

From the time when Artaxerxes declared this in 457 BC until AD 27 was 483 years. In AD 27, Jesus came onto the scene, exactly as this prophecy indicates. In fact the renowned commentator Matthew Henry, wrote of this prophecy that: "We have [in Daniel 9:24–27] the most illustrious prediction of Christ and gospel-grace that is extant in all the Old Testament."[2]

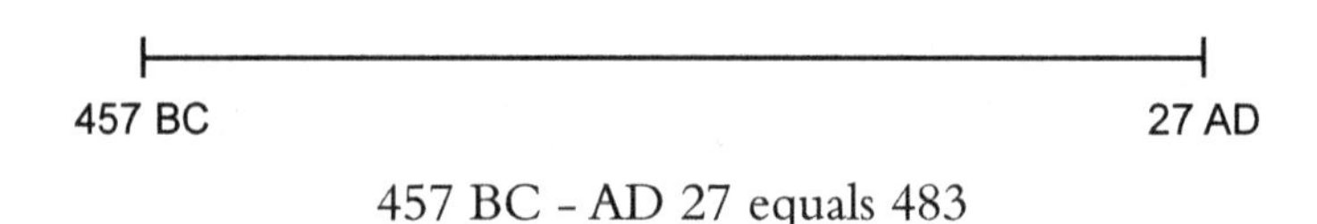

457 BC - AD 27 equals 483

The prophecy continues, even telling of the Messiah's death, *"After the sixty-two 'sevens,'* [including the previous seven sevens, thus sixty-nine weeks or 483 years] *the Anointed One* [Jesus] *will be put to death and will have nothing..."* (Dan. 9:26).

After the prophecy finishes speaking about the 490 years of mercy being extended to Israel, telling the exact date of the Messiah's coming and prophesying His death, it then declares the coming destruction of Jerusalem.

> ...*The people* [the Roman armies] *of the ruler* [Titus] *who will come will destroy the city and the sanctuary. The end will come like a flood: War will continue until the end* [of Jerusalem], *and desolations have been decreed* (Daniel 9:26).

After this, God backs up for a moment to bring clarity to the last seven years of the 490 years of mercy. He states that halfway through the last seven years, the Messiah will confirm a new covenant (see Matt. 26:28) and put an end to the Old Covenant and its sacrificial system.

> *He* [Jesus] *will confirm a covenant with many for one "seven." In the middle of the "seven" he will put an end to sacrifice and offering...* (Daniel 9:27).

This prophecy tells exactly when the Messiah will show up (AD 27), that the Messiah will die, and that He will end the sacrificial system halfway through the last seven years of the 490 years. Jesus did this by His death on the cross exactly three and a half years after AD 27.

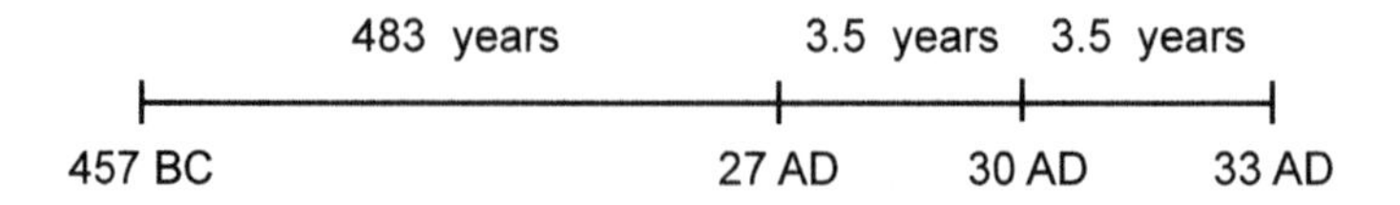

The last seven years and Jesus' death

This brings us to a fascinating point from the Gospels. When Peter asked Jesus how many times he had to forgive his brother, suggesting that seven times might be forgiving enough, Jesus replied that he should forgive seventy times seven, which is 490 times. Jesus was alluding to this prophecy from Daniel, and He was telling Peter to be as forgiving as God had been toward His wicked people (see Matt. 18:21).

Let's recap: Daniel heard the prophecy of 490 years of mercy being extended. He heard that the 490 years would start when the edict to rebuild Jerusalem went forth. After the edict was released and the clock started ticking, 483 years would go by, and then the Messiah would appear, which happened in AD 27, when Jesus began His ministry. Then during the last seven years of the 490 years of mercy, the Messiah would end animal sacrifice, and He would also be put to death. This happened in AD 30. Out of the 490 years, this timeline still leaves us with three and a half years left on the clock.

Approximately, three and a half years after Jesus' death and resurrection, Stephen was stoned to death, which was approved of by the chief ruler of the synagogue (see Acts 7:1,54–60). This was the end of God's mercy clock for Jerusalem. Not long after, God gave Peter the vision of the unclean animals and sent him to evangelize Cornelius' house (see Acts 10), as well as converting Paul and sending Him to the Gentiles (see Acts 9:1–5). This completed the 490 years of mercy God extended to His people.

Those who follow the teachings of Darby believe the last seven years of Daniel 9's prophecy haven't happened yet. I agree with DeMar's assessment of such obvious error.

> The idea of separation and the placement of an indeterminable gap between the two sets of weeks is one of the most unnatural and nonliteral interpretations of Scripture found in any eschatology system. This interpretation is taught by those who insist on a literal hermeneutic, if dispensationalists were consistent in their literalism, they would never manipulate Scripture to fit an already established prophetic system.[3]

The Abomination of Desolation

In Matthew 23, we read of Jesus in the Temple declaring woes and judgments against the wicked Israelites of His day. He declares destruction upon them and upon Jerusalem. Then in Matthew 24:15, Jesus referred to the last verse in this passage from Daniel 9.

> *So when you see standing in the holy place "the abomination that causes desolation,"* **spoken of through the prophet Daniel**—*let the reader understand—then let those who are in Judea flee to the mountains* (Matthew 24:15).

The last half of Daniel 9:27, which Jesus was referring to, says *"And on the wing of abominations shall come one who makes desolate, until the decreed end is poured out on the desolator"* (Dan. 9:27 ESV).

We see from what Jesus is saying in Matthew 24:15 that when His listeners in the first century saw the "abomination that causes desolation," they should flee Judea to the mountains. Fortunately for us, Jesus told us exactly what the abomination was in the parallel Gospel of Luke: *"When you see Jerusalem being surrounded by armies, you will know that its desolation is near"* (Luke 21:20). The Roman army, which surrounded Jerusalem and brought utter desolation in AD 70, was the great abomination.

The prophecy from Daniel 9 is, as Matthew Henry wrote, "most remarkable." It contains amazing predictions of Jesus' arrival and death, the end of sacrifice, and the confirming of the New Covenant. Yet it also contains the predicted destruction of Jerusalem. It is imperative that the modern Church teaches believers about the AD 70 destruction, as it is literally a predicted part of the Messianic gospel of Jesus Christ. Although it is unpleasant, this is not a good reason to avoid teaching it. Obviously, the cross of Christ was an unpleasant scene, yet all good preachers keep it central to their message.

The destruction of Jerusalem, the Temple, and the priesthood is a major part of understanding the gospel of Jesus Christ. To not understand the significance of the AD 70 destruction is to miss a major component of the redemption story. The destruction of Jerusalem is akin to the virgin birth, the cross, and the resurrection. I know that is a huge statement, but I believe it is absolutely true. Even though many Christians have not been taught about this event, it is still an essential component.

The Gospel of Doom?

The redemption message prophesied from the Old Testament (see Dan. 9:24–27) included:

- The Messiah's arrival
- The Messiah's death
- The end of the Old Covenant
- The confirming of a New Covenant
- The coming destruction of Jerusalem

The fifth point, the destruction of Jerusalem, was the final removal of the Old Covenant and the confirmation that the New Covenant had fully arrived. Most Christians have never heard about the AD 70 destruction and, thus, are literally missing a major piece of the redemption message. This is quite shocking to most people because it is similar to being a Christian for fifty years and then hearing for the first time that Jesus was born of a virgin!

Throughout Jesus' ministry, we can observe the emphasis that He put on the coming destruction. In fact, one of the few and definitely the longest recorded prophetic words from Jesus is the Olivet Discourse (see Matt. 24; Mark 13; Luke 21). As we have seen, this passage is Jesus decreeing the destruction of Jerusalem.

As we saw earlier, when Jesus was anointed for ministry, He quoted from Isaiah 61:1–2 in Luke 4:18–19, leaving off the final phrase *"and the day of vengeance of our God."* Later, He finished quoting the Isaiah passage in Luke 21:21, foretelling the coming destruction. For three years, He focused on the first part of His mission; then in Luke 21:21, He declared the last part of His mission, the day of vengeance upon Jerusalem.

> *The Spirit of the Sovereign LORD is on me, because the LORD has anointed me to proclaim good news to the poor. He has sent me to bind up the brokenhearted, to proclaim freedom for the captives and release from darkness for the prisoners, to proclaim the year of the LORD's favor* [this is the quote from Luke 4:18-19, then He finishes quoting the passage in Luke 21:21] ***and the day of vengeance of our God...*** (Isaiah 61:1-2).

Jesus also spoke of this in several of His parables. In Matthew 22:5–7, Jesus told a parable to the Pharisees, saying when the king returned to deal with those who killed his son, he would set their city on fire, which is a clear reference of the coming judgment upon Jerusalem. Earlier in Matthew 21:33–46, Jesus gave another parable in which God *"destroy*[ed] *those wicked men miserably"* (NKJV).

When John the Baptist prophesied that Jesus was coming, he said that Jesus would baptize (immerse) with the Holy Spirit and with fire.

> *I baptize you with water for repentance. But after me will come one who is more powerful than I, whose sandals I am not fit to carry. He will baptize you with the Holy Spirit and with fire* (Matthew 3:11).

It is reasonable to understand the immersion with the Holy Spirit as the day of Pentecost, whereas the immersion with fire happened when Jerusalem was burned to the ground. As we will see in a moment, even Peter confirmed this in Acts 2.

In Matthew 24, Jesus' disciples asked Him about the end of the Age (of Moses), and Jesus responded about the coming destruction. For three years, Jesus had reached out to His people, and they had received Him not. Near the end of His ministry, He specifically focused on the destruction of the old system. In Matthew 22, He spoke of coming to set their city on fire. In Matthew 23, He gave a whole chapter of rebukes against the religious leaders, which ended with a statement of how He longed to gather them under His wings, but they would not let Him (see Matt. 23:37). Then He declared that all the blood of the Old Testament would come in judgment upon that generation's head (see Matt. 23:31–36). Then in Matthew 24, Jesus gave very precise, detailed answers to the disciples regarding the coming judgment. As we can see, the coming destruction is a very large part of the gospel story.

Likewise, at the end of the Book of Hebrews, we find a contrast between the physical worship in earthly Jerusalem and the spiritual worship in the Heavenly Jerusalem. At the end of the contrast, the writer says that everything that can be shaken will be shaken (a clear reference to the AD 70 destruction) and that only the spiritual worship will remain.

> *..."Yet once more I will shake not only the earth, but also heaven."* [Quoting from Haggai 2:6] *Now this, "Yet once more,"* ***indicates the removal of those things that are being shaken, as of things that are made, that the things which cannot be shaken may remain.*** *Therefore, since we are receiving* ***a kingdom, which cannot be shaken,*** *let us have grace, by which we may serve God acceptably with reverence and godly fear. For our* ***God is a consuming fire****"* (Hebrews 12:26-29 NKJV).

Notice again the reference to fire and specifically the statement that God is a consuming fire. This passage is foreshadowing the fact that God was about to come upon Jerusalem and the earthly worship system as a consuming fire!

All throughout the New Testament, we find that the early Church was focused on the coming destruction of Jerusalem. It was an integral part of the Good News that Jesus brought. That judgment would begin first at the house of God (see 1 Pet. 4:17). God was going to clean out His house and fully establish His spiritual Kingdom upon the removal of the previous establishment. The early Church referred to this coming (AD 70) event as the "last days," the "end of the age" and the "Day of Judgment." This is a major part of understanding Jesus' message and the mindset of the early Church.

The End of the Age

Matthew 13:39	The harvest is the end of the age.
Matthew 13:40	So it will be at the end of this age.
Matthew 13:49	So it will be at the end of the age.
Matthew 24:3	What will be the sign of Your coming, and of the end of the age?
Hebrews 9:26	But now, once at the end of the ages, He has appeared.

The End

Matthew 10:22	He who endures to the end will be saved.
Matthew 24:6	But the end is not yet.
Matthew 24:13	He who endures to the end shall be saved.
Matthew 24:14	The the end will come.

1 Corinthians 1:8	Who will also confirm you to the end.
1 Corinthians 10:11	On whom the ends of the ages have come.
Hebrews 3:6	Firm to the end.
Hebrews 3:14	Hold the beginning of our confidence steadfast to the end.
Hebrews 6:11	Show the same difigence...until the end.
1 Peter 4:7	The end of all things is at hand.

The Last Times, Days, etc.

1 Timothy 4:1	In latter times some will depart from the faith.
2 Timothy 3:1	In the last days perilous times will come.
Hebrews 1:2	[God] has in these last days spoken to us.
James 5:3	You have heaped up treasure in the last days.
1 Peter 1:5	Salvation ready to be revealed in the last times.
1 Peter 1:20	[Who] was made manifest in these last days.
2 Peter 3:3	Scoffers will come in the last days.
1 John 2:18	It is the last hour.
Jude 18	That there would be mockers in the last time.

The Day of the Lord, God, etc.

2 Peter 3:12	Looking for and hastening the coming of the day of God.
1 Thessalonians 5:2	The day of the Lord so comes as a thief in the night.
1 Corinthians 1:8	That you may be blameless in the day of our Lord Jesus Christ.
1 Corinthians 5:5	That his spirit may be saved in the day of our Lord Jesus Christ.
2 Corinthians 1:14	You also are ours, in the day of the Lord Jesus.
Acts 2:20	The great and notable day of the Lord.
Jude 6	The judgment of the great day.
Romans 2:5	Treasuring up for yourself wrath in the day of wrath.

The "end of the age," "the end," "the last times," "the last days," and "the day of the lord" are very specific references to the days between Jesus' prophecy of Matthew 24 and its fulfillment in AD 70. These were the "last days" of Judaism and Jerusalem. (In contrast, references to "the day of judgment, "the day of redemption," or "the last day" are references to the final judgment, which will be addressed in detail in Chapter 14, "The Big Three.") Many don't understand that the Old Covenant age ended with the AD 70 destruction and that the whole New Testament speaks of that end. We are now living in the Kingdom Age, which grows without end (more on that later).

The baptism of the Holy Spirit, which John the Baptist prophesied, occurred on the Day of Pentecost in Acts 2. At that event, Peter spoke specifically about the yet-to-come baptism of fire, the destruction of Jerusalem.

> *No, this is what was spoken by the prophet Joel* [see Joel 2:28-32]*: "**In the last days,** God says, I will pour out my Spirit on all people. Your sons and daughters will prophesy, your young men will see visions, your old men will dream dreams. Even on my servants, both men and women, I will pour out my Spirit in those days, and they will prophesy. **I will show wonders in the heavens above and signs on the earth below, blood and fire and billows of smoke. The sun will be turned to darkness and the moon to blood before the coming of the great and glorious day of the Lord.*** [The coming destruction upon Jerusalem] *And everyone who calls on the name of the Lord will be saved"* [The rest of Joel 2:32 finishes with: "for on Mount Zion and in Jerusalem there will be deliverance, as the LORD has said, even among the survivors whom the LORD calls."] (Acts 2:17-21).

In this message, Peter was clearly referring to the same destructive event that Jesus spoke of in Matthew 24:29–30 (I discussed this in detail in Chapter 3). Peter said the day of Pentecost was the fulfillment of this prophecy from Joel, and in the next breath, he referenced the coming destruction. By this, Peter was saying the pouring out of the Holy Spirit was confirmation that they were in the last days, and the next thing to take place would be the destruction of Jerusalem. Then He said all who called upon the Lord would be saved, referring not only to salvation in Jesus, but also to protection from the destruction of Jerusalem for the first-century Christians.

This brings up an amazing point about speaking in tongues. Speaking in tongues was a prophetic sign that pointed to the coming destruction of Jerusalem.

Speaking in Tongues

The idea that the advent of speaking in tongues was confirmation of the coming destruction of Jerusalem might be a new concept for some readers. Yet we find that the apostle Paul also confirmed this idea in First Corinthians 14:21–22:

> *In the Law it is written: "**With other tongues and through the lips of foreigners I will speak to this people, but even then they will not listen to me, says the Lord.**"* [Quoting from Isaiah 28:11] *Tongues, then, are a sign, not for believers but for unbelievers; prophecy, however, is not for unbelievers but for believers* (1 Corinthians 14:21-22).

Here Paul quotes from Isaiah 28:11, showing that Isaiah had prophesied the coming gift of tongues. When we read the rest of Isaiah's prophecy, we can see that he foretold not only speaking in tongues, but also apostasy, Jesus' coming, and God's judgment upon Israel. Here are the three passages from Isaiah 28 that speak about these three events:

Apostasy

> *So then, the word of the LORD to them will become: Do this, do that, a rule for this, a rule for that; a little here, a little there—so that as they go **they will fall backward; they will be injured and snared and captured.** Therefore hear the word of the LORD, you scoffers who rule this people in Jerusalem. You boast, "We have entered into a covenant with death, with the realm of the dead we have made an agreement. When an overwhelming scourge sweeps by, it cannot touch us, for **we have made a lie our refuge and falsehood our hiding place"*** (Isaiah 28:13-15).

Jesus, the Chief Cornerstone

> *So this is what the Sovereign LORD says: "See, I lay a stone in Zion, a tested stone, a precious cornerstone for a sure foundation [see Matthew 21:42]; the one who relies on it will never be stricken with panic. I will make justice the measuring line and righteousness the plumb line..."* (Isaiah 28:16-17).

God's Judgment

> *"...Hail will sweep away your refuge, the lie, and water will overflow your hiding place. Your covenant with death will be annulled; your agreement with the realm of the dead will not stand. When the overwhelming scourge sweeps by, you will be beaten down by it. As often as it comes it will carry you away; morning after morning, by day and by night, it will sweep through."* ***The understanding of this message will bring sheer terror*** (Isaiah 28:17-19).

By reading this extended passage from Isaiah 28, we can clearly see that the advent of the gift of speaking in tongues was a sign of the coming destruction of Jerusalem. Along these lines, regarding the gift of speaking in tongues, the scholar David Chilton writes:

> The miracle of Pentecost was a shocking message to Israel. They knew what this meant. It was the sign from God that the Chief Cornerstone had come, and that Israel had rejected Him to its own damnation (Matthew 21:42-44; 1 Peter 2:6-8). It was *the sign of judgment and reprobation*, the signal that the apostates of Jerusalem were about to "stumble backward, be broken, snared, and taken captive." [See Isa. 28:13.] The Last Days of Israel had come: the old age was at an end, and Jerusalem would be swept away in a new flood to make way for God's New Creation. As St. Paul said, the gift of tongues was "for a sign, not to those who believe, but to unbelievers" (1 Corinthians 14:22)—*a sign to the unbelieving Jews of their approaching doom.*

> The early Church looked forward to the coming of the new [Kingdom] age. They knew that, with the visible end of the Old Covenant system, the Church would be revealed as the new, true Temple; and the work Christ came to perform would be accomplished. This was an important aspect of redemption, and the first-generation Christians looked forward to this event *in their own lifetime.* During this period of waiting and severe trial, the apostle Peter assured them that they were "protected by the power of God through faith for a salvation ready to be revealed in the last time" (1 Peter 1:5). They were on the very threshold of the new world.[4]

This quote sums up the major shift between the Old and New Covenants that happened, beginning with Jesus' death and resurrection and culminating in the destruction of Jerusalem. In this way, the early believers received the Kingdom in their day, and the Church has been advancing the Kingdom ever since, as we will discuss in the next chapter.

CHAPTER POINTS

- Daniel 9 prophesies the exact date of:
  - The Messiah's arrival
  - The Messiah's death
  - The end of the Old Covenant
  - The confirming of a New Covenant
  - The coming destruction of Jerusalem
- The destruction of Jerusalem is part of Messianic prophecy.
- Jesus' coming immersed Jerusalem in a baptism of fire.
- Jesus shook the old system and left only the unshakeable Kingdom.
- To the early Church, the "last days" meant the time before AD 70 occurred.
- The advent of the gift of tongues on the day of Pentecost was a confirmation of the coming destruction of Jerusalem.

DISCUSSION QUESTIONS

1. The seventy weeks of Daniel 9 equals how many years?

2. When Jesus began His ministry at thirty years of age, how many years of the prophecy were left?

3. When Jesus was crucified after three and a half years of ministry, how many years of the prophecy were left?

4. What events finished the 490 years of the prophecy?

5. How does Matthew 18:21 tie into this prophecy?

6. What are the five main components of the Daniel 9 prophecy?

7. How was speaking in tongues a sign of the coming judgment?

chapter ten

THE KINGDOM WITHOUT WRATH

"If Jesus took the wrath of God on the cross, how come He brought about the destruction of Jerusalem in AD 70?"

I get this question a lot nowadays, especially from those grappling with the reality of grace and stepping into optimistic eschatology. Unfortunately, a lot of misconceptions about grace and wrath are floating around the Church. For example, some branches of the Church teach that Jesus was the sponge that soaked up all of God's wrath at the cross. Some go even farther, saying that God no longer has any wrath after the cross.

On the opposite end of the spectrum, many other Christians believe that God poured out His wrath at the cross, and the Church is currently living in a period of unprecedented grace. However, at the onset of the endtimes, the Church will be suddenly raptured away so that God can pour out His wrath again upon the earth, as recorded in the Book of Revelation.

In the previous two paragraphs, there are as many theological errors as there are words!

Not surprisingly, I will present another perspective. I have looked up every reference for *wrath* from Matthew to Jude. As a result of my study, here is what I have come to understand: *God has no more wrath to pour out in the future. He finished pouring out His entire wrath in the first century and is not storing wrath for our future.*

What I am about to explain will likely be foreign to many of my readers, but it is not foreign to orthodox teaching and Church history. In brief:

1. The cross of Christ had nothing to do with the wrath of God.
2. God's wrath was connected to the Old Covenant.
3. The Old Covenant coexisted with the New Covenant during the New Testament (see Heb. 8:13).
4. The Old Covenant was removed by the destruction of Jerusalem in AD 70, as described in Revelation and Matthew 24 (and as we've already discussed in this book).
5. Revelation 15:1 and First Thessalonians 2:16 indicate that AD 70 was the complete removal of God's wrath with the passing away of the law.

God's Wrath and the Old Covenant

The first thing we must recognize is that the crucifixion of Christ did nothing to assuage the wrath of God. Jesus was not the Father's "wrath sponge" soaking up His anger toward sin on the cross. Although it is a popular notion, we have absolutely no indication of this in Scripture.[1] The reality of what Christ did on the cross was that He operated as a perfect lamb sacrifice, thus creating a brand new covenant through which the Father could forgive sin once and for all. The cross was not the punishment of sin; the cross made a way for the Father to forgive sin. God did not punish our debt of sin; He forgave our debt of sin through the perfect sacrifice. No lamb sacrifice was ever punished for sin. Rather, the lamb's death simply enacted covenantal forgiveness. The animal merely stood between the owner and God, and its shed blood brought covenantal forgiveness. Jesus, the perfect lamb, released perfect forgiveness (see Heb. 8:6–13).

Considering that no Scriptures point to God's wrath being poured out at the cross, we must consider another question: *What do we understand from the New Testament regarding the wrath of God?* By studying every passage on wrath in the New Testament, I found that wrath is connected to the Law (the Old Covenant). This is seen very clearly, for example, in Romans 4:15, which says, *"For* ***the law brings wrath****, but where there is no law there is no transgression."*

Clearly, the wrath of God is an Old Covenant Law-based concept. When *wrath* is mentioned in the New Testament, it is consistently used to point to the coming destruction of Jerusalem, the final outpouring of

God's wrath. For example, in Matthew 3:7 and Luke 3:7, John the Baptist rebukes the Pharisees and speaks of their future destruction in AD 70, saying that the axe is already laid to the root and they won't be saved by claiming Abraham as their father. He goes on to say of AD 70, *"Who warned you to flee from the wrath to come?"* Similarly, in Luke 21:23, Jesus speaks of the AD 70 massacre of Jerusalem and refers to it as the great distress and the "wrath upon the people."

Thus, we can see that the wrath of God was *not* poured out on the cross, but it was poured out at the destruction of Jerusalem. The death of the perfect Lamb on the cross has provided us with a New Covenant of forgiveness. By contrast, the Old Covenant provided Laws that, when broken, caused the wrath of God to come upon people. For those standing inside Christ in the New Covenant, there is absolutely *no* wrath, judgment, or anger. Yet for those in the first century who were not willing to enter into the New Covenant, who rather killed Jesus and persecuted the early Church, an accumulation of wrath was building up against them. In fact, Jesus went so far as to essentially say that all the sin of the Old Testament would be held to the account of the AD 70 generation (see Matt. 23:35–36).

It was that contemporary generation that Paul referred to as the children of disobedience who were destined for God's wrath.

> *Let no man deceive you with vain words: for because of these things cometh the* ***wrath*** *of God upon the children of disobedience* (Ephesians 5:6).

> *For which things' sake the* ***wrath*** *of God cometh on the children of disobedience* (Colossians 3:6 KJV).

The Book of First Thessalonians gives us the clearest indicators that the wrath of God was not poured out at the cross upon Jesus but was actually being filled up until the Days of Vengeance (see Luke 21:22). Then God took His vengeance out on those who killed His Son (see Matt. 22:41). They had even declared the judgment upon their own heads (see Matt. 27:25), and He avenged the early Church for the persecution they faced between AD 30 and AD 70 (see Rom. 12:19). Let's look more closely at several verses from First Thessalonians (being sure to notice their first-century relevance):

> *Jesus, who rescues* ***us*** *from the coming* ***wrath*** (1 Thessalonians 1:10b).

> *For God did not appoint* ***us*** *to suffer* ***wrath*** *but to receive salvation through our Lord Jesus Christ* (1 Thessalonians 5:9).

> *For you, brothers and sisters, became imitators of God's churches in Judea, which are in Christ Jesus: You suffered from your own people the same things those churches suffered from the Jews who killed the Lord Jesus and the prophets and also drove us out. They displease God and are hostile to everyone in their effort to keep us from speaking to the Gentiles so that they may be saved.* ***In this way they always heap up their sins to the limit. The wrath of God has come upon them at last*** (1 Thessalonians 2:14–16).

This last passage clearly speaks of the children of disobedience, who clung to the Law, which brings wrath (Rom 4:15), and continued to persecute the first-century Church until the wrath of God was filled up (see 1 Thess. 2:14–16) and poured out upon them in AD 70. In other words, God judged the Old Covenant, and those who clung to the sinking ship drowned with it. Those who turned to the New Covenant of Christ were saved from the Day of Wrath. As I mentioned previously, out of the approximately 1.1 million Jews who were killed in the slaughter of AD 70, not one Christian died.

To further understand the period of time between Jesus' death on the cross (the inauguration of the New Covenant) and the wrath of God poured out at the destruction of Jerusalem (the end of the Old Covenant), let's look at a sometimes confusing reality: The Old and New Covenants coexisted for forty years.

The Old and New Covenants Coexisted

Most Christians do not have clarity regarding the Old Covenant and the Old Testament, the New Covenant and the New Testament. The lines between these terms are blurry. The general tendency is to draw the dividing line between the end of Malachi and the beginning of Matthew and declare the Old Testament as the Old Covenant and the New Testament as the New Covenant; yet that is a very inaccurate formula that leads to major interpretive problems.

A good starting point is to understand that not all of the New Testament is New Covenant and not all of the Old Testament is Old Covenant. For example, the New Covenant did not start in Matthew 1:1. It wasn't until Jesus inaugurated the New Covenant by His death that a New Covenant was formed. Also, from Genesis 1:1 until Exodus 20 (when Moses met with God on Mount Sinai), the Law had not yet been given, and the Old Covenant had not yet been formed. Therefore, understanding the covenant interactions with human timelines is of great importance.

This can feel foundation-shaking for many Christians, who only recognize the division between the Old and New Testaments. When many first grasp that not all of the New Testament is New Covenant, the first response is to try to draw a new line between the Old and New Covenants—perhaps after John the Baptist (representative of the Old Covenant) is beheaded, or after the Mount of Transfiguration, or after the Last Supper, or after Jesus' death, or after His resurrection, or after Pentecost, and so forth. Ultimately the truth sets in: There is no simple line to be drawn between the Old and the New.

This is because they coexisted, side-by-side from the crucifixion until the Old Covenant was completely removed in AD 70. That is why Hebrews 8:13 says *"By calling this covenant 'new,' he has made the first one obsolete; and what is obsolete and outdated* ***will soon disappear.****"* The Book of Hebrews was written decades after Jesus' death and resurrection. Yet in Hebrews 8:13 we learn that the Old Covenant had been made obsolete and outdated (because of the perfect Lamb's sacrifice on the cross) but was still in existence, still clinging on for a little longer.

Jesus came as the King in the manger and demonstrated His Kingdom during His ministry. He spoke of the New Covenant at the Last Supper and inaugurated it upon the cross by declaring that the establishing of the New Covenant was now finished. However, the Old Covenant, although obsolete and outdated, had not yet disappeared, as Hebrews 8:13 makes clear. Therefore, throughout the New Testament we see Jesus the King, His established and growing Kingdom (see Matt. 13:31–33), and the New Covenant inaugurated at the cross—*but, the Old Covenant had not disappeared yet.*

For this reason, I believe the second most significant event in Christian history (the death and resurrection being foremost) was the destruction of Jerusalem in AD 70. From Christ's prophecy of the destruction of the Temple in Matthew 24 until its fulfillment, there was a forty-year period of transition (AD 30–70). Theologians refer to this time as a transition generation, a time when the Old Covenant was fading out and the New Covenant was rising. This was exemplified in the Old Testament by Israel's wilderness journey, which allowed time (also forty years) for the older slave-minded generation to die away and for the next generation to take their place.

We can also see this picture in the story of King Saul, who remained king for forty years after God rejected him. During the same forty years, God anointed David and prepared him to take Saul's place. Lastly, we find an example in what Paul writes in Galatians regarding Ishmael and Isaac see (Gal. 4:21–31). He clearly shows that Ishmael represents the Old Covenant and Isaac represents the New Covenant—and that Ishmael and Isaac have an overlapping time of coexistence. The same is true of the New and Old Covenants in the New Testament. Because of these forty years of coexistence (AD 30–70), we lose any chance of drawing a simple and clean line between the Old and New Covenants.

With this in mind, as we approach the New Testament, we must review each passage with new lenses because not everything is New Covenant. For example, Jesus says that we must forgive or else the Father will not forgive us (see Matt. 6:15), yet Paul writes that we forgive because we are forgiven (see Eph. 4:32). These two statements directly contradict each other. This difference can be reconciled by understanding that Jesus' statement was rooted in the Old Covenant, which no longer has personal application, whereas Paul's verse is the reality of the New Covenant, in which we dwell. This may be hard for some to swallow, but we must remember that *part* of Jesus' mission on earth was to show His listeners the futility of trying to hold up the Law. His statement in Matthew 6:15 falls into that category, and we know that because it contradicts the gospel of the New Covenant.

We must also recognize that (as we've already discussed) the Church from AD 30–70 was looking toward and anticipating the coming destruction of Jerusalem as the removal of the Old Covenant. As Ishmael persecuted Isaac, so the Old Covenant persecuted the New Covenant (see Gal. 4:21–31). Clearly, the two coexisted during that forty-year period leading up to the destruction of Jerusalem.

The End of God's Wrath in AD 70

The destruction of Jerusalem introduced the end of God's wrath, as First Thessalonians 2:16b so clearly describes: *"...the wrath is come upon them* ***to the uttermost.****"* Also in Revelation 15:1, it says, *"Then I saw another sign in heaven, great and amazing, seven angels with seven plagues, which are the last, for with them* ***the wrath of God is finished****"* (ESV). Here we see that, as God poured out His wrath on Jerusalem in AD 70, He put an end to the Old Covenant once and for all. At His coming in judgment against Jerusalem, Jesus made war against the apostate Old Covenant system and completely annihilated it. Once He poured out His wrath on the Old Covenant system, we entered the Kingdom Age accompanied by the glorious truth that God does not have any more wrath to pour out on the earth, ever.[2]

What about Deliberate Sin?

This revelation of God's grace and the end of wrath has led to much confusion among believers. Some wonder, "But what if someone deliberately keeps on sinning?" Won't that bring wrath upon them?

The confusion comes from a few passages in the Book of Hebrews. For example: *"If we deliberately keep on sinning after we have received the knowledge of the truth, no sacrifice for sins is left"* (Heb. 10:26).

The issue is that these passages in Hebrews have not been put into their biblical/historical context. Specifically, Hebrews 8, 9, and 10 require a contextual understanding for proper interpretation; without it, we can easily end up with a God who is very judgmental toward His very own stumbling children.

The first thing we must understand is that the Book of Hebrews was written somewhere between AD 30 and AD 70. As we just discussed, during that time period, the King, the Kingdom, and the New Covenant had been established, yet the Old Covenant continued to linger until the AD 70 destruction of Jerusalem.

Hebrews 9:1–9, speaking of the Old Covenant tabernacle, repeats this key concept again: *"They are only a matter of food and drink and various ceremonial washings—external regulations* ***applying until the time of the***

new order. *"* Again the author declares that the Old is only going to last until the time of the *"new order."*

The rest of chapter 9 goes on to show the blood of Jesus is the New Covenant, which replaces the blood of the goats and bulls of the Old Covenant. In chapter 10, the theme continues with Jesus as the high priest that replaces all the Old Covenant high priests. In verse 9 we find again *"Then He said, 'here I am, I have come to do your will.'* ***He sets aside the first to establish the second.*** *"* The theme of the Old being replaced by the New is inescapable. Yet, unfortunately, many today are trying to drag the Old into the New.

Chapter 10 continues to speak of this amazing New Covenant until we get to verse 25: *"Not giving up meeting together, as some are in the habit of doing, but encouraging one another-and all the more* ***as you see the Day approaching.*** *"* This fascinating verse has been used by pastors for years to encourage people to keep going to church, but this is a false application. The context here is that the early Church was meeting from house-to-house daily until AD 70, when every one of their houses would have been burned to the ground in the destruction of Jerusalem, which was the *"day"* they saw *"approaching."*

Directly following Hebrews 10:25 is verse 26, which we began this discussion with: *"If we deliberately keep on sinning after we have received the knowledge of the truth, no sacrifice for sins is left"* (Heb. 10:26). The context of this verse is Jesus' delivery of this amazing New Covenant, along with the promise that the lesser, outdated, and obsolete Old Covenant is about to be destroyed and removed by the *"approaching Day"* of judgment.[3]

From Hebrews 10:26–39, the rest of the chapter speaks of those who go back from the New Covenant to the Old Covenant. It says that God is coming to *"judge His people"* (the Jews) (Heb. 10:30) and that *"In just a little while, He who is coming will come and will not delay"* (Heb. 10:37). This is not a reference to the final return of the Lord (that is in our future), but to Jesus' coming to bring destruction upon Jerusalem. Thus we see that this promise of judgment against God's people referred to a specific and unique period of time, when the Old and New Covenants coexisted, and it referred to people who, after accepting the New Covenant, later turned back to the Law.

If we don't put Hebrews 10:26 into its proper context, as I have done here, we end up very confused by the way it contradicts other passages in the Bible, such as:

> *My dear children, I write this to you so that you will not sin.* ***But if anybody does sin, we have an advocate with the Father—Jesus Christ, the Righteous One*** (1 John 2:1).

So when we sin, is Jesus our advocate or is our sin being counted against us and building up wrath? For years, I was terrorized by the Hebrews 10:26–39 passage until I understood the context. God's judgment, spoken of in these passages and others, was for the Jews of the first century who would not accept what Jesus' blood did on our behalf and, thus, trampled the Son of God under foot. Now, under the New Covenant, if we sin, Jesus is our lawyer. He is on our side, standing as our defender against the accuser of the brethren. We are not now and never will be the subjects of God's wrath. He poured it out on the earth, once and for all, when He judged the Old Covenant at the AD 70 destruction of Jerusalem. Yes, at the end of time, there will be a final judgment before God's throne, but this is not something believers need to fear. We are not destined for wrath; we are forever covered by His grace!

CHAPTER POINTS

- God's wrath was connected to the Old Covenant.
- God did not pour out His wrath on Jesus on the cross. The cross was not the *punishment* for sin, but it made a way for God to *forgive* sin by cutting a New Covenant of forgiveness.
- The New Testament references to *wrath* are primarily speaking of the destruction of Jerusalem that was coming in AD 70. This was the final pouring out of God's wrath on the earth.
- The first-century Jews who received witness of their Savior, but refused to accept Him, were the "children of disobedience." They clung to the Law and the Old Covenant and, therefore, chose to be judged with it, bringing the wrath of God upon themselves.
- The Old Covenant and the New Covenant coexisted during the New Testament (AD 30–70), in the time between Jesus' death and resurrection (inauguration of the New Covenant) and the destruction of Jerusalem (elimination of the Old Covenant).
- Some of the statements in the New Testament were written from the perspective of the Old Covenant and the Law rather than the gospel of grace.
- The Old Covenant was forever destroyed by the destruction of Jerusalem in AD 70 (as described in Revelation and Matthew 24).
- Revelation 15:1 indicates the complete removal of God's wrath and the passing away of the law. God does not have any more wrath to pour out on the earth, ever. (All that remains is the final judgment before the throne of God.)
- When a believer sins, God responds with grace, not judgment.

DISCUSSION QUESTIONS

1. Explain the "wrath sponge" perspective and its fatal flaw in approaching the Book of Revelation.

2. What covenant creates the wrath of God? What verse of Romans 4 points this out?

3. Was the wrath of God poured out at the cross or at on the destruction of Jerusalem in AD 70?

4. When did the Old and New Covenants overlap?

5. Israel in the wilderness, King Saul and David, and Isaac and Ishmael are three shadow examples of what period of time?

6. If the Old Covenant is gone and the New Covenant is a covenant of forgiveness, how much wrath does Father God still have?

chapter eleven

THE NEW COVENANT OF LIGHT

Many Christians have been taught that the light of God's people and the darkness of satan's kingdom will both increase simultaneously. This teaching developed from what I believe to be a misunderstanding of Isaiah 60:

> *Arise, shine, for your light has come, and the glory of the LORD rises upon you. See, darkness covers the earth and thick darkness is over the peoples, but the LORD rises upon you and His glory appears over you. Nations will come to your light, and kings to the brightness of your dawn* (Isaiah 60:1–3).

I can understand where the confusion has come from. It would seem, from a surface reading, that Isaiah was observing darkness and light together as parallels. Yet upon closer inspection, we find that Isaiah was not observing them together. Look again at verse 1.

> *Arise, shine, for your light has come, and the glory of the LORD rises upon you* (Isaiah 60:1).

Notice the verb tense, *"Arise, shine."* These are commands telling someone who is currently not standing to arise, spoken in the future tense. *Arise and shine* is something that the hearer is commanded to do in the momentary future. The next verse is a comment on the current state of affairs and speaks to the present tense. *"See, darkness covers the earth and thick darkness is over the peoples..."* (Isaiah 60:2a).

The word *see* means "to look around or observe" in the present. Picture with me that Isaiah was perhaps in a vision. In this vision, he sees that in the present *"darkness covers the earth and thick darkness is over the peoples."* Then he hears the voice of the Holy Spirit declare, *"Arise! Shine! For your light has come and the glory of the Lord rises upon you!"* Because of the order of these two sentences, we have overlooked the fact that the verb tenses actually reverse their order. By putting verse 2 before verse 1, we receive much clarity.

To paraphrase these verses in chronological order, it would go something like this, "Hey Isaiah, look around and notice all the darkness. Now look over there and see the light that is rising from the glory of the Lord. Soon My glory will dispel the darkness and the nations will come to My light."

What Was Isaiah Seeing?

Another problem that has come from this passage is the interpretation of the phrase, *"darkness covers the earth and thick darkness is over the peoples."* Throughout history doom-and-gloom prophets have been declaring that the end is near because of how thick the spiritual darkness is. Yet perhaps Isaiah was not even talking about *spiritual* or *metaphorical* darkness. What if he was prophetically seeing a time of physical darkness? If so, we must ask: *Was there a time in history when darkness covered the whole earth?* If we can find an answer to that question, we can find the time that Isaiah was seeing. I suggest that Isaiah was actually seeing and prophesying about the following event.

> *It was now about the sixth hour, and darkness came over the whole land until the ninth hour, for the sun stopped shining. And the curtain of the temple was torn in two* (Luke 23:44–45).

The Jewish day starts at 6 a.m. Thus, the sixth hour would be 12 noon, and the ninth hour would be 3 p.m. This means that the sun stopped shining from noon until 3 p.m., the brightest three hours of the day, which are especially bright in the desert climate of Israel. I would like you to consider that Isaiah was prophetically seeing a specific day when literal darkness covered the earth (see Luke 23), and then he saw God speaking to His people saying, *"Arise, shine, for your light has come, and the glory of the LORD rises upon you"* (Isa. 60:1).

When did this glory of the Lord come upon His people? I believe that the day of Pentecost fits the description perfectly.

> *When the day of Pentecost came, they were all together in one place. Suddenly a sound like the blowing of a violent wind came from heaven and filled the whole house where they were sitting. They saw what seemed to be tongues of fire that separated and came to rest on each of them. All of them were filled with the Holy Spirit and began to speak in other tongues as the Spirit enabled them* (Acts 2:1–4).

This fulfills Isaiah 60:3–5, which prophesies that once the glory had risen upon His people, the nations will turn to the light.

> *Nations will come to your light, and kings to the brightness of your dawn. Lift up your eyes and look about you: All assemble and come to you; your sons come from afar, and your daughters are carried on the arm. Then you will look and be radiant, your heart will throb and swell with joy; the wealth on the seas will be brought to you, to you the riches of the nations will come* (Isaiah 60:3–5).

This is why Jesus instructed His disciples to *"...make disciples of all nations..."* (Matt. 28:19). He knew Luke 23 would fulfill the prophecy of darkness Isaiah saw and the day of Pentecost would release the glory of the Lord as Isaiah had prophesied. Soon the disciples would see Isaiah 60:3–5, when the nations turn toward the light, take place. Therefore, they needed to be ready to disciple those nations.

New Covenant Light

In light of this historical fulfillment of Isaiah 60, we must consider how this passage applies to us now. Even though the day of Pentecost brought glory into the Church, she still had to "Arise and shine." That process took a time of transition from darkness into light. For example, Jesus inaugurated the New Covenant at the cross and declared the inauguration of that covenant as finished. Yet the Old Covenant lingered throughout the New Testament until it was finally removed by the AD 70 destruction of Jerusalem. That is why Hebrews 8:13 says *"By calling this covenant "new," he has made the first one obsolete; and what is obsolete and outdated will soon disappear."*

That is why, throughout the New Testament, the days before the New Covenant are spoken of as being the ***darkness*** and the New Covenant is called the ***light***. For example:

> *The god of this age has blinded the minds of unbelievers, so that they cannot see* ***the light of the gospel*** *that displays the glory of Christ, who is the image of God... For God, who said,* ***"Let light shine out of darkness,"*** *made* ***his light shine*** *in our hearts to give us the* ***light of the knowledge*** *of God's glory displayed in the face of Christ* (2 Corinthians 4:4,6).

> *When Jesus spoke again to the people, he said, "I am the* ***light of the world****. Whoever follows me will* ***never walk in darkness****, but will have* ***the light of life*** (John 8:12).

> *In him was life, and that life was the* ***light of all mankind****. The* ***light shines in the darkness,*** *and the darkness has not overcome it* (John 1:4–5).

> *because of the tender mercy of our God, by which* ***the Sunrise from on high*** *shall visit us,* ***to shine on those living in darkness*** *and in the shadow of death, to guide our feet into the path of peace* (Luke 1:78–79).

The gospel of Jesus is light that burst forth out of the darkness! Jesus is literally the light of the world! He is the light of all humankind; He is the sunrise from on high!

Before the New Covenant of light was established, the world stumbled around in spiritual darkness. The ancient pagans lived in constant fear of angering the gods, which would bring a lack of rain, storms of devastation, crop failure, barrenness, and so forth. The apostle Paul, in his debate with the philosophers in Athens, refers to this previous era of darkness in terms of people groping about without God:

> *The God who made the world and everything in it is the Lord of heaven and earth and does not live in temples built by human hands. And he is not served by human hands, as if he needed anything. Rather, he himself gives everyone life and breath and everything else. From one man he made all the nations, that they should inhabit the whole earth; and he marked out their appointed times in history and the boundaries of their lands.* ***God did this so that they would seek him and perhaps reach out for him*** *["Grope and find him," Weymouth Literal Translation]* ***and find him, though he is not far from any one of us.*** *'For in him we live and move and have our being.' As some of your own poets have said, 'We are his offspring.' ...In the past God overlooked such ignorance, but now he commands all people everywhere to repent* (Acts 17:24–28, 30).

The theologian David Chilton has also written compellingly on the dawn of the light in an era of deep darkness:

> The New Covenant age is regarded in Scripture as progressively an era of Light, in contrast to the relative darkness of pre-Messianic times. In the absolute and ultimate sense, the Light will come only at the end of the world, at the return of Christ. But, as the apostles contemplated the end of the Old Covenant era, during which the nations were enslaved to demons, they spoke of the imminent Dawn as *the* age of righteousness, when the power of the Gospel would sweep across the earth, smashing idolatry and flooding the nations with the Light of God's grace. Relatively speaking, the whole history of the world: from Adam's fall to Christ's Ascension was Night; relatively speaking, the whole future of the world is bright Day. This follows the pattern laid down at creation, in which the heavens and earth move from evening darkness to morning light.[1]

> The era of the Old Covenant was the time of the world's dark Night; with the Advent of Jesus Christ has come the age of Light, the great Day of the Lord, established at His Ascension and His full inauguration of the New Covenant.[2]

With transition from dark to light in mind, we see the power inherent in Paul's command to us to wear the armor of the New Covenant, which is the armor of light:

> *But you, brothers and sisters, are not in darkness so that this day should surprise you like a thief.* ***You are all children of the light and children of the day. We do not belong to the night or to the darkness.*** *So then, let us not be like others, who are asleep, but let us be awake and sober. For those who sleep, sleep at night, and those who get drunk, get drunk at night. But* ***since we belong to the day,*** *let us be sober, putting on faith and love as a breastplate, and the hope of salvation as a helmet* (1 Thessalonians 5:4–8).

> *And do this, understanding the present time: The hour has already come for you to* ***wake up*** *from your slumber, because our salvation is nearer now than when we first believed.* ***The night*** *is nearly over; the day is almost here. So let us put aside the* ***deeds of darkness and put on the armor of light*** (Romans 13:11–12).

This is our present reality! The light of the Kingdom is ever increasing, pushing back the darkness. When Christians speak about how dark it is in the world—about the "gross, dense darkness" and the political darkness making way for a future dark day—they simply have not yet understood that the darkness was long ago replaced by the bright new day of the New Covenant! The glory and brightness of Jesus is on the scene, and darkness is being dispelled more and more every day.

CHAPTER POINTS

- Isaiah 60 does *not* teach that the light of the Kingdom and the darkness in the world increase simultaneously
- Isaiah saw a present deep darkness that would be dispelled by a coming light. After this, the nations would come to that light. These prophecies were fulfilled in Luke 23 and Acts 2.
- The days prior to the New Covenant are often referred to in the Bible as the *darkness,* while the time of the New Covenant is referred to as the *light.*
- Ever since the first century, the light has been increasing, and the darkness has been decreasing.

DISCUSSION QUESTIONS

1. Does light and darkness grow together? If you can, give an example in the natural.

2. So what was Isaiah really saying in chapter 60?

3. How would you explain the first-century transition from an age of darkness into an age of light?

4. Is light growing? Is darkness decreasing? Can you give a few examples from the last 2,000 years?

THE KINGDOM NOW

At 4 in the morning, King Nebuchadnezzar awoke from a deep sleep. He was drenched in sweat and visibly shaken—speaking rapidly and incoherently about a dream he had just had. Clearly this was no ordinary dream. He demanded all the magicians and wizards be brought to the palace so they might help him understand the dream. He made an unusual request of them, however. The king told them he'd had a troubling dream, and he demanded the interpretation. But when the magicians asked the king to tell them the dream so they could interpret it for him, he refused. Instead, he promised he would kill all of them and destroy their households unless they both told him his dream and then interpreted it. The magicians, not surprisingly, were astounded that the king would ask such a thing. *"There is no one on earth who can do what the king asks!"* they said. *"No king, however great and mighty, has ever asked such a thing of any magician..."* (Dan. 2:10). In response to this, the king became so angry he ordered the execution of all of Babylon's magicians.

Fortunately, Daniel, one of the Hebrew captives in Babylon, who had also been trained as a magician, had tremendous wisdom and insight. He was able to accurately tell the king his dream and its interpretation. King Nebuchadnezzar had dreamed about a large and dazzling statue. The head was made of gold, its chest and arms of silver, its belly and thighs of bronze, its legs of iron, and its feet partly of iron and partly of baked clay. As the king looked upon this statue, a large rock, *"not* [cut out] *by human hands"* rolled into the statue, smashing its feet of iron and clay. Successively, the iron, clay, bronze, silver, and gold all broke into pieces and blew away, leaving no trace. However, the rock grew into an enormous mountain that filled the entire earth.

As the king and his court listened, Daniel told Nebuchadnezzar that the various metals represented various earthly kingdoms. The Babylonian Empire under Nebuchadnezzar was the pinnacle of splendor and power, the head of gold. After him would come another inferior kingdom, the silver chest and arms. A third kingdom, symbolized by the bronze belly and thighs, would then rule.

Lastly, a fourth kingdom would rise, depicted as iron because iron breaks and smashes everything, which is what this kingdom will do to all the others. The fact that the feet and toes were partly clay and partly iron indicated that the final kingdom would become a divided kingdom; it would have some of the strength of iron, but also be brittle as clay. Just as iron and clay cannot be mixed, so the people of this kingdom would not be unified.

During that final, divided kingdom, God would establish a Kingdom—symbolized by the rock not cut by human hands—that would never be destroyed or left to another people. It would crush all the previous kingdoms, bringing them to an end, but it would endure forever (see Dan. 2:31–45).

In this prophetic dream, God revealed to Nebuchadnezzar *what would take place in the future*. However, it is important for us to remember that, though this reveals events "in the future" to the original listeners, this passage doesn't necessarily speak about *our future*. In fact, this dream clearly has been fulfilled in *our past*.

Five eras make up the statue from the dream:

- The Babylonian
- The Medeo-Persian
- The Greek
- The Roman
- The Divided Roman Empire (represented by ten toes)

King Nebuchadnezzar was the ruler of the Babylonian kingdom. After him, Daniel served under King Darius the Mede (see Dan. 6) and King Cyrus the Persian (see Dan. 10). After the Medeo-Persian kingdom came the Greek kingdom and then finally the Roman Empire, which fiercely took control of the civilized world of that day.

The fifth kingdom, which was represented by clay and iron toes in the dream, occurred when the Roman Kingdom was divided into ten provinces under Augustus Caesar, who ruled from 27 BC to AD 14. The famed commentator F.W. Farrar lists the following as the ten provinces of the divided Roman Empire of the first century: Italy, Achaia, Asia, Syria, Egypt, Africa, Spain, Gaul, Britain, and Germany.[1] During Augustus' rule, the ten toes were established, and then Jesus came as the Rock and crashed into the toes in 3 BC.

As prophesied by this dream, during the divided Roman Empire, Jesus came and established His Kingdom as the rock that would fill the whole earth. This is consistent with other passages of Scripture where Jesus is referred to as the chief cornerstone and the rock that the builders rejected (see Luke 20:17), as well as the rock that followed the Hebrews in the wilderness (see 1 Cor. 10:4). Jesus also told Peter that on this rock (the revelation that Jesus is the Messiah) He would build His Church (see Matt. 16:18). Clearly, we can see that the rock in this dream speaks of Jesus.

His First Coming

The future return of Jesus is popularly referred to as the "second coming." Although it is a minor detail, I refer to that event as the final return of Jesus. I believe that the popular phrase—second coming—has the numbering wrong.

Jesus' first coming was the manger in the stable at Bethlehem. His second coming was when He came back from the dead at His resurrection. His third coming was when He came in judgment upon Jerusalem in AD 70. That is why I refer to His future coming as the final return. We have already examined how Daniel 2 prophesies of Jesus coming into the earth as the rock that crushed the divided Roman Empire and that Jesus' Kingdom began to grow and is continuing to grow even to this very day. This naturally leads to the question: *When did Jesus' Kingdom arrive?* Was it at the manger? Was it when Jesus began His ministry at thirty years of age? Was it when He died on the cross? Was it at the AD 70 destruction of Jerusalem? Just as knowing which "coming" we are looking forward to is an important detail, so too, understanding the arrival of the Kingdom is also important.

We have seen that Caesar Augustus (AD 27–14) divided Rome into ten provinces that are represented in Daniel 2 as the ten toes of the statue. Daniel 2:44 says:

In the time of those kings, the God of heaven will set up a kingdom that will never be destroyed, nor will it be left to another people. It will crush all those kingdoms and bring them to an end, but it will itself endure forever.

Thus we know the rock, which represents Jesus and His Kingdom, arrived during the 27 BC–AD 14 rule of Augustus in 3 BC. (Jesus was technically born in 3 BC, not in AD 0; our calendars are slightly off.)

Jesus the King came in the manger at Bethlehem and brought His Kingdom with Him. Then thirty years later, John the Baptist began to proclaim that King Jesus was about to be revealed. *"Repent the Kingdom of God is at hand"* (Matt. 3:2).

As Jesus ministered for three and a half years, His constant theme was teaching and demonstrating what it looks like to be in His Kingdom. During the last supper, Jesus stood and said, *"This is my blood of the covenant, which is poured out for many for the forgiveness of sins"* (Matt. 26:28). This was a confirmation of His Kingdom being transferred to His followers as they transitioned from the Old Covenant into the New Covenant.

At His death on the cross, He declared, *"It is finished!"* (John 19:30). In the eyes of God, through the removal of the need for Old Covenant animal sacrifice, this was the end of the Age of Moses and the inauguration of the Kingdom of Jesus. Though the Jews continued the Temple practices after the death of Jesus, it had no value in the eyes of God.

Even after His resurrection, Jesus took of His precious time to continue training His ambassadors about the Kingdom they had just inherited:

After his suffering, he presented himself to them and gave many convincing proofs that he was alive. He appeared to them over a period of forty days and spoke about the kingdom of God (Acts 1:3).

Jesus' birth, ministry, last supper, death, resurrection, and ascension message all centered on the removal of the Old Covenant and the inauguration of the New Covenant. Jesus is the rock of Daniel 2 and has established His Kingdom in the earth. This Kingdom is founded on the New Covenant of forgiveness (see Matt. 26:28; Heb. 8:8–12) rather than the Old Covenant of blessings and curses (see Deut. 28).

Jesus declared that His Kingdom had come as the smallest seed and would grow to be the largest tree in the garden, that it came as a measure of yeast and would work its way through the whole loaf (see Matt. 13:31–33). Some have taught Jesus' Kingdom will someday arrive in the future and be established all at once with complete dominion, yet Jesus taught His Kingdom would be established gradually.

According to God, what Jesus accomplished on the cross removed the need for the old sacrificial system. The Father went so far as to rip the veil in the Temple, revealing that the Ark of the Covenant was no longer there and that the old system had been superseded. Yet between AD 30 and AD 70, the Jewish non-Christians carried on with the Old Covenant ways in the Temple. To the Father God, who had just laid down His only Son as the perfect lamb sacrifice, this was an obstinate abomination. The apostle John even refers to those Jews as the synagogue of satan (see 1 John 2:9; 3:9).

Likewise, the author of Hebrews refers to the Old Covenant system as *"obsolete and outdated* [because of the Cross] *and will soon fade away* [because the AD 70 destruction, which would completely destroy Jerusalem, the Temple, the Jews as a nation, and the priesthood]" (Heb. 8:13).

The Kingdom came in the manger and was proclaimed by John the Baptist, explained and demonstrated by Jesus, confirmed in the covenant of forgiveness at the last supper, established more fully by the finishing of the Old Covenant on the cross, and passed to the apostolic ambassadors before His ascension. Then it grew throughout the Book of Acts to reach the entire inhabited and civilized world before the AD 70 destruction removed the Old Covenant ways entirely.

At this point, the Kingdom is here and now; it has been here for two thousand years, and it is growing and will continue to grow.

CHAPTER POINTS

- Jesus is the Rock that crashed into the Roman Empire in the first century.
- His Kingdom was established at His first coming, not at a future coming.
- His Kingdom will continue to grow without end (see Isa. 9:7).

DISCUSSION QUESTIONS

1. What four kingdoms were prophesied in the statue of Daniel 2?

2. Who is the rock cut out of the mountain?

3. What did the ten toes of the statue represent?

4. Was the kingdom established at Jesus first coming or are we waiting for it to be established at His second coming? Explain your perspective.

chapter thirteen

THE KINGDOM ADVANCING

As I wrote in the last chapter, some people believe the Kingdom will arrive all at once in the future. They say God's Kingdom will instantly triumph over all the powers of the devil when it finally appears. This idea comes from thinking we are currently in the so-called Church Age. However, as I have already shown, the Kingdom arrived with the King in 3 BC. With that foundation, in this chapter we will look at the nature of this gradually advancing and ever-increasing Kingdom.

The Ever-Increasing Kingdom

Jesus came to set up His Kingdom, and He said it would continually grow. He used these two analogies to describe this aspect of the Kingdom:

> *The Kingdom of Heaven is like a mustard seed planted in a field. It is the smallest of all seeds, but it becomes the largest of garden plants; it grows into a tree, and birds come and make nests in its branches* (see Matt. 13:31-32).

> *The Kingdom of Heaven is like the yeast a woman uses in making bread. Even though she puts only a little yeast in three measures of flour, it permeates every part of the dough* (see Matt. 13:33).

As Daniel 2:44 says:

In the time of those kings, the God of heaven will set up a kingdom that will never be destroyed, nor will it be left to another people. It will crush all those kingdoms and bring them to an end, but it will itself endure forever.

This verse is reminiscent of Isaiah 9:7, which says, *"Of the increase of His government and peace there shall be no end..."* (Isa. 9:7 NKJV). The nature of the Kingdom of God is ever progressing—always expanding, never retreating, and continually growing. Take, for example, the following five progressive statements from Scripture. The Word says that we move from:

1. Brighter to Brighter
The path of the righteous is like the first gleam of dawn, shining ever brighter till the full light of day (Proverbs 4:18 NIV).

2. Grace to Grace
And of His fullness we have all received, and grace for grace (John 1:16 NKJV).

3. Strength to Strength
They go from strength to strength... (Psalm 84:7 NKJV).

4. Faith to Faith
For in it the righteousness of God is revealed from faith to faith; as it is written, "The just shall live by faith (Romans 1:17 NKJV).

5. Glory to Glory
But we all, with unveiled face, beholding as in a mirror the glory of the Lord, are being transformed into the same image from glory to glory, just as by the Spirit of the Lord (2 Corinthians 3:18 NKJV).

According to these verses, we can accurately say that the Church is currently walking in the greatest brightness, grace, strength, faith, and glory it ever has. This is very hard for some to accept, but it is true. Jesus set in motion a Kingdom that is still progressing and being established more and more each day. *"Of the increase of His government and peace there shall be no end..."* (Isa. 9:7 NKJV). It will continue to progress until it has fulfilled the following verses:

> *...For the earth will be filled with the knowledge of the LORD as the waters cover the sea* (Isaiah 11:9 NKJV).

> *For the earth will be filled with the knowledge of the glory of the LORD, as the waters cover the sea* (Habakkuk 2:14 NKJV).

> *But truly, as I live, all the earth shall be filled with the glory of the LORD* (Numbers 14:21 NKJV).

As I have already noted, it is very important to understand that Jesus set up His Kingdom upon His first visit. Many have been taught that Jesus set up the Church Age and that we are not currently living in the Kingdom Age, but that the Church Age continues until Jesus' return, at which point He will initiate the Kingdom Age. Scripture does not support this point of view in any way; Jesus clearly brought His Kingdom (see Matt. 4:17) and sent His disciples to preach the gospel of the Kingdom (see Matt. 10:7), not the gospel of the Church Age. The whole concept of a Church Age cannot be found in Scripture. The Kingdom arrived in the first century when *the rock cut without hands*, Jesus, crashed into the Roman Empire, and it has been growing ever since.

Many who don't understand that Jesus and His Kingdom (as established during the first century) are *"the rock cut without hands"* from Nebuchadnezzar's dream also believe the Roman Empire has to be rebuilt so that Jesus can crash into it *in the future* in order to set up His Kingdom. Fortunately, this has already been accomplished. Jesus completely fulfilled Daniel 2 in the first century, and there is no reason to revive the Roman Empire so that Jesus can fulfill this prophecy twice!

What of the "Remnant"?

We have established that the Kingdom that Jesus set up is progressing and advancing all the time. The next question that typically arises is about remnant theology. In the Old Testament, we observe a pattern of the "faithful remnant." In other words, often only a minority of a group of people was actually faithful to God. For example, out of all the people on the face of the earth, only eight survived the flood on Noah's ark (see Gen. 8). Out of all of Gideon's men, only 300 fought in the battle (see Judg. 7). Out of all the inhabitants of Sodom and Gomorrah, only Lot and his daughters survived (see Gen. 19). This is a common pattern in the Old Testament.

Many people have carried the idea of the remnant over from the Old Testament into the New Testament, yet this is not the nature of the Kingdom that Jesus established in the New Testament. Rather, the remnant concept is reversed in the Kingdom of God. Under Jesus, out of twelve disciples, He only lost one, Judas (see John 17:12). The Kingdom starts as a seed and grows to the biggest tree; it starts as a little leaven and works through the whole loaf (see Matt. 13:31–33); it starts as a stone cut without hands and grows into a mountain that fills the whole earth (see Dan. 2:35).

The New Testament holds no room for remnant thinking. This type of defeatist thinking, which sees only a portion of the whole Church as good, needs to be set aside with animal sacrifice and certain other Old Testament realities that are no longer valid.

Historical Perspective

Many Christians have a hard time viewing the future optimistically because they have a lack of perspective regarding the past. When they look back, they think that they are seeing "the good ol' days." However, with a better grasp on history, we will see that God's Kingdom has, in fact, been steadily progressing forward. To see this improvement, we must lift ourselves to a higher perspective, from which we can look over the course of history. We know what life is like today; let's compare it to the conditions of society in the past.

The Early 1800s

First, let's look at what life was like in the United States 200 years ago—in the early 1800s. At that time, the population was slightly over 5 million, but 20 percent of those people were slaves (that's more than 1 million slaves). Abortion was legal during most of the nineteenth century, and according to the records, one fifth of all pregnancies were aborted (Michigan had the highest rate at 34 percent). Also, in many states, the age of sexual consent was as low as nine or ten years old, and prostitution was commonplace. New York City estimated having a ratio of one prostitute to every sixty-four men, and Savannah estimated a ratio of one to thirty-nine.

This was also the time of the pioneers and covered wagon trains heading westward. Thousands relocated to the wild west looking for gold and a fresh start. When gold was discovered, the gold rushes created the most despicable and dangerous of communities. In fact, throughout the West, murder was so common that most people carried a gun for protection. Even in safer frontier communities, no organized churches were formed until years after settlements had been established. At the same time, tens of thousands of American Indians were murdered or forced from their lands, and thousands of Chinese people were imported on the western coast as slaves.

During that time period, women had virtually no rights. Not only were women not allowed to vote, but their husbands were legally allowed to beat them as long as they avoided maiming or killing them. Also, alcoholism occurred at a much higher rate than it does today.

Although some godly people were laying the foundations for the United States government and other good things were happening, from these simple statistics, we can plainly see that morally, ethically, and spiritually the climate of the United States was far worse than it is today.

The Time of Jesus' Childhood

Looking even farther back in time, let's examine the climate of the whole world approximately 2,000 years ago—the time when Jesus was a child. As we know, the Roman Empire ruled the world, with its primary cultural centers being in Europe, the Middle East, and Northern Africa. Throughout the empire, slavery was commonplace—to the point that in Italy, the hub of the empire, about 40 percent of the population was slaves. Homosexuality was also the norm, especially between masters and slaves. Also, many babies were killed after birth because of being deformed or sickly or even simply female.

Obviously, at that time, since Jesus was still a child, the gospel had not yet arrived on the scene. The Jews had a revelation of God, yet they lived in disobedience, and it had been 400 years since a prophet had spoken on God's behalf. Rather, most people worshipped a multitude of cruel and capricious gods, including Jupiter, Juno, and Neptune. Temple prostitution and ritual child sacrifice were a regular part of this religious system. This was also the era of the gladiators, and in the Roman arenas, people were regularly tortured to death or mauled by wild animals. Later, under Nero, this fate befell many of the early Christians. It is hard for us to understand, but the philosophers that Western society so praises—Plato, Aristotle, and Socrates—saw nothing wrong with these practices.

Ernest Hampden Cook, in his book *The Christ Has Come*, wrote:

> The fact is that bad as the world still is, yet morally it is vastly better than it was when Jesus was born in Bethlehem of Judea.... Few people in these days have an adequate conception of the misery and degradation which were then the common lot of almost all mankind, owing the monstrous wickedness of the times, to continual wars, to the cruelties of political despotism, and of everywhere-prevailing slavery.
>
> Outside of the Roman Empire, things were no better. In Africa, Asia, and Australia, people worshipped nature, demons, and their deceased ancestors. In North America, the American Indians had many forms of worship, and in South America, tens of thousands of people were regularly sacrificed to a bloodthirsty god. Yet throughout the whole world, no one knew the Messiah.[1]

Truly, as we can see from this brief overview, the world was lost in darkness beyond what most of us can even imagine. This is what the apostle Paul meant when he wrote, *"...formerly you, the Gentiles...were at that time separated from Christ...having no hope and without God in the world"* (Eph. 2:11–12).[2]

Today

By comparison, let's examine the world today. The gospel is reaching even the remotest places in the world, and Christianity is experiencing phenomenal growth globally. In fact, worldwide, more than 80,000 people are being born again daily. That adds up to more than a half million people who are becoming Christians every week. The tiny seed that came into the earth in that little nation of Israel has grown to permeate the earth. Christianity is, in fact, the largest, most influential force of humanity in the world today.

Certainly, I am not saying our world is perfect or that global peace and utopia are just around the corner. Until Jesus' return, the struggle between light and dark will continue. Difficult times of war, famine, disease, and poverty may yet happen in the future, and during such times, people are often capable of the most inhumane acts. I am not denying the reality that life is sometimes tragic and excruciatingly painful. But I also want to highlight the definite reality that, though it is not anywhere near perfect living here on earth, it is consistently becoming morally, ethically, and spiritually better. We must be watchful and hard at work, for we still have much to accomplish before Christ's return, but we must do this with the understanding that we are gaining ground, not losing it. The increase of God's government and peace is truly without end.

Many of you may have been stretched by the historical facts that you just read. You may need to read it a few more times to grasp the shift in thinking required of you. But when you are ready to be stretched some more, here are some additional enlightening statistics.

Status Update

The number of Christians around the world has nearly quadrupled in the last 100 years, from about 600 million in 1910 to more than 2.3 billion as of 2011, representing 33 percent of the world population.[3]

In his book *Mega Shift, Igniting Spiritual Power*, author James Rutz points out that when the Spirit was first poured out on the early Church, 3,000 people were saved in one day. That was amazing. Back then, it was a huge number. However, today approximately 3,000 people get saved, somewhere in the world, every 54 minutes! The math is almost overwhelming. He further states that until 1960, western evangelicals outnumbered non-Western (Latino, black, and Asian) evangelicals two to one. In 2000, non-western evangelicals had surpassed westerners four to one.

According to Rutz, often these numbers happen though large events, such as the crusade that Reinhard Bonnke held in Lagos, Nigeria, in November 2000. During those six days and nights, almost 6 million people attended, and 3.4 million registered decisions to follow Christ, over 1 million of them being on the final night. One important element of such events is the widespread healing of all kinds of physical deformities, diseases, and illnesses through the power of the Holy Spirit. At Bonnke's Nigeria event, over 1,000 physicians were present to examine people and confirm healings. Bonnke also had 30,000 ushers and spent the six months prior training 200,000 counselors to assist the many converts.

Such massive influxes of new believers are not isolated events, but are becoming increasingly common occurrences. Some have even estimated the advent of a billion new converts within ten years.

Rutz goes on to say:

> From our vantage point in North America and Europe, where church membership is going nowhere, this sounds like a cooked-up fantasy, but it is true. This is the biggest mega shift in history. Can you think of any time when over a billion people eagerly changed their lives and loyalties in one generation?" Looking at the statistics, we can clearly see that, if growth continues at this rate, whole nations will experience transformation on all levels. In fact, as Rutz predicts, "We are in the early stages of a total transformation of our planet.[4]

Christianity today—unlike a century ago—is truly a global faith. Here are the stats to prove it. Since 1900, the number of Latin American Christians has grown by an incredible 877 percent. Three of the top ten countries in Christian population are in the Americas (the United States, Brazil, and Mexico). Two are in Europe (Russia and Germany), two are in the Asia-Pacific region (the Philippines and China), and three are in sub-Saharan Africa (Nigeria, DR Congo, and Ethiopia), reflecting Christianity's global reach.[5] Christians are so far-flung and geographically widespread, in fact, that no single continent or region can indisputably claim to be the center of global Christianity.[6]

A century ago, this was not the case. In 1910, about two-thirds of the world's Christians lived in Europe, where the bulk of Christians had been for a millennium, according to historical estimates by the Center for the Study of Global Christianity.[7] Today, while about a quarter of all Christians live in Europe (26 percent) and more than a third now live in the Americas (37 percent); about one in every four Christians lives in sub-Saharan Africa (24 percent) and about one-in-eight is found in Asia and the Pacific (13 percent).[8]

Africa, where there were relatively few Christians at the beginning of the twentieth century, has been the most stunning area of Christian growth over the past century. The Christian population in sub-Saharan Africa climbed from 9 percent in 1910 to 63 percent in 2010, or from 8.5 million to 516 million. The number of Christians in the Asia-Pacific region also jumped from 27 million in 1910 to 285 million in 2010. Most remarkably, in 1950 China had 1 million believers, but by 1980, it had 40 million, and by 2010, it had 75 million.[9]

Another astonishing growth spurt, measured typologically, has been among Pentecostals and charismatics—from 981,000 in 1900 to 612 million in 2011. With an average of 37,000 new adherents every day, it is the fastest-growing group of Christians in the two millennia of Christian history.[10]

The point of these statistics is clear. The "good ol' days" were not as good as many of us have assumed they were. When we remove our romanticized lenses in order to see what really was, as well as what really is happening *now,* we can clearly see that God's Kingdom is markedly advancing.

What's Left?

After reading the contents of this book thus far, many will likely make the exclamation, "Then what's left?!" That is the natural response when a person finds out the Great Tribulation has already happened, there is no one-world ruler coming to take over, we aren't waiting for a Jewish revival as the sign of the end, and there is no secret rapture. For some who have made the endtimes the major focus of their Christian walk, if they have come to agree with the contents of this book, it is likely that their theology has been shaken as if by an earthquake.

Many may feel like they are losing a major portion of the New Testament—which they thought related to them personally—when they find out it had a historical and prophetic fulfillment. This would be the wrong assessment. We don't lose any of the 360 Old Testament messianic prophecies that Jesus fulfilled; in fact, these fulfillments build our faith and knowledge of the Word. To realize that Matthew 24 has occurred does not mean that we lose Scripture; it means that we can affirm how amazing of a prophet Jesus is! Everything that He said would happen within a generation (forty years) did happen within that generation (forty years). Once people find out there is no future Tribulation or antichrist, they shouldn't feel loss; they should be rejoicing because of what they lost!

Discovering the optimistic view of the endtimes is one of the most exciting and wonderful bits of news the modern Christian can hear. The inability to receive this as good news often arises from an unhealthy place in the hearts of individuals, especially the ones who want to see God rain down judgment upon their surroundings. Many will not receive this book as good news because they, like James and John, want to see the destruction of sinners, yet Jesus would say, *"You know not what spirit you are of"* (Luke 9:55).

The Kingdom and the Church

Although a lot of the passages that are taught as future are actually past, I do also believe there are many passages of Scripture that remain to be fulfilled. These passages mainly fall into two categories: The Kingdom of God and the Church.

I define the Kingdom of God as His ruler-ship, in other words, the King's domain (i.e., King-dom). Therefore, the Kingdom is God's sphere of ruler-ship. Jesus taught that the Kingdom of God is growing and expanding (see Matt. 13:31–33; Isa. 9:7), that God's ruler-ship is ever increasing from glory to glory. The primary way the Kingdom grows is through God's representatives in the earth, His Church. Jesus placed the keys of the Kingdom into the hands of Peter as the representative of the Church (see Matt. 16:18–19). Therefore, the Church in the earth is working as God's representatives to expand and increase the Kingdom and see His government grow without end—the ultimate end being that it would be on earth as it is in Heaven (see Matt. 6:10).

With this understanding, let's examine a few passages that remain to be fulfilled, first about the Kingdom and then regarding the Church.

The Kingdom

In Luke 19, Jesus told a parable:

> *He said therefore, A certain nobleman went into a far country to receive for himself a kingdom, and to return. And he called his ten servants, and delivered them ten pounds, and said unto them,* ***Occupy till I come*** (Luke 19:12-13 KJV).

Jesus is the one who went to a far country (Heaven) to receive for Himself a Kingdom, and He will someday return. When Jesus left, He put stewardship into the hands of His servants (the Church). To *occupy* is to aggressively expand. The servants took the finances they were given and multiplied them. We are called to occupy the Kingdom, to advance it in the earth, to be a part of its growth from glory to glory. W*e are to occupy until He comes, not be pre-occupied with His coming.* As the prophet Isaiah wrote:

> ***Of the increase of his government and peace there shall be no end,*** *upon the throne of David, and upon his kingdom, to order it, and to establish it with judgment and with justice from henceforth even for ever. The zeal of the LORD of hosts will perform this* (Isaiah 9:7 KJV).

The Kingdom of God started growing at Jesus first coming and will continue to grow until it culminates in His final return. As Jesus put it in another parable:

> *Another parable put he forth unto them, saying, The kingdom of heaven is like to a grain of mustard seed, which a man took, and sowed in his field: Which indeed is the least of all seeds:* ***but when it is grown,*** *it is the greatest among herbs, and becomes a tree, so that the birds of the air come and lodge in the branches thereof. Another parable spoke he unto them; The kingdom of heaven is like unto leaven, which a woman took, and hid in three measures of meal,* ***till the whole was leavened*** (Matthew 13:31-33 KJV).

The Kingdom will continue to grow until His glory and knowledge fill the whole earth.

> *...For the earth will be filled with the knowledge of The Lord as the waters cover the sea* (Isaiah 11:9).

> *For the earth will be filled with the knowledge of the glory of the LORD, as the waters cover the sea* (Habakkuk 2:14).

Currently, Jesus is sitting on the throne, waiting until all His enemies are made into His footstool, as the following passages make clear:

> *When the Lord Jesus had finished talking with them, he was taken up into heaven* ***and sat down*** *at God's right hand* (Mark 16:19 TLB).

> *But when this Priest had offered for all time one sacrifice for sins, He sat down at the right hand of God.* ***Since that time He waits*** *for His enemies to be made His footstool* (Hebrews 10:12-13).

> *Then the end will come, when He hands over the kingdom to God the Father after He has destroyed all dominion, authority and power. For He must reign until He has* ***put all His enemies under His feet. The last enemy to be destroyed is death*** (1 Corinthians 15:24-26).

Jesus has been sitting at the right hand of God for 2,000 years waiting while His Church builds Him a divine ottoman of sorts. The assignment of the Church for the last 2,000 years has been to crush satan under our feet—*"The God of peace will soon crush Satan under your feet"* (Rom. 16:20a)—and thus put Jesus' enemies under His feet. As delegated authorities, by crushing satan under our feet, we are placing him under Jesus' feet. We are part of a progressive destruction of the demonic kingdom, which will continue until death, the final enemy, is destroyed.

The ultimate goal is that His *"Kingdom would come"* and His *"will be done on earth as it is in heaven"* (Matt. 6:10). The "signs of the times" that Jesus listed in Matthew 24 were only in reference to AD 70; therefore, *the true "signs" we can be looking for in these days are the evidence of the growth of His Kingdom within the earth.*

The Church

The Scriptures also contain several prophecies about the Church that are yet unfulfilled. Here I will cover three aspects of the Church's destiny we have to work toward and look forward to—our calling to walk in unity, to be a mature body for Christ, and to produce the sons of God.

1. The Church in Unity

Jesus' famous prayer for unity in the Church is recorded in John 17:

> ***That they all may be one,*** *as You, Father, are in Me, and I in You; that they also may be* ***one in Us****, that the world may believe that You sent Me. And the glory which You gave Me I have given them,* ***that they may be one*** *just as We are one: I in them, and You in Me;* ***that they may be made perfect in one****, and that the world may know that You have sent Me, and have loved them as You have loved Me* (John 17:21-23 NASB).

The apostle Paul also echoed Jesus' call for unity in his description of the fivefold ministry:

> *So Christ himself gave the apostles, the prophets, the evangelists, the pastors and teachers, to equip his people for works of service, so that the body of Christ may be built up* ***until we all*** *reach* ***unity in the faith*** *and in the knowledge of the Son of God and become mature, attaining to the whole measure of the fullness of Christ* (Ephesians 4:11-13).

According to David B. Barrett's *World Christian Encyclopedia*, there are 33,830 Christian denominations in the world today.[11] I would say we have not reached *"unity in the faith."*

One of the largest hindrances to arriving at the "unity of the faith" is an expectancy of the "last days apostasy." If a church believes there must be a massive falling away from the faith, then that church avoids partnering with other ministries for fear of contamination. Also, if a church believes the one-world ruler will come and take over a one-world government and a one-world religion, then all progress toward unity is seen as a supposed "sign of the end." Yet, here we have two very clear passages regarding the Church walking in unity. I am not sure what this will look like, but I believe it still is in our future.

2. The Church Grows to Carry the Head

Connected to the mandate of unity is the promise that the Church will mature into a fitting "body" for Christ as the "head":

> *And he gave some, apostles; and some, prophets; and some, evangelists; and some, pastors and teachers; For the perfecting of the saints, for the work of the ministry, for the edifying of the body of Christ:* ***Till*** *we all come in the unity of the faith, and of the knowledge of the Son of God, unto a* ***perfect*** [complete] ***man, unto the measure of the stature of the fullness of Christ*** (Ephesians 4:11-13).

Throughout the New Testament, the physical body is used as a metaphor to explain the relationship between Christ and His Church. The writers refer to Christ as the head and the Church as His body. The above passage from Ephesians is making reference to this metaphor and declaring that the apostles, prophets, evangelists, pastors, and teachers are working toward the goal that the Body of Christ would be "perfect" and the "measure of the stature of Christ."

Essentially, this is saying that Jesus' body will someday match His head. Jesus is not going to come back for a weak and sickly body to attach to His head. The Body of Christ will continue to grow and mature, to become healthy and strong, and then Jesus will have a body that is capable of carrying His head.

3. The Church Brings Forth the Sons of God

The "sons of God" is a term that applies to all who are His children, both male and female. We are the sons of God, and we have a crucial role to fulfill in relation to creation. As the apostle Paul wrote:

> *I consider that our present sufferings are not worth comparing with the glory that will be revealed in us. The* ***creation waits in eager expectation***

> ***for the sons of God to be revealed.*** *For the creation was subjected to frustration, not by its own choice, but by the will of the One who subjected it,* ***in hope that the creation itself will be liberated from its bondage to decay and brought into the glorious freedom of the children of God*** (Romans 8:18-21).

When we see earthquakes, tsunamis, tornados, wildfires, floods, and many other natural disasters, I believe this is the most important passage to keep in view. Rather than immediately asking, *"What sin is God judging?"* or *"What gave the devil access to bring such destruction?"* or simply concluding (wrongly), *"It must be a sign of the times,"* we can find a better understanding of what is taking place in the earth through this passage. The earth is *subjected to frustration*. Romans 8:22 says that *"the whole earth groans"* (NKJV). And it is the children of God who are meant to bring it into glorious freedom.

I believe the children of God will continue to grow into a greater understanding of their identity, which will result in them living in glorious freedom in a way that has not yet been experienced. Where the Spirit of the Lord is, there is freedom! (See 2 Corinthians 3:17.) Someday in the future, the heart of the Church will be filled with glorious freedom, and this will impact the entire planet!

The Big Three

I do not believe Jesus will return to earth during my lifetime. I will choose to work as if He is returning soon, but I believe the Church and the Kingdom have a lot farther to go. Acknowledging that we have a way to go, I am also convinced by Scripture that Jesus absolutely, without a shadow of a doubt, will return to earth in the future to resurrect the dead and bring the final judgment. *The Big Three* is what I call the idea that Jesus will still do three things in the future: return, resurrect, and judge. I will address these in detail in the next chapter.

CHAPTER POINTS

- Remnant theology is not valid in the New Testament; instead, we have an ever-advancing Kingdom of God.
- The Bible contains some promises regarding the Church and the Kingdom that are yet to be fulfilled.
- We are to occupy until He comes, not be preoccupied with His coming.
- The Kingdom will continue to grow until the knowledge of God and His glory fill the whole earth.
- All of Jesus' enemies will be made His footstool prior to His return. The Church enacts this as His delegated authorities on earth.
- The true "sign of the times" is when we see His Kingdom coming and His will being done on earth as it is in Heaven.
- True unity in the Church is a promise that has not yet been fulfilled, but will be before Christ's return.
- Before Christ's return, the Church will mature into a "body" that is capable of carrying its "head"—Christ.
- The Church will bring forth the "sons of God," who will help release freedom to the earth prior to Christ's return.

DISCUSSION QUESTIONS

1. Does the Kingdom come at the end of time, or is it present and growing?

2. How is this different than what you grew up believing?

3. What is remnant teaching? What fruit have you seen from this teaching?

4. Is remnant teaching compatible with Kingdom teaching? Why or why not?

5. How did you feel when you read about the tremendous advancement of the Kingdom?

chapter fourteen

THE BIG THREE

I get asked the same question very often: "If there is no rapture, no future Great Tribulation, and no antichrist, then do you believe in the return of Jesus Christ?"

The answer is, *absolutely yes!* Jesus will return to earth in the future.

I have come to understand that a lot of verses that speak of Jesus coming on the clouds of heaven are actually about the AD 70 destruction of Jerusalem (as we covered in Chapters 2 and 3). Yet a significant number of verses still speak about events in our future. Although I believe a majority of Bible prophecy has been fulfilled, I still see three major prophetic events as remaining unfulfilled. I refer to these as *The Big Three*: the physical return of Christ, the resurrection of the dead, and the final judgment.

What you have read in this book stands in total agreement, not only with the Scripture, but also with the historical creeds of the Church. The early Church leaders gathered in Nicaea in AD 325, and once they reached a consensus, they wrote the Nicene Creed. We see in the creed that they believed in a physical, future return of Jesus to earth.

The Nicene Creed

Here's the creed in full:

We believe in one God the Father Almighty, Maker of heaven and earth, and of all things visible and invisible.

> And in one Lord Jesus Christ, the only-begotten Son of God, begotten of the Father before all worlds, God of God, Light of Light, Very God of Very God, begotten, not made, being of one substance with the Father by whom all things were made; who for us men, and for our salvation, came down from heaven, and was incarnate by the Holy Spirit of the Virgin Mary, and was made man, and was crucified also for us under Pontius Pilate. He suffered and was buried, and the third day he rose again according to the Scriptures, and ascended into heaven, and sits on the right hand of the Father. **And he shall come again with glory to judge both the quick and the dead,** whose kingdom shall have no end.
>
> And we believe in the Holy Spirit, the Lord and Giver of Life, who proceeded from the Father and the Son, who with the Father and the Son together is worshipped and glorified, who spoke by the prophets. And we believe one holy catholic and apostolic Church. We acknowledge one baptism for the remission of sins. And we look for the resurrection of the dead, and the life of the world to come. Amen.[1]

We see three things in this one sentence that I've highlighted: He shall come again, He shall judge, and His judgment will be of the quick (living) and the dead (which refers to resurrection). These are the three things even those in AD 325 realized were future unfulfilled events.

The Return of Christ

Although Jesus used the Hebrew phrase "coming upon clouds" in reference to the destruction that God brought on Jerusalem in AD 70, Jesus also prophesied that He would physically return one day in the future. The majority of the New Testament verses about Jesus' coming are about the AD 70 destruction. Keep in mind that Jews in AD 30 were much more focused on the immediate destruction of the Temple, the end of sacrifice, and the removal of the Holy City. The idea that Jesus would return physically someday in the future was not their major focus. The early Church's thoughts were more consumed with surviving the Jewish persecution and looking forward to Christ's coming to punish their persecutors.

Yet, several passages do speak of Jesus' future, physical return to earth. Here are the main passages:

> *After he said this, he was taken up before their very eyes, and a cloud hid him from their sight. They were looking intently up into the sky as he was going, when suddenly two men dressed in white stood beside them. "Men of Galilee," they said, "why do you stand here looking into the sky? This same Jesus, who has been taken from you into heaven, will come back in the same way you have seen him go into heaven"* (Acts 1:9-11).

> *So Christ was sacrificed once to take away the sins of many; and he will appear a second time, not to bear sin, but to bring salvation to those who are waiting for him* (Hebrews 9:28).

> *While we wait for the blessed hope—the appearing of the glory of our great God and Savior, Jesus Christ* (Titus 2:13).

At His return, the following two events will occur: the resurrection of the dead and the final judgment.

The Resurrection of the Dead

> *Do not be amazed at this, for a time is coming when all who are in their graves will hear his voice and come out—those who have done what is good will rise to live, and those who have done what is evil will rise to be condemned* (John 5:28-29).

A time is coming—it is still in our future—when all graves will be emptied out and the dead will be sorted into two different categories: the good and the evil, those who will live and those who will be condemned. This is typically called the final judgment; I will address that more in the next section. For now, simply notice that the resurrection occurs first, then the sorting. In the next two passages, we can see more detail regarding what happens to the believers when they are resurrected for the sorting.

> *Brothers and sisters, we do not want you to be uninformed about those who sleep in death, so that you do not grieve like the rest of mankind, who have no hope. For the Lord himself will come down from heaven, with a loud command, with the voice of the archangel and with the trumpet call of God, and the dead in Christ will rise first* (1 Thessalonians 4:13,16).

When the Lord speaks and blows His trumpet, the dead in Christ will rise first. The apostle Paul gives us more details in this next passage:

> *So will it be with the resurrection of the dead. The body that is sown is perishable, it is raised imperishable; it is sown in dishonor, it is raised in glory; it is sown in weakness, it is raised in power; it is sown a natural body, it is raised a spiritual body....*
>
> *I declare to you, brothers and sisters, that flesh and blood cannot inherit the kingdom of God, nor does the perishable inherit the imperishable. Listen, I tell you a mystery: We will not all sleep, but we will all be changed—in a flash, in the twinkling of an eye, at the last trumpet. For the trumpet will sound, the dead will be raised imperishable, and we will be changed. For the perishable must clothe itself with the imperishable, and the mortal with immortality. When the perishable has been clothed with the imperishable, and the mortal with immortality, then the saying that is written will come true: "Death has been swallowed up in victory." "Where, O death, is your victory? Where, O death, is your sting?"* (1 Corinthians 15:42-44,50-55).

Believers will become immortal, and we will have imperishable bodies. This is likely similar to what happened to Jesus on the Mount of Transfiguration or after His resurrection. The dead in Christ will be changed in the twinkling of an eye (really fast). Death will be swallowed up in victory.

Now we will look at the third event of the Big Three.

The Final Judgment

Many verses throughout the New Testament clearly teach about the final judgment, including these words from Jesus:

> *And he has given him authority to judge because he is the Son of Man. Do not be amazed at this, for a time is coming when all who are in their graves will hear his voice and come out—those who have done what is good will rise to live, and those who have done what is evil will rise to be condemned* (John 5:27-29).

Here we can clearly see that Jesus has been given the authority to be the judge. Paul confirmed this in his speech to the people of Athens:

> *"For he has set a day when he will judge the world with justice by the man he has appointed. He has given proof of this to everyone by raising him from the dead." When they heard about the resurrection of the dead, some of them sneered, but others said, "We want to hear you again on this subject"* (Acts 17:31-32).

This is an affirmation that Jesus will be the judge, but it also says that the *proof* that Jesus is God is in the fact that He was raised from the dead.

> *When the Son of Man comes in his glory, and all the angels with him, he will sit on his glorious throne. All the nations will be gathered before him, and* ***he will separate the people one from another*** *as a shepherd separates the sheep from the goats. He will put the sheep on his right and the goats on his left.... Then they will go away to eternal punishment, but the righteous to eternal life* (Matthew 25:31-33,46).

As we've discussed before, Jesus "coming in His glory" is different than the Hebrew idiom "coming in clouds," which is a reference to the destruction of a nation or city. When Jesus "comes in His glory," it will be as a judge on the throne, bringing the final judgment.

It is important, also, to notice that Jesus is not judging the character of nations in Matthew 25. The phrase *"all nations"* indicates that everyone will be gathered before Him, but the judge clearly separates *the people,* the individuals. Some have created strange doctrines on the idea that God will separate "sheep and goat nations," but that is not stated in any passage of Scripture. This is about separating individuals. Individuals are personally accountable before God, not nations. I know this is stretching for some of you doctrinally, but I would ask you to reread the Matthew 25 passage a few times and notice that the "sheep and goat nations" teaching is not supported by this passage.

Here are five thoughts about the "sheep and goat nations" teaching:

1. Yes, it is our mission to disciple the nations (see Matt. 28:19).
2. Yes, this mission will be successful (see Rev. 11:15).
3. No, Christian nations are not considered "sheep nations." Matthew 25 uses the Greek word *ethnos* in reference to the nations. That means it is referring to individuals of all ethnicities, not citizenship.
4. Yes, we are to pray that we would inherit the nations (see Ps. 2:8). Again here *nations* is the same root word as *ethnicities*. God is not looking for sheep countries; He is looking for all ethnicities to be discipled so He has countries full of sheep individuals.
5. Some might say to me, "Seriously, Jonathan, why does this matter? Aren't you splitting hairs on this?" For many years, I have sat in church and heard "prophetic" teachers speak of our nation as a "sheep nation," warning that we must stay the course or else we might become a "goat nation." This led me to think through the implications of this teaching:

- How does one become a goat nation? Does this require 51 percent being non-Christian?
- What if the population is 51 percent Christian? Are we then a sheep nation?
- What denominations count toward the 51 percent needed to keep ourselves as a sheep nation?
- What if you are a sheep living in a goat nation? What happens to you on judgment day?

- If I am a Christian in a goat nation on judgment day, will God send me to hell? (Of course, I would assume that none of these preachers would say so, but if judgment is national—not individual—then how could they disagree?)
- If judgment day is based on national citizenship, should I get citizenship in multiple countries and be better prepared for God's national sheep/goat "roulette" on judgment day?

My conclusion about the "sheep and goat nations teaching" is that God is no respecter of country borderlines. His New Covenant (see Heb. 8) has nothing to do with countries and neither does judgment day. Judgment day will be individuals standing before God as individuals. It does not matter what country you live in.

Now of course, the well-intentioned goal of those teaching the "sheep and goat nations" is that we are called to disciple all nations, which I agree with.

We can find further confirmation for individual (not national) judgment in the following passage:

> *If anyone builds on this foundation using gold, silver, costly stones, wood, hay or straw, their work will be shown for what it is, because the Day will bring it to light. It will be revealed with fire, and the fire will test the quality of each person's work. If what has been built survives, the builder will receive a reward. If it is burned up, the builder will suffer loss but yet will be saved—even though only as one escaping through the flames* (1 Corinthians 3:12-15).

The final judgment will divide righteous people from evil people, and the evil will receive their punishment. Yet the righteous will also receive varying rewards. Christians typically don't like to talk about being rewarded, but Jesus and the early Church had no qualms about rewards. In this passage, Paul spoke of the rewarding of Christians at the final judgment. In fact, it seems like, according to Paul, this is something that should be on our minds.

At the final judgment, all humankind will be resurrected and appear before the throne of God. Then individuals are sorted out as good or evil, sheep or goats. Then the good, righteous sheep will have a further judgment, which is to examine them for reward. This is pictured as each individual having a large pile of wood, hay, and straw piled in front of them, as well as gold, silver, and jewels mixed into the pile. I picture each believer standing by a pile, which represents his or her life; then a runner with a torch comes and begins to set fire to each person's pile. As the pile burns, all the wasted time in one's life burns as the wood, hay, and straw. Then finally the fire burns out, the pile is gone, and all that remains is a smaller pile of ash. Among the ash is gold, silver, and jewels. These represent the rewards.

Some teach that every sinful action in a Christian's life will be projected on a giant screen in Heaven for all to see; then God will forgive that Christian, allowing admission into Heaven. This is an evil and foolish teaching that promotes shame to try to stop Christians from sinning. According to the Bible, God has forgiven us, and He chooses to remember our sins no more (see Heb. 8:12; 10:17). This idea of judgment comes from the dark ages, not from the Bible. There is a judgment for Christians, but not for shame and guilt over sins that God has already forgiven and doesn't even remember. The only reason to judge Christians is to dole out the varying rewards.

> *Therefore judge nothing before the appointed time; wait until the Lord comes. He will bring to light what is hidden in darkness and will expose the motives of the heart. At that time each will receive their praise from God* (1 Corinthians 4:5).

This judgment is not a matter of salvation; it is a matter of how much praise or how little praise one will receive. As Paul wrote in another place,

> *You, then, why do you judge your brother or sister? Or why do you treat them with contempt? For we will all stand before God's judgment seat... so then, each of us will give an account of ourselves to God* (Romans 14:10,12).

Again, this accounting is about reward, not about shame and punishment. Although, there won't be much praise for some Christians who stand before His throne, this is not about shame and punishment. Of course, it would be better to live a life that God can praise and reward with gold, silver, and jewels rather than a life that will burn up leaving nothing but a pile of ash.

When most people think of the final judgment, this is the passage that comes to mind:

> *Then I saw a great white throne and him who was seated on it. The earth and the heavens fled from his presence, and there was no place for them. And I saw the dead, great and small, standing before the throne, and books were opened. Another book was opened, which is the book of life. The dead were judged according to what they had done as recorded in the books. The sea gave up the dead that were in it, and death and Hades gave up the dead that were in them, and each person was judged according to what they had done. Then death and Hades were thrown into the lake of fire. The lake of fire is the second death. Anyone whose name was not found written in the book of life was thrown into the lake of fire* (Revelation 20:11-15).

This is a very descriptive passage and gives more detail to the picture of judgment, while basically encapsulating the previously examined passages. Simply stated, one day Jesus will return in glory with His angels and bring judgment based on whose names are and are not written in the Lamb's book of life. Those who are not in the book of life will be thrown into the lake of fire. Those who are in the book of life will then have their lives burned down as wood, hay, and straw or silver, gold and jewels. Then each Christian will receive the due praise from God. This is what will take place in the future and directs how we should choose to live.

CHAPTER POINTS

- There are yet three major prophetic events remaining to be fulfilled: the physical return of Christ, the resurrection of the dead, and the final judgment.
- In the future, when Christ returns, all of the dead will be resurrected for judgment. After their resurrection, the good and evil people are sorted.
- At the resurrection of the dead, believers will receive imperishable bodies.
- Jesus will be the judge at the final judgment, and He will judge individuals, not nations.
- At the judgment, evil people (unbelievers) will receive punishment and righteous people (Christians) will receive rewards.
- Christians will be rewarded based on how they lived their lives for the Kingdom. However, God forgives all who repent, even those whose lives receive little or no reward. His purpose in this is not humiliation or condemnation, and our sins will not be projected on a screen for all to see.

DISCUSSION QUESTIONS

1. Does the Bible teach a future return of Jesus?
2. Does Church history affirm this? Does Jonathan Welton affirm this?
3. When Jesus returns, what two other major events will occur?
4. Have you heard the sheep and goats as *nations* teaching?
5. Have you understood the sheep and goats *as individuals*? Which makes sense and why?

chapter fifteen

THE APOSTOLIC MISSION

So what is God waiting for?

Think about it. Why hasn't Jesus come back yet? For nearly 2,000 years, the Church has eagerly awaited the final return of Jesus Christ. Yet for the same two thousand years, I believe Jesus Christ has been waiting for the Church.

Many Christians have no idea what God is waiting for. Yet if we don't understand what He is waiting for, it is impossible for us to partner with Heaven in order to bring Jesus back to earth! This has resulted in an incredible amount of theological confusion regarding the return of the Lord. One of the most prevalent misconceptions is that Jesus could return at any moment. This teaching is present in so many Christian novels and low-budget end-times films, yet it is not a sound doctrine of the Bible.

When teachers lift verses out of their intended historical context, they can easily create a doctrine of Jesus' "any moment" return. Yet this is not taught anywhere in the New Testament. When a historical, contextual understanding of the New Testament is put into place, the modern any-moment-return doctrine crumbles.

While many liberal theologians would say differently, John A. T. Robinson has written a masterpiece that correctly demonstrates that the entire New Testament was written before the AD 70 destruction of Jerusalem.[1] This context is important because it gives a foundation for interpreting the New Testament. With that truth in mind, we can understand that the backdrop to everything recorded in the New Testament was the impending doom that was about to fall upon the city of Jerusalem. Here are a few examples:

- *Why would the early disciples sell their property?* (See Acts 4:32–37.) They did this because they had insider information that the city was about to be destroyed.
- *What was Stephen accused of that led to his stoning?* (See Acts 6:13–14.) Stephen was declaring the impending destruction. (*A false witness* typically meant a bribed witness.)
- *Why, instead of building large churches, did the early Church chose to meet in the temple courts and from house to house?* (See Acts 2:46.) They did this because they knew their city was about to be destroyed. If you knew destruction was coming, would you start building a large church facility? Of course not! Instead, you would logically meet in homes and lecture halls (see Acts 2:46; 19:9).
- *Why did James encourage his readers to take their plans lightly?* (See James 4:13–17.) He did this because he knew that at any moment the destruction of Jerusalem could begin (see James 5:1–9).

The "Any-Moment" Doctrine

As we discussed previously, when the New Testament refers to Jesus' coming, it is a clear reference to the impending judgment upon Jerusalem in AD 70. Once we understand that, we can shine light upon the passages that are used to teach the any-moment return of Christ:

> *Therefore be on the alert, for you do not know which day your Lord is coming* (Matthew 24:42).

> *Be on the alert then, for you do not know the day nor the hour* (Matthew 25:13).

> *Be on guard! Be alert! You do not know when that time will come* (Mark 13:33).

But let us be alert and sober (1 Thessalonians 5:6b).

The first-century Christians had to be prepared for and watchful of the impending judgment. We are informed through the historical record that not one Christian died in the destruction of Jerusalem. To put that in context, 1.1 million Jews were killed in the slaughter, but every Christian of the first century understood that the prophecy of Matthew 24 was about their generation, and they literally kept watch and ran for the mountains of Pella to escape the destruction.

In Matthew 24:15–18, Jesus gave very practical advice to His followers about how to stay alive during the AD 70 destruction. We can tell from this passage that Jesus was speaking of a local destruction (flee Judea) and a historical setting (not on a Sabbath). The natural tendency, upon seeing an approaching army, would have been to flee into Jerusalem for safety. Yet Jesus told them to fight their natural instincts and flee the city. Because of Jesus' command to flee, His followers were protected.

It was important for the first generation Church to be alert and watchful so that they wouldn't die in the AD 70 destruction. These verses applied to them, but they do not apply to us. We are not called to live on the edge of our seats believing Jesus could come at any moment. We are called to pray it would be *"on earth as it is in heaven"* (Matt. 6:10). We are to occupy until He comes, not be preoccupied with His coming!

Righteous Thinking Is Long-Term Thinking

One of the "Seven Core Values" that guides my ministry is investing. Here is how I have stated it for my team:

> Investing is long-term thinking. This impacts every aspect of life. Although it may cost more, buying quality only hurts you once. It is better to do something right the first time rather than to do it twice.
>
> We believe time is an un-renewable resource. There is always more money, but there is not more time. Operating in long-term thinking is kingly thinking, whereas short-term thinking is poverty thinking.

Let's focus on that last sentence: *Operating in long-term thinking is kingly thinking.* The Bible gives us the stories of two very different kings, one who thought long-term and one who thought short-term.

1. King David stored up vast resources and wealth for his son Solomon to reign and build a temple unto the Lord (see 1 Chron. 22). He was thinking of future generations, and he prepared for a temple he would never live to see.
2. Later in Israel's history, King Hezekiah came into power. When Isaiah the prophet told King Hezekiah he would have a peaceful reign but after him the kingdom would fall into utter ruin and captivity, Hezekiah didn't care (see Isa. 39). King Hezekiah operated in a poverty mindset. He cared only about himself and his own life and generation.

We learn from King Solomon, who wrote the Book of Proverbs, *"A righteous man leaves an inheritance for his children's children"* (Prov. 13:22). It is amazing to ponder that Solomon was able to write this proverb because of witnessing his father, King David, living as a righteous man and thinking of his children's children. This proverb is not simply a wise saying; it was something Solomon observed and appreciated about his father, the righteous King David.

The larger context of the Bible teaches that the righteous think long term. Yet much of modern Christianity has been infected with short-term thinking. Consider the following quote from *The Days of Vengeance:*

> First, have you ever wondered why Christians in the United States are clearly in the majority, and always have been, yet they have so little cultural influence?
>
> Here are three good reasons: (1) They have no plan; (2) they have little or no personal incentive; (3) they see no long-run hope of success.[2]

I believe volumes have been said in this quote. It is a statement worth pondering until we (1) have a plan; (2) understand what motivates us to pursue it; and (3) understand that we are called to build the Kingdom of Heaven in the earth and think long-term!

Although there are moments in time, such as AD 70, when God gave a warning and told the early Christians to keep watch, this is not the posture of all Christians for all time. We are not called to live on the edge of our seats and bite our nails hoping for (or fearing) the rapture. Actually, for much of Church history, Christian leaders have taught and believed we are called to think and live long-term. Take, for example, the *Book of Common Prayer.* We can see from the fact that it contains tables for finding Holy Days all the way through AD 8400 that its compilers were not expecting Christ to return in the near future![3] This is just one example from a multitude throughout history that the idea of thinking long-term and building the Kingdom of God in the earth realm until the final return of Christ has been the predominant view of the Church in history. Consider also the words of the following leaders:

> All unprejudiced persons may see with their eyes, that He is already renewing the face of the earth: And we have strong reason to hope that the work He hath begun He will carry on unto the day of the Lord Jesus; that He will never intermit this blessed work of His Spirit until He has fulfilled all His promises, until He hath put a period to sin and misery, and infirmity, and death; and re-established universal holiness and happiness, and caused all the inhabitants of the earth to sing together "Hallelujah." —John Wesley[4]

> The visible kingdom of Satan shall be overthrown, and the kingdom of Christ set up on the ruins of it, everywhere throughout the whole habitable globe. —Jonathan Edwards[5]

> I myself believe that King Jesus will reign, and the idols be utterly abolished; but I expect the same power which turned the world upside down once, will still continue to do it. The Holy Ghost would never suffer the imputation to rest upon His holy name that He was not able to convert the world. —Charles Spurgeon[6]

Long-term thinking is not only seen in the writings of great leaders, but also even in something as mundane as Church architecture. For example, if a leader believes the Church is called to think long-term and establish the Kingdom of God upon the earth, it is easy to commission the building of a church of stone that will take a hundred years to complete—as many of the ancient cathedrals did. Even though that leader will not live to see the completion, he is intentionally planning toward a future generation. The massive stone cathedrals across Europe are a testament of leaders who thought long-term.

Once we settle into the fact that the Kingdom has been here since the manger in Bethlehem and is growing and being established more and more through the Church in the earth, we can begin to understand our calling. The Church no longer needs to live on the edge of her seat, as if she will float away any second! She no longer has to wait with an identity crisis—"Why won't my groom come back for me?" Instead, she can get on with her calling to build the Kingdom of God upon the earth.

For this reason, it is vitally and profoundly important that the Church abandon the any-moment-return doctrine and embrace the long-term thinking of the righteous person (see Prov. 13:22).

Completing the Apostolic Mission

In summary, Jesus came to earth as the King over all creation. He established His Kingdom, and it began to grow from the first century through to the present day. Now the Church, as the Bride of Christ, is God's ambassador to further establish His Kingdom in the earth. I refer to the Church's calling as the Apostolic Mission. Bill Johnson and Randy Clark provide an excellent definition of what it means to be an *apostle* in their book, *The Essential Guide to Healing*:

> The word *apostle* in the New Testament means "sent one." *Apostle* was originally a secular term used by both the Greeks and the Romans to refer to the leader of a special envoy. That leader had the job of establishing the culture of the empire he represented into the daily lives of the citizens the empire conquered. Leaders had discovered

> that the citizens of conquered lands went back to their previous way of life rather quickly without transforming influence. It was extremely frustrating to see no change result in a conquered nation, which nullified the purpose of the conquest. For this reason, they came up with a strategy to transform the culture of a conquered city so that when the empire's leaders visited, it would feel the same as home. The position of apostle was created in response to this need.
>
> Jesus adopted the term to reveal His intentions. His apostles lead a special envoy of people who have the job of establishing the culture of the empire of heaven into the daily lives of the citizens they serve.[7]

As citizens of Heaven (see Phil. 3:20) and as ambassadors of Heaven (see 2 Cor. 5:20), we are here with a mission. Jesus is not coming back until we finish the Apostolic Mission—the mission of the *apostolos* to implement the culture of Heaven into the culture of the earth.

Someday the Church will complete this mission. Sons and daughters of King Jesus will know who they are and will live out their identity as righteous people. Suffering will be brought to a minimum in the earth realm. Sin will massively decrease. The sex industry will collapse, and broken families will be restored. People will live longer, healthier, and more joy-filled lives. There will be no more orphans, no more starvation, and sickness will be rare. All the enemies of God will bow under Jesus' feet until finally death is put under His feet as the last foe (see 1 Cor. 5:26). All other foes will be subdued as we put them under our feet (see Rom. 16:20).

The day will come when the culturing of the *apostolos* has completed the Apostolic Mission. On that day, Jesus will be able to touch His toe to earth in physical form and finally say, as the Roman Emperors did in days past, "This place feels a lot like home!"

CHAPTER POINTS

- God is waiting for the restoration of all things (see Acts 3:19–21).
- The Early Church (AD 30–70) seemed to live and think very short term because they were focused on the time they were living in before the destruction of Jerusalem.
- The "any-moment return" doctrine is not healthy or applicable to all Christians at all times of history.
- Righteous thinking is long-term thinking.
- We have an apostolic mission to culturize earth with the culture of Heaven.

DISCUSSION QUESTIONS

1. Are we waiting for Jesus, or is He waiting for the Church? Discuss.

2. With the AD 70 destruction in the background of the New Testament, how much does this affect the way you read the New Testament?

3. What do the any-moment verses actually refer to?

4. What if you didn't live the rest of your life on the edge of your seat but began to think long term? What would you do differently starting today?

5. What did the word *apostle* originally mean, and how does it apply to your life?

BOOK THREE

THE ART OF REVELATION

JONATHAN WELTON

PART ONE

Imagine we are standing together at an art museum. Before us is a large, magnificent painting of grass surrounded by a tall forest and interspersed with wildflowers and deer. I turn to you and say, "I will explain this painting to you."

You nod in agreement and suddenly step extremely close to the painting. Pointing at one tiny blotch of color, you ask, "What is this patch of color? What does it mean? What does it represent?"

Like this painting, the Book of Revelation is a beautiful tapestry of images and symbols. In order to understand it, we first need to step back and look at the entire piece of art—at the big picture. Yet often people do exactly the opposite. Like you did in our imaginary scenario, they move too close to the painting and point at tiny patches of color, demanding isolated interpretations of those particles.

As one who would like to explain this painting, I ask that we start by standing back and taking in the painting at once, as a whole. Then I will tell you about the artist who painted it, why He painted it, and the historical context that surrounded this painter and influenced the way He created His painting.

Allow yourself to understand these points surrounding the painting before you step closer to examine the details. If you don't do this first, any interpretation of the details will be slanted by personal preference rather than an understanding of what the artist was trying to convey.

Because it is most important for us to understand what exactly the Holy Spirit was conveying when He wrote the Book of Revelation, let us begin with the big picture, which is encapsulated in the answers to four important questions—*when, how, why,* and *where.*

1. When Was This Painting Created?

The first question that must be answered for any work of art is the question of *when* it was written. This is an especially important question for the Book of Revelation because the *when* determines whether or not to applies to the AD 70 destruction of Jerusalem. As you may guess, I have come to believe the majority of the Book of Revelation was written regarding events that took place at the destruction of Jerusalem in AD 70. In order to believe that, we must first address the date of authorship. If the book was written in AD 96, as many modern teachers claim, then my point of view cannot be valid. Yet, I believe the overwhelming body of evidence proves beyond reasonable doubt that Revelation was more likely written before AD 68. Let's look at the proofs to establish the date of writing.

THE PROOFS

The primary reason some Bible teachers claim the Book of Revelation was written around AD 96 is because John noted in Revelation 1:9 that he was on the island of Patmos at the time he received the Revelation. There is some historical evidence that John was exiled to Patmos under the reign of Domitian between AD 81 and AD 96. Therefore, the book might have been written during that time—or so some claim. In reality, there are also historical documents that tell us John was exiled to Patmos at a much earlier date. Here I will share ten evidences that Revelation was written before AD 68.

1. The Syriac

We have the witness of one of the most ancient versions of the New Testament, called *The Syriac.* The second-century Syriac Version, called the *Peshitto*, says the following on the title page of the Book of Revelation:

> Again the revelation, which was upon the holy John the Evangelist from God when he was on the island of Patmos where he was thrown by the emperor Nero.

Nero Caesar ruled over the Roman Empire from AD 54 to AD 68. Therefore, John had to have been on the island of Patmos during this earlier period. One of the oldest versions of the Bible tells us when Revelation was written! That alone is a very compelling argument.

2. Revelation 17:10

When we look at the internal evidence, we find a very clear indicator of the date of authorship in Revelation 17:10: *"They are also seven kings.* ***Five have fallen, one is, the other has not yet come****; but when he does come, he must remain for only a little while"* (Rev. 17:10). This passage, which speaks of the line of rulers in Rome, tells us exactly how many rulers had already come, which one was currently in power, and that the next one would only last a short while. Take a look at how perfectly it fits with Nero and the Roman Empire of the first century.

The rule of the first seven Roman Emperors is as follows:

"Five have fallen..."
Julius Caesar (49–44 BC)
Augustus (27 BC–AD 14)
Tiberius (AD 14–37)
Caligula (AD 37–41)
Claudius (AD 41–54)

"One is..."
Nero (AD 54–68)

"the other has not yet come; but when he does come, he must remain for only a little while."

Galba (June AD 68–January AD 69, a six-month rulership)

Of the first seven kings, five had come (Julius Caesar, Augustus, Tiberius, Gaius, and Claudius), one was currently in power (Nero), and one had not yet come (Galba), but would only remain a little time (six months). The current Caesar at the time of John's writing was the sixth Caesar, Nero.

3. Those Who Pierced Him

As I discussed in depth in *Raptureless*, the Hebrew idiom "coming on clouds" speaks of God coming to bring judgment on a city or nation. That is what Jesus came to do in AD 70. Revelation 1:7 tells us whom His judgment is against:

> *Lo, he doth come with the clouds, and see him shall every eye, even* ***those who did pierce him,*** *and wail because of him shall* ***all the tribes of the land****. Yes! Amen* (Revelation 1:7 YLT).

Here, the phrase *"those who did pierce him"* refers to the people of the first century. According to this passage, they were expected to be alive at the time of Revelation's fulfillment. The fact that "those who did pierce him" were not alive in AD 96, because they were killed in the slaughter of AD 70, is a clear indicator that Revelation was written before AD 70.

4. Jewish Persecution of Christians

The Jewish persecution of Christianity in Revelation 6 and 11 indicates a pre-AD 70 authorship. After the slaughter of AD 70, the Jews were not in a position to persecute the early Church. In fact, since AD 70, the Jews have *never* been in a position to be able to persecute Christians.

5. Judaizing Heretics in the Church

The activity of the Judaizing heretics in the Church (see Rev. 2:6,9,15; 3:9) is emphasized in the letters to the churches in Revelation. This tells us something about the dating of the letter, because the Judiazing heretics lost a great deal of influence after Paul's epistles were circulated. Also, it makes sense that the heresy would have been a much smaller issue after so many

Jews were slaughtered in AD 70. Only an early date of authorship allows for the heretics to be a significant problem.

6. Existence of Jerusalem and the Temple

The existence and integrity of Jerusalem and the Temple (see Rev. 11) suggest a date before the destruction of AD 70. If the Book of Revelation was written in AD 96, only twenty-six years after the destruction of the Temple and the Holy City, it is shocking John didn't mention the recent massacre of the city and Temple.

7. Time-related Passages

The internal time-related portions of Revelation indicate that the events it foretells will come to pass shortly (see Rev. 1:1,3; 22:10,20). If this is read with an unbiased perspective, we can easily conclude Revelation was not written about events two thousand years in the future. The time texts are bookends that frame the contents of the book.

8. John's Appearance in AD 96

Another reason to believe the Book of Revelation was written at the earlier date is because Jerome noted in his writings that John was seen in AD 96 and that he was so old and infirm that "he was with difficulty carried to the church, and could speak only a few words to the people."[1] We must put this fact together with Revelation 10:11, which says John must *"prophesy again concerning many peoples and nations and tongues and kings."* It is difficult to imagine John would be able to speak to many nations and many kings at any date after AD 96 since he was already elderly and feeble.

9. Timetable Comparison with Daniel

In Daniel, the author was told to *"seal up the vision, for it is a long way off"* (Dan. 12:4)—which referred to a 483-year wait until Jesus came to fulfill the prophecy. By contrast, in Revelation, John was told to *"not seal up the vision because it concerns things which must shortly come to pass"* (Rev 22:10). If 483 years was considered a long way off, meaning that the vision should be sealed, it makes no sense that two thousand plus years would be considered *"shortly to come to pass"* and not to be sealed up. Clearly, the obvious answer is Revelation shouldn't be sealed because it was about to happen at the AD 70 destruction of Jerusalem.

10. Only Seven Churches

The existence of only seven churches in Asia Minor (see Rev. 1) also indicates a writing date before the greater expansion of Christianity into that region, which occurred after the fall of Jerusalem.

THE OTHER PERSPECTIVE

Those who believe in the later date of authorship for the Book of Revelation mainly lean on the fact that Irenaeus the Bishop of Lyons (AD 120–202) claimed John wrote while on Patmos under Domitian's reign. This alone could seem compelling, except Irenaeus is noted for making mistakes in recording dates and times in his writings. Irenaeus is the same Church father who claimed Jesus' ministry lasted nearly twenty years, from the age of thirty until the age of fifty.

Because Revelation contains no internal evidence for a later date of authorship, proponents of the later date must lean only upon external evidence to force this conclusion. Even the external evidence of Irenaeus is not a reliable source, and many scholars have even picked apart Irenaeus' quote about the date of authorship as possibly being a very misunderstood quotation.

Kenneth Gentry has done the world an invaluable service by writing his doctoral dissertation on the dating of Revelation. His irrefutable paper is easily purchasable as a book under the title: *Before Jerusalem Fell.* John A.T. Robinson has also graced us all with his book, *Redating the New Testament,* in which he proves all the books of the New Testament were written before AD 70.

Considering these strong proofs for an early date of writing alongside the very poor evidence in favor of a later date, I believe it is common sense to date the writing of Revelation prior to AD 70.

2. How Was the Painting Painted? What Medium Did the Artist Use?

Now that we have examined the masterpiece before us and determined the date it was painted, we must examine it within its larger context to understand the medium used and the backdrop on which it was created. The context of the big picture of Revelation is the entire Bible and the history of Israel from Abraham to Jesus.

We struggle to understand the Book of Revelation because we struggle to understand the history of the Old Testament. If I asked a well-studied Christian to sketch out a rough timeline of the Old Testament, it would look something like this:

- Adam and Eve (the Garden of Eden)
- Noah (the Flood)
- Abraham
- Isaac
- Jacob
- Joseph
- Egyptian slavery
- Moses (the Exodus)
- Joshua
- the Judges
- King Saul
- King David
- King Solomon

Overall, this rough timeline is excellent. The problem is not with what is written but with where it ends—with Solomon. After Solomon, the story gets too complicated for the modern teacher and preacher, and therefore, the modern pew-sitter never gets a handle on the Old Testament past the reign of King Solomon. However, to understand the Book of Revelation, one must *especially* understand the Old Testament after Solomon.

For the average Bible reader, the timeline breaks down after Solomon into a jumble of major and minor prophets, a divided kingdom, Elijah and Elisha, the exile to Babylon, and the return to rebuild Jerusalem. This whole section of texts becomes troublesome and challenging to relate to or understand. Allow me to iron out the timeline after Solomon, at least a little bit.

- After Solomon dies, Israel divides into two kingdoms, which spiritually and morally enter into drastic decline. Many evil rulers come and go in both kingdoms.
- Elijah and Elisha fight against the tide of wickedness flooding into the divided kingdom.
- Isaiah, Ezekiel, and Jeremiah prophesy a coming destruction upon Jerusalem for her wickedness.
- Babylon brings destruction upon the kingdom of Judah and takes Daniel and others as captives. Assyria destroys the Northern Kingdom, whose ten tribes are now essentially lost to history.
- Daniel writes the Book of Daniel while in Babylonian captivity.
- Esther protects her people from destruction while still in captivity.
- Finally the exile in Babylon ends, and the Israelites return to Jerusalem. They rebuild the city and the Temple under Ezra and Nehemiah.
- Interspersed with the story from Solomon to Ezra and Nehemiah are the smaller books of the minor prophets.

The most important Old Testament book to a proper understanding of the Book of Revelation is Ezekiel. Ezekiel prophesied the destruction of Jerusalem in the Old Testament and gives a most stunning parallel of the Book of Revelation.

Examine carefully the following list of parallels between the contents of Revelation and Ezekiel:

CONTENT	REVELATION	EZEKIEL
The Throne Vision	4	1
The Book	5	2-3
The Four Plagues	6:1-8	5
The Slain under the Altar	6:9-11	6
The Wrath of God	6:12-17	7
The Seal on the Saints' Foreheads	7	9
The Coals from the Altar	8	10
No More Delay	10:1-7	12
The Eating of the Book	10:8-11	2
The Measuring of the Temple	11:1-2	40-43
Jerusalem and Sodom	11:8	16
The Cup of Wrath	14	23
The Vine of the Land	14:18-20	15
The Great Harlot	17-18	16, 23
The Lament over the City	18	27
The Scavengers' Feast	19	39
The First Resurrection	20:4-6	37
The Battle with Gog and Magog	20:7-9	38-39
The New Jerusalem	21	40-48
The River of Life	22	47

Ezekiel is to the Old Testament what the Book of Revelation is to the New Testament. Ezekiel laid out the coming destruction of Jerusalem (by the Babylonians) in the Old Testament, and John used the same prophetic language to speak of the imminent coming destruction of Jerusalem in the New Testament. With that framework, the symbolism of Revelation is set in place and becomes simpler to interpret.

Also, Ezekiel is the turning point of the Old Testament. Before Ezekiel, from Adam to Solomon, the kingdom of Israel continually gained momentum. This momentum began to slow with the divided kingdom, but Ezekiel brought any remaining momentum to a screeching halt. His prophecy was followed by captivity, exile, a post-exilic return to Jerusalem, and a painful rebuilding process while still under a measure of captivity. After four hundred years of silence, the story of the Jews is resumed in the New Testament with Jerusalem under Roman oppression.

One crucial difference exists between Ezekiel's (as well as Jeremiah's and Isaiah's) prophecies of the coming destruction of Jerusalem and the apostle John's prophecy of the destruction of Jerusalem. Ezekiel, Jeremiah, and Isaiah all prophesied a future return to Jerusalem, which manifested through Ezra and Nehemiah. In contrast, John declared the utter devastation of Jerusalem with *no re-gathering* to the land.

- Ezekiel prophesied the destruction of Jerusalem in 586 BC.
- John prophesied the destruction of Jerusalem in AD 70.
- Ezekiel prophesied the post-exilic return and rebuilding of Jerusalem (see Ezek. 34–37).
- John prophesied no such return and no rebuilding of Jerusalem.

Many scholars have struggled with and debated over the somewhat odd and choppy version of Greek the apostle John used to write the Book of Revelation. I believe this is simply solved by observing that John was taking on a different prose and style in order to prophesy in the manner of Ezekiel, Isaiah, and Jeremiah, his Old Testament shadows.

Thus we can see the backdrop of the whole Bible is needed to understand the point and purpose of Revelation. The painting is painted *in this manner* because of the biblical surroundings and backdrop of John's day and the historical precedent of Ezekiel. John's readers in the first-century Church would have known the recent history of the Jews and would have recognized the parallels between Ezekiel's prophecy and John's. The fact that the modern Church has so poorly understood the meaning of Revelation demonstrates our lack of understanding regarding these very things.

3. Why Did the Artist Choose to Paint This Painting?

Now for the third question—*Why?* Matthew, Mark, and Luke all record in their gospels an event referred to as the Olivet Discourse (see Matt. 24, Luke 21, Mark 13), Jesus' longest recorded prophecy in the gospels. In it, Jesus declared the coming destruction of Jerusalem within a generation (forty years), which was fulfilled exactly by AD 70.

The gospel of John does not include this notable prophecy. Matthew, Mark, and Luke are named the synoptic gospels because they are somewhat parallel eyewitness accounts of the life, death, and resurrection of Jesus Christ. In contrast, the gospel of John records many events that have no parallel in the synoptic gospels—for example, the Samaritan woman at the well in John 4 or the unpopular "eat my flesh, drink my blood" sermon in John 6. John's gospel is known as the more esoteric of the gospels, recording statements, sayings, encounters, and events that are much more mystical than the synoptic gospels; even a cursory reading makes this self-evident. Also, John's letters—First, Second, and Third John—are similar, maintaining a heavenly and somewhat ethereal approach.

Therefore, when we get to John's version of the Olivet Discourse, why would we expect anything different? Surely John heard the Olivet Discourse at the same time the synoptic writers did, yet he didn't include this long prophecy in his gospel. Then, many years later, while on the Isle of Patmos, Jesus visits him with a much more detailed and dramatic version of the Olivet Discourse. Thus John wrote his version of the Olivet Discourse as a direct vision on Patmos, likely within a decade of the actual fulfillment of Jesus' prophecy.

One of the main reasons John was finally writing this Olivet Discourse was because Jesus needed to give His Church a comforting update. From AD 30–70, the Church suffered terrible persecution at the hands of the Jewish Temple leaders. This greatly intensified in AD 64–68 under Nero, who made it his goal to completely annihilate Christianity. During this very difficult time, the Church needed encouragement from Jesus. They needed reassurance that He would be coming back soon, and that is just what Revelation gave them. Throughout Revelation, God tells His followers to be patient because His justice, wrath, and vengeance are coming very soon.

When the city of Babylon is destroyed in Revelation 18, the people of earth mourn, but in Revelation 19, all of Heaven rejoices at the destruction of the evil harlot-city. In this we see that Revelation was also intended to give the early Church Heaven's perspective regarding the impending doom of Jerusalem in AD 70. God was saying, in essence, "Don't mourn with the sinners over that wicked city, but rejoice that My justice is poured out. I have been patient to allow all people a chance to come to repentance, but now justice has been served. Rejoice!"

The purpose of the painter's painting is to express his version of the Olivet Discourse, to give the early Church an update on the coming destruction, and to remind them of Heaven's perspective regarding the impending events.

4. Where Was the Painting Painted? What Location Does it Reference?

Finally, we must consider the region the painting was painted in and also the region it refers to. Was our painting painted in France during the French Revolution or in Colonial America during the American Revolution? Is it a modern piece, or was it upon the wall of a cave in ancient times?

TIME TEXTS

To do this, we must first briefly revisit the topic of timing. Earlier, we established that the Book of Revelation was written before AD 68. After the early date of authorship is established, the next important key is the time-texts regarding the content of the book. As we noted previously, Revelation is an unsealed book (see Rev. 22:10) because the events were soon to take place, whereas Daniel is a sealed book (see Dan. 12:4) because its contents were regarding events in the *then* distant future—five hundred years later.

Here is what the Book of Revelation says about the timing of its fulfillment:

- What must *shortly* take place (see Rev. 1:1)
- For the time is *near* (see Rev. 1:3)
- I am coming to you *quickly* (see Rev. 2:16)

- I am coming *quickly* (see Rev. 3:11)
- The third woe is coming *quickly* (see Rev. 11:14)
- The things which must *shortly take place* (see Rev. 22:6)
- Behold, I am coming *quickly* (see Rev. 22:7)
- For the time is *near* (see Rev. 22:10)
- Behold, I am coming *quickly* (see Rev. 22:12)
- Yes, I am coming *quickly* (see Rev. 22:20)

An important principle of biblical interpretation is stated by the scholar Gordon Fee, "A text cannot mean what it never could have meant to its author or his or her readers."[2] In other words, we cannot simply look at the texts that say *soon* and conclude it couldn't be so because it was written two thousand years ago and we haven't identified anything in history that fits what we think it should look like! This should not be. Instead, we must diligently treat the text with respect. Our ignorance of history gives us no allowance for such a conclusion.

The text says *soon*; therefore, we must look for a soon fulfillment that respects the text. We also must not do violence to the text by forcing it to fit into history. If it fits into history, it should fit beautifully and with such smoothness as to not violate the conscience in the least. I believe Revelation does just that—if we understand it in its proper location, which is not the entire globe but the small region of the world where it was created and where its original audience lived.

LOCATION

The modern reader has been trained to read Revelation as if it was written about a global catastrophe. Unfortunately, our English translations are careless with the details regarding location. For example, when Revelation writes about a third of the grass, a third of the trees, and a third of the earth (see Rev. 8), the modern reader imagines this on a global scale. Yet the original wording of the Greek manuscripts paints an extremely different picture.

In the Greek, we must understand two words regarding location. The first word is *ge*, which is used sixty-seven times in Revelation. It refers to a local inhabited civilization or the land of a particular nation.[3] The second word is *kosmos*, which is used three times in Revelation (see Rev. 11:15; 13:8; 17:8). It refers to the entire globe, the entirety of planet earth and the heavens.[4]

The apostle John often used this word, *kosmos*, in his other writings—a whopping fifty-seven times in his gospel and seventeen times in First John alone. Yet he chose not to use it in Revelation because *he was not writing about a global event.* This is an incredibly important point!

From this simple study of these two words translated as "world," we can see that the Book of Revelation was not written about a global catastrophe but a *local* catastrophe. The contents of the entire Book of Revelation refer to local (*ge*) events, not global (*kosmos*) events.

SUMMARY

We have taken a step back and observed the large painting of Revelation, noting the timing, method, purpose, and context of its creation. With this framework—the *when, how, why*, and *where*—in place, we can now look at the particulars and interpret them in the context they were meant to be understood in.

PART TWO

NAMING THE PAINTING

When you hear about Vincent Van Gogh's painting named "Starry Night," what do you expect to see? What about Monet's "Lillypads" or da Vinci's "Mona Lisa"? Don't you expect to see a starry night sky, lillypads, and a young woman? Of course! Similarly, to properly understand John's vision, we must grasp the name of the vision. Just this simple piece will go a long way toward a correct understanding.

John's vision is not named The Book of Revelations, The Book of Revelation, or even The Revelation. Its full name is: The Book of the Revelation of Jesus Christ.

I have read many books about John's vision that begin with a statement about how the vision is about Jesus and then spend hundreds of pages writing about the antichrist, the Tribulation, and the end of the world. While I agree with their opening statements, I find what follows in their writing to be inconsistent with their introduction.

I believe this inconsistency stems from the fact that, although they know the vision is supposed to unveil Jesus, it seems like much of it is actually about the destruction of the planet. This confusion comes in when people don't understand the shift in the first century from the Mosaic Covenant to the New Covenant. The Revelation of Jesus Christ is about the removal of the Old Covenant and the fully unveiled New Covenant.

All through the New Testament, we find the apostles writing of a soon-approaching day when Jesus would be fully revealed. For example:

> *These have come so that the proven genuineness of your faith—of greater worth than gold, which perishes even though refined by fire—may result in praise, glory and honor* **when Jesus Christ is revealed** (1 Peter 1:7).

> *Therefore, with minds that are alert and fully sober, set your hope on the grace to be brought to you* **when Jesus Christ is revealed** *at his coming [in the AD 70 destruction, not His final return]* (1 Peter 1:13).

> *God is just: He will pay back trouble to those who trouble you and give relief to you who are troubled, and to us as well. This will happen* **when the Lord Jesus is revealed** *from heaven in blazing fire with his powerful angels* (2 Thessalonians 1:6–7).

> *Therefore you do not lack any spiritual gift as you eagerly wait for our* **Lord Jesus Christ to be revealed** (1 Corinthians 1:7).

> *But because of your stubbornness and your unrepentant heart, you are storing up wrath against yourself for the day of God's wrath, when his righteous judgment will* **be revealed** (Romans 2:5).

Notice in this last passage, the day of wrath (AD 70) was also to be the day of revealing. The idea that Jesus needs to be revealed is based on the presupposition that He is hidden or unrevealed. So the obvious question is, *What hid Him?* The modern Christian would probably answer, "Jesus is in the invisible heavens." But that is not how the first-century Christians would have logically answered that question. Jesus was very active through His early Church with the manifestations of the Holy Spirit, and they did not view Him as being hidden in that sense.

To properly answer this question, then, we must clarify the terms. When the New Testament says *revealed*, it uses the Greek word *apocalypsis*, which means "to unveil." This means Jesus was veiled and needed to be unveiled.

So the more precise question is, *What was veiling Jesus, and when was it removed?*

The apostle Paul gives us an incredibly clear answer to this question:

> *Now if the ministry that brought death, which was engraved in letters on stone, came with glory, so that the Israelites could not look steadily at the face of Moses because of its glory, transitory though it was, will not the ministry of the Spirit be even more glorious? If the ministry that brought condemnation was glorious, how much more glorious is the ministry that brings righteousness! For what was glorious has no glory now in comparison with the surpassing glory. And if what was transitory came with glory, how much greater is the glory of that which lasts!*
>
> *Therefore, since we have such a hope, we are very bold. We are not like Moses, who would put a veil over his face to prevent the Israelites from seeing the end of what was passing away. But their minds were made dull,* **for to this day the same veil remains when the old covenant is read.** *It has not been removed, because only in Christ is it taken away.* **Even to this day when Moses is read, a veil covers their hearts.** *But whenever anyone turns to the Lord,* **the veil** *is taken away. Now the Lord is the Spirit, and where the Spirit of the Lord is, there is freedom. And we all, who with* **unveiled** *faces contemplatethe Lord's glory, are being transformed into his image with ever-increasing glory, which comes from the Lord, who is the Spirit* (2 Corinthians 3:7–18).

The Old Covenant, the Mosaic Covenant, was a veil that kept Jesus hidden.

As I have addressed in *Raptureless* and many of my blog posts, what Jesus did on the cross established the New Covenant and made the Old Covenant *"obsolete and outdated* [and it] *will soon disappear"* (Heb. 8:13). Yet as long as the Temple stood in Jerusalem until AD 70, the Old Covenant continued to operate in obstinacy to the New Covenant. From the cross until the destruction of Jerusalem, AD 30–70, the earthly Jerusalem became a "New Egypt," and the Christians experienced a new exodus from the earthly Jerusalem into the New Covenant heavenly Jerusalem (see Gal. 4:24–27).

The Old Testament contains a book about the Old Covenant

(Deuteronomy) that says, *"You shall not add to the word which I command you, nor take from it, that you may keep the commandments of the Lord your God which I command you"* (Deut. 4:2 NKJV).

The New Testament contains a book about the New Covenant (Revelation) that says:

> *For I testify to everyone who hears the words of the prophecy of this book: "If anyone adds to these things, God will add to him the plagues that are written in this book; and if anyone takes away from the words of the book of this prophecy, God shall take away his part from the Book of Life, from the holy city, and from the things which are written in this book"* (Revelation 22:18–19 NKJV).

Since the New Covenant is a covenant of forgiveness, how is it that people can still receive plagues under the New Covenant? It only happens one way—by adding to the New Covenant. In other words, when we add the Old Covenant into the New Covenant, we add curses to the New Covenant, which has no curses! To take away from the New Covenant is to take away forgiveness, which is what grants entry into the holy city, the heavenly Jerusalem.

In the earthly Jerusalem, the Ark of the Covenant (which symbolized the Old Covenant) had disappeared and was revealed as missing when the temple veil was torn (see Matt. 27:50–51; Mark 15:37–38; Luke 23:45–46).

In the heavenly Jerusalem, the Ark of the Covenant (which symbolizes the New Covenant) is found in Heaven with God:

> *Then God's temple in heaven was opened, and within his temple was seen the ark of his covenant. And there came flashes of lightning, rumblings, peals of thunder, an earthquake and a severe hailstorm* (Revelation 11:19).

Therefore, John's vision is the apocalypse of Jesus because it is about the destruction of the Old Covenant system (see Rev. 4–19) and the finalization of the New Covenant as the only covenant in existence (see Rev. 20–22). It is the unveiling (*apocalypsis*) of Jesus Christ and His New Covenant by the removal of the veil, which was the Old Covenant system (see 2 Cor. 3).

With this proper foundation, Revelation 1:1 makes sense. If we can understand the first verse of the book properly, the rest of the book can come into right focus.

The revelation of Jesus Christ*, which God gave him to show to his servants the things that must soon take place. He made it known by sending his angel to his servant John* (Revelation 1:1).

PART THREE

THE NINE MAJOR COMPONENTS

Now, join me as I take two steps closer to the painting and begin pointing out its major elements. No longer are we looking at the bigger picture, but neither are we looking at the minute details. The painting before us has nine major components: trees, grass, a pond, fences, flowers, deer, rabbits, sky, and the sun. Similarly, the Book of Revelation is comprised of nine main elements—an introduction, seven visions, and an epilogue. Each of these visions is added on top of the previous vision so that the painting has a layering effect.

Here's the breakdown:

- The Introduction (Rev. 1:1–7)
- First Vision—The Seven Churches (Rev. 1:8–3:22)
- Second Vision—The Seven Seals (Rev. 4:1–8:5)
- Third Vision—The Seven Trumpets (Rev. 8:6–11:19)
- Fourth Vision—Followers of the Lamb or the Beast (Rev. 12–14)

- Fifth Vision—The Seven Bowls of Wrath (Rev. 15-16)
- Sixth Vision—The Babylonian Harlot (Rev. 17–19:21)
- Seventh Vision—The New Heavens and New Earth (Rev. 20:1–22:11)
- The Epilogue (Rev 22:12–21)

Although I will not be able to examine the specific colors or brushstrokes used within these nine major components, I will give you some major interpretive keys that will give you a lens you can use to effectively study the book in more depth. This short book is intended merely as an introduction to get you pointed in the right direction.

THE INTRODUCTION

REVELATION 1:2–7

After naming the work, the painter continues by giving a general context; this is done by creating a frame. The frame denotes, in subtle ways, the type of painting that will be placed within it (a rustic frame versus a gold-guilded frame). In the same way, the introduction and epilogue of Revelation are bookends that frame the context of the book itself. Although they are often overlooked, these two sections give us important buttresses for our edifice. Let's look briefly at the text:

> *The revelation from Jesus Christ, which God gave him to show his servants* **what must soon take place.** *He made it known by sending his angel to his servant John, who testifies to everything he saw—that is, the word of God and the testimony of Jesus Christ. Blessed is the one who reads aloud the words of this prophecy, and blessed are those who hear it and take to heart what is written in it,* **because the time is near** (Revelation 1:1–3).

We have been so trained to read Revelation as if it was only written to us and about our future, yet the opening lines are so clear, obvious, and emphatic. The time *was* near for those first readers right before the destruction of Jerusalem. The time of Revelation is not near for us; it happened long ago.

> *John, to the seven churches in the province of Asia: Grace and peace to you from him who is, and who was, and who is to come; and from the seven spirits before his throne, and from Jesus Christ, who is the faithful witness, the firstborn from the dead, and the ruler of the kings of the earth. To him who loves us and has freed us from our sins by his blood, and has made us to be a kingdom and priests to serve his God and Father—to him be glory and power forever and ever! Amen.*
>
> *"Look, he is coming with the clouds," and "every eye will see him,* **even those who pierced him**"*; and* **all peoples on earth** *"will mourn because of him." So shall it be! Amen* (Revelation 1:4–7).

Those who pierced Him were the Roman soldiers living in the first century. And in fact, the Roman soldiers did watch God come upon Jerusalem in judgment during the destruction of AD 70. (As I discussed in *Raptureless*, the phrase "*coming on clouds*" is a Hebrew idiom for God coming in destruction on a city or region.) If we believe, instead, that Revelation is about our future, we are faced with a difficult question. How will those soldiers who have been dead for two thousand years be alive to witness His return?

Further, many translations of verse 7 have failed to accurately portray what the Greek language says. The phrase "*all peoples on earth*" is a very deceptive and inaccurate translation. It implies this will be a global event and every person on earth will see Him. In actuality, the Greek word translated as "earth" here is *ge*, not *kosmos*; therefore, this verse is about the earth of Israel, or more accurately, the *land* of Israel.

As usual, Young's Literal Translation is much more accurate and phrases the translation this way: *"Lo, he doth come with the clouds, and see him shall every eye, even those who did pierce him, and wail because of him shall all the tribes of the land. Yes! Amen"* (Revelation 1:7 YLT).

VISION I

THE SEVEN CHURCHES

REVELATION 1:8-3:22

In Revelation 1:19, we behold three time periods: past, present, and future. In fact, as scholar David Chilton demonstrates, Revelation 2–3 is actually an overview of Old Testament history from the Garden of Eden to the AD 70 destruction of Jerusalem. In this way, Revelation 2–3 covers the past and present mentioned in Revelation 1:19. (Then Revelation 4–22 covers the future aspect of Revelation 1:19).

Though this idea may be surprising to many readers, it is naturally found within the text itself. Chilton expresses it well in his book, *The Days of Vengeance*:

> 1. *Ephesus* (2:1–7). The language of Paradise is evident throughout the passage. Christ announces Himself as the Creator, the One who holds the seven stars; and as the One who walks among the lampstands to evaluate them, as God walked through the Garden in judgment (Gen. 3:8). The "angel" of Ephesus is commended for properly guarding the church against her enemies, as Adam had been commanded to guard the Garden and his wife from their Enemy (Gen. 2:15). But the angel, like Adam, has "fallen," having left his first love. Christ therefore threatens to come to him in judgment

and remove his lampstand out of its place, as He had banished Adam and Eve from the Garden (cf. Gen. 3:24). Nevertheless, Eden's gate is open to those who gain victory over the Tempter: **"To him who overcomes, I will grant to eat of the Tree of Life, which is in the Paradise of My God."**

2. *Smyrna* (2:8-11). The situation of the Patriarchs (Abraham, Isaac, Jacob, and Joseph) and of the children of Israel in Egypt appears to be reflected in the words of this message. Christ describes Himself as He "who was dead, and has come back to life," a redemptive act foreshadowed in the lives of Isaac (Gen. 22:1–14; Heb. 11:17–19) and Joseph (Gen. 37:18–36; 39:20–41:45; 45:4–8; 50:20), as well as in the salvation of Israel from the house of bondage. The Smyrnaeans' condition of seeming poverty and actual riches is analogous to the experience of all the patriarchs, who "lived as aliens in the land of promise" (Heb. 11:9). False "Jews" are persecuting the true heirs of the promises, just as Ishmael persecuted Isaac (Gen. 21:9; cf. Gal. 4:22–31). The danger of imprisonment at the instigation of a slanderer is paralleled in the life of Joseph (Gen. 39:13–20), as is the blessing of the crown of life for the faithful (Gen. 41:40–44); Aaron too, as the glorious image of Man fully redeemed, wore a crown of life (Ex. 28:36–38). **The "tribulation of ten days" followed by victory reflects the story of Israel's endurance through the ten plagues before its deliverance.**

3. *Pergamum* (2:12–17). The imagery in this section is taken from the sojourn of Israel in the wilderness, the abode of demons (Lev. 16:10; 17:7; Deut. 8:15; Matt. 4:1; 12:43); the Christians of Pergamum also had to dwell "where Satan's throne is...where Satan dwells." **The enemies of the church are described as "Balaam" and "Balak," the false prophet and evil king who tried to destroy the Israelites by tempting them to idolatry and fornication (Num. 25:1–3; 31:16).** Like the Angel of the LORD and Phineas the priest, Christ threatens to make war against the Balaamites with the sword (cf. Num. 22:31; 24:7–8). To those who overcome, He promises a share in the "hidden manna" from the Ark of the Covenant

(Heb. 9:4), and a white stone with a "new name" inscribed on it. The emblem of the redeemed covenant people worn by the High Priest (Ex. 28:9–12).

4. *Thyatira* (2:18–29). St. John now turns to imagery from the period of the Israelite monarchy and the Davidic covenant. Christ announces Himself as "the Son of God," the greater David (cf. Ps. 2:7; 89:19–37; Jer. 30:9; Ezek. 34:23–24; 37:24–28; Hos. 3:5; Acts 2:24–36; 13:22–23). He rebukes the angel of Thyatira, whose toleration of his "wife, Jezebel," is leading to the apostasy of God's people (cf. 1 Kings 16:29–34; 21:25–26). She and those who commit adultery with her (cf. 2 Kings 9:22) are threatened with "tribulation," like the three and one-half years of tribulation visited upon Israel in Jezebel's day (1 Kings 17:1; James 5:17); she and her offspring will be killed (cf. 2 Kings 9:22–37). But he who overcomes will be granted, like David, "authority over the nations" (cf. 2 Sam. 7:19; 8:1–14; Ps. 18:37–50; 89:27–29). **The concluding promise alludes to David's rod of iron; like the vessels of a potter they shall be broken to pieces, as I also have received from My Father" (cf. Ps. 2:9).**

5. *Sardis* (3:1–6). The imagery of this section comes from the later prophetic period (cf. the references to the Spirit and the "seven stars," speaking of the prophetic witness) leading up to the end of the monarchy, when the disobedient covenant people were defeated and taken into captivity. **The description of the church's reputation for "life" when it is really "dead," the exhortations to "wake up" and to "strengthen the things that remain," the acknowledgement that there are "a few people" who have remained faithful, all are reminiscent of prophetic language about the Remnant in a time of apostasy** (Isa. 1:5–23, 6:9–13, 65:8–16; Jer. 7:1–7, 8:11–12; Ezek. 37:1–14), as in the warning of imminent judgment (Isa. 1:24–31, 2:12–21, 26:20–21; Jer. 4:5–31, 7:12–15, 11:9–13; Mic. 1:2–7; Zeph. 1).

6. *Philadelphia* (3:7–13). The Return from the Exile under Ezra and Nehemiah is reflected in this message, which speaks in the imagery of

the synagogue and the rebuilding of Jerusalem and the Temple (cf. the prophecies of Haggai, Zechariah, and Malachi). The Philadelphians, like the returning Jews, have "a little power." The reference to the "synagogue of Satan, who say they are Jews, and are not" recalls the conflicts with "false Jews" in Ezra 4 and Nehemiah 4, 6, and 13. The warning of a coming "hour of testing... which is about to come on the whole world, to test those who dwell upon the Land" reminds us of the tribulation suffered under Antiochus Epiphanes (cf. Daniel 8 and 11). **But Christ promises the overcomer that he will be made "a pillar in the Temple" and share in the blessings of the "New Jerusalem."** [By mentioning the New Jerusalem, the picture is likened to the New Jerusalem under Ezra and Nehemiah.]

7. *Laodicea* (3:14–22). The period of the Last Days (A.D. 30–70) [i.e., Last Days of Israel and the Mosaic Covenant] provides the motifs for the seventh and last message. The "lukewarm" church, boasting of its wealth and self-sufficiency yet blind to its actual poverty and nakedness, is a fitting image of the Pharisaical Judaism of the first century (Luke 18:9–14; cf. Rev. 18:7). **Warned that she is about to be spewed out of the Land (the curse of Lev. 18:24–28; cf. Luke 21:24),** Israel is urged to repent and accept Christ, offered in the Eucharistic meal. Those who overcome are granted the characteristic blessing of the age brought in by the New Covenant: dominion with Christ (cf. Eph. 1:20–22; 2:6; Rev 1:6).[1]

Here John is referring to Israel in the Old Testament as the Church. He is using the same teaching tool that Paul employed in First Corinthians 10:1–13, using the story of Israel as an example to the Church. Also, at Steven's trial Israel at Mount Sinai was referred to as "the church in the wilderness" (see Acts 7:38).

Thus we can see the Revelation 2–3 timeline runs from the Garden to AD 70:

Garden – Ephesus

Patriarchs – Smyrna

Wilderness – Pergamum

Monarchy – Thyatira

Prophets – Sardis

Rebuilding – Philadelphia

First Century – Laodicea

Most examinations of Revelation 2–3 fall into two categories. While Chilton (whom I agree with) matches the letters with periods in the history of Israel leading up to the destruction of Jerusalem, many Christians wrongly try to align these letters to match different times in the history of the Church, beginning with the first-century Church and ending with a future Great Tribulation. This is the earmark of Dispensational eschatology. But to the original readers, it would have been clear from the indicators inside the text itself that John was writing a timeline from the Garden of Eden to the AD 70 destruction (I have put the indicators in bold above for easy reference).

The other method applies a very close focus to examining the details of each letter, often causing readers to overlook the forest by examining the trees. A well-known example of this is found in the interpretation of the church of Laodicea. Many teachers have expounded upon the *hot, cold,* and *lukewarm* dynamics of this church. Typically, *hot* is said to represent a fervent Christian being "on fire" for God, whereas *cold* indicates someone who is anti-God (i.e., an atheist). Following these lines, *lukewarm* falls on the scale between the fervent Christian and the atheist as the mediocre Christian. If you have grown up in the American Church, most likely this is exactly how you have always heard this passage explained.

Yet there is no reason to interpret this passage in this manner. Consider what this interpretation says to the mediocre Christian: "God would rather have you be an atheist and go to hell than to be a mediocre Christian." What an outrageous message of condemnation! Fortunately, this is not what Jesus was saying. Let's look at what *hot, cold*, and *lukewarm* are really all about:

> Laodicea was situated between two other important cities, Colossae and Hierapolis (see Colossians 4:13–16). Colossae, wedged into a

> narrow valley in the shadow of towering mountains, was watered by icy streams, which tumbled down from the heights. In contrast, Hierapolis was famous for its hot mineral springs, which flowed out of the city and across a high plain until it cascaded down a cliff, which faced Laodicea. By the time the water reached the valley floor, it was lukewarm, putrid, and nauseating. At Colossae, therefore, one could be refreshed with clear, cold, invigorating drinking water; at Hierapolis, one could be healed by bathing in its hot, mineral-laden pools; but at Laodicea, the waters were neither **hot** (for health) nor **cold** (for drinking).[2]

In other words, the basic accusation against Laodicea's spirituality is that it is putrid and good for nothing. The Laodicean church brings neither a cure for illness nor a cool drink to soothe dry lips and parched throats. This is not about the condition of some "end of the world" church that is mostly mediocre and bothersome to God. This is about the condition of the first-century church in Laodicea.

VISION 2

THE SEVEN SEALS

REVELATION 4:1-8:5

In Revelation 1, John meets Jesus on Patmos. Then in Revelation 2–3, Jesus gives letters to seven literal churches in the first century while also giving a metaphoric overview of Israel's history from Genesis to the first-century nation of Israel that was about to be vomited out of the land.

Now we are going to step a little closer to the painting and examine some of the more challenging components. Most scholars interpret chapters 4 and 5 similarly. There are a few differences, but we will pass over them for the sake of clarity.

In Revelation 4 and 5, we find God the Father enthroned in Heaven similarly to the visions of Isaiah 6 and Ezekiel 1. A scroll of judgement is brought forth that cannot be opened until Jesus, as the Lamb slain, appears and begins to open the scroll of judgment. This shows that judgment was not to be poured out until after the New Covenant had been established by Jesus' death on the cross and His ascension into Heaven.

Most scholars agree Revelation 6–8 is a parallel of Matthew 24, although they debate the timing of Matthew 24's fulfillment. Since I have already proven beyond reasonable doubt in *Raptureless* that Mathew 24 was perfectly fulfilled in AD 70, Revelation 6–8 easily becomes very clear.

Let's briefly look at the major components of these chapters and how they parallel Matthew 24:

Seal 1: Horseman 1

The first seal and horseman symbolize conquest, a parallel to *"nation rising against nation"* in Matthew 24:7. This refers to the fragmenting of the Pax Romana (Roman Peace) of the first century.

Seal 2: Horseman 2

The first seal and horseman clearly lead to the second seal and horseman, which symbolize the *"wars and rumors of war"* in Matthew 24:6.

Seal 3: Horseman 3

The third seal and horseman clearly symbolize famine, mirroring Matthew 24:7's prophecy of the widespread first century famines. Interestingly, in this picture, John hears this detail:

> *Then I heard what sounded like a voice among the four living creatures, saying, "Two pounds of wheat for a day's wages, and six pounds of barley for a day's wages, and do not damage the oil and the wine"* (Revelation 6:6).

According to Robert Mounce, this means the price had risen 1,000 percent from its former price. Josephus recorded much regarding the unbelievable famine that occurred in AD 67–70.[1] From his records, we know this famine lived up to these awful predictions.

Seal 4: Horseman 4

The fourth seal and horseman symbolize the sword, plagues, famine, and death—the natural outcomes caused by the first three horsemen of conquest, war, and famine.

Seal 5: Martyrs

The fifth seal gives a picture of martyrs crying out to God for judgment. These are the Christians who were persecuted and martyred during AD 30–70. In this vision, they cry out to God, "How much longer?" The implication in the first century (as we have already discussed) was "How much longer until the AD 70 destruction occurs?" They were calling for God's jugement against the Old Covenant and the apostate nation of Israel, not for Jesus' final return. They reappear in their white garments in the sixth seal.

Seal 6: An Earthquake, the Heavens Shaken, the 144,000 Sealed, and the Great Multitude in White Robes

The sixth seal contains several events that together symbolize the destruction of Jerusalem in AD 70. First, an earthquake shakes the heavens and the earth. This parallels Matthew 24:7, 29, which I have explained in detail in *Raptureless*.

Second, the 144,000 are sealed. This number symbolizes wholeness and represents the entire first-century Christian community, which followed Jesus' instructions in Matthew 24:15–21 by fleeing to the nearby mountains of Pella. As a result, not one Christian died in the destruction of AD 70. (This also parallels Ezekiel 9.)

Third, we get another glimpse of the martyred saints, this time post-judgment. Since the sixth seal pictures the destruction of Jerusalem, with the shaking of the heavens and earth and the 144,000 (the entire Christian community) fleeing to Mount Pella for protection, we know this group in white robes is the same as the group in the fifth seal. Now they are pictured after their pleas for justice have been fulfilled in the AD 70 destruction.

Seal 7: Silence for Thirty Minutes

This symbolizes the rest that came after the AD 70 destruction. In fact, this is the quietest period in Church history. Very little is recorded about the period directly following the destruction of Jerusalem. The persecution of the Church by the Jewish Temple leaders completely halted, and the Church enjoyed a short period of peace at Mount Pella, which the seventh seal depicts as silence.

VISION 3

THE SEVEN TRUMPETS

REVELATION 8:6-11:19

Reading the Book of Revelation can be very confusing because it is filled with symbols that require interpretation, *and* it is also filled with repetition. The seals, the trumpets, the seven figures, and the bowls all depict the same events of the AD 70 destruction in different ways and from different angles. They are not exact parallels, but each repeating picture emphasizes something new.

Some might wonder, *Why would the artist paint the picture with repeating patterns? What does this represent?* David Chilton gives a great explanation of why we find four pictures of seven judgments:

> St. John's prophecy is related to the message of Leviticus 26. Like Deuteronomy 28, Leviticus 26 sets forth the sanctions of the [Mosaic] Covenant: If Israel obeys God, she will be blessed in every area of life (Lev. 26:1–13; Deut. 28:1–14); if she disobeys, however, she will be visited with the Curse, spelled out in horrifying detail (Lev. 26:14–39; Deut. 28:15–68). (These curses were most fully poured out in the progressive desolation of Israel during the Last Days, culminating in the Great Tribulation of A.D. 67–70, as punishment for her apostasy and rejection of her True Husband, the Lord Jesus

Christ.) One of the striking features of the Leviticus passage is that the curses are arranged in a special pattern: Four times in this chapter God says, "I will punish you seven times for your sins." (Lev. 26:18, 21, 24, 28). The number *seven*, as we will see abundantly throughout Revelation, is a Biblical number for completeness or fullness (taken from the seven-day pattern laid down at the creation in Genesis 1). [The number seven alone is used fifty-four times in Revelation.] The number *four* is used in Scripture in connection with the earth, especially the Land of Israel; thus four rivers flowed out of Eden to water the whole earth (Gen. 2:10); the Land, like the Altar, is pictured as having four corners (Isa. 11:12; cf. Ex. 27:1-2), from which the four winds blow (Jer. 49:36); the camp of Israel was arranged in four groups around the sides of the Tabernacle (Num. 2); and so on (see your concordance and Bible Dictionary). So by speaking of four seven-fold judgments in Leviticus 26, God is saying that a full, complete judgment will come upon the Land of Israel for its sins. This theme is taken up by the prophets in their warnings to Israel: *"I will send* **four kinds of destroyers** *against them," declares the Lord, "the sword to kill and the dogs to drag away and the birds and the wild animals to devour and destroy."* (Jer. 15:3)

"For this is what the Sovereign Lord says: How much worse will it be when I send against Jerusalem my **four dreadful judgments**—*sword and famine and wild beasts and plague—to kill its men and their animals!"* (Ez. 14:21)

The imagery of a sevenfold judgment coming four times is most fully developed in the Book of Revelation, which is explicitly divided into four sets of seven. In thus following the formal structure of the covenantal curse in Leviticus, St. John underscores the nature of his prophecy as a declaration of covenant wrath against Jerusalem.[1]

In the light of Old Testament prophecy, Chilton's explanation makes perfect sense. With this foundation in mind, then, let's look at the seven trumpets and how they parallel the seven seals and the Olivet Discourse in Matthew 24.

Trumpet 1: Hail and Fire Rain Down

After the first trumpet, hail and fire rain down upon the *local land* of Israel (ge). I will examine the hail more specifically when when I discuss the parallel seventh bowl judgment.

Trumpet 2: A Mountain Thrown into the Sea

The symbol of the second trumpet has been distorted by many over the last two thousand years. The most popular theory recently projects an asteroid will crash into the ocean and kill a third of the sea creatures and destroy a third of all ships. In reality, if an asteroid that big is going to crash into the earth, the Book of Revelation should end right there; such an asteroid would literally move earth off its axis, and all life on earth would immediately either burn up or freeze because of the planet moving closer to or away from the sun. Clearly, we are dealing with a symbol. So we must ask ourselves, *What would the mountain represent to John's readers?*

The most obvious answer is that the first-century Jewish believers would have interpreted this mountain in Revelation as a symbol of Jerusalem, God's holy mountain (see Exod. 15:17).

Again Chilton gives stunning insight:

> Connect this [Revelation 8:8] with the fact that Jesus, in the middle of a lengthy series of discourses and parables about the destruction of Jerusalem (Matt. 20–25), cursed an unfruitful fig tree, as a symbol of judgment upon Israel. He then told His disciples, "Truly I say to you, if you have faith, and do not doubt, you shall say to this mountain, 'Be taken up and cast into the sea,' it shall happen. And all things you ask in prayer, believing, you shall receive' (Matt. 21:21–22). Was Jesus being flippant? Did He really expect His disciples to go around praying about moving literal mountains? Of course not. More importantly, Jesus was not changing the subject. He was still giving them a lesson about the fall of Israel. What was the lesson? Jesus was instructing His disciples to pray imprecatory prayers, beseeching God to destroy Israel, to wither the fig tree, to cast the apostate mountain into the sea.

And that is exactly what happened. The persecuted Church, under the oppression from the apostate Jews, began praying for God's vengeance upon Israel (Rev. 6:9–11), calling for the mountain of Israel to "be taken up and cast into the sea." Their offerings were received at God's heavenly altar, and in response God directed His angels to throw down His judgments to the Land (Rev. 8:3-5).[2]

Thus in amazing simplicity, the mountain falling into the sea is a symbol of Jerusalem's destruction.

Trumpet 3: A Star Falling

The first-century Jewish reader would have grasped this key to understanding the third trumpet: The star is named Wormwood and turned a third of the water into wormwood. Modern readers seem to gloss over the mention of wormwood and focus entirely on the falling star. As I mentioned before, Revelation has four repetitions within its judgments. This star connects to the sixth seal and the stars that fell to the earth (see Rev. 6:13). But even more important to understanding this passage is the definition of *wormwood.*

Wormwood is a specific term used in the Old Testament to warn Israel of its destruction as a punishment for apostasy. The following passages demonstrate this clearly:

> *So that there may not be among you man or woman or family or tribe, whose heart turns away today from the LORD our God, to go and serve the gods of these nations, and that there may not be among you a root bearing bitterness or wormwood* (Deuteronomy 29:18 NKJV).

> *Therefore thus says the LORD of hosts, the God of Israel: "Behold, I will feed them, this people, with wormwood, and give them water of gall to drink"* (Jeremiah 9:15 NKJV).

> *Therefore thus says the LORD of hosts concerning the prophets: "Behold, I will feed them with wormwood, and make them drink the water of gall; for from the prophets of Jerusalem profaneness has gone out into all the land"* (Jeremiah 23:15 NKJV).

He has filled me with bitterness, He has made me drink wormwood.... Remember my affliction and roaming, the wormwood and the gall (Lamentations 3:15, 19 NKJV).

You who turn justice to wormwood, and lay righteousness to rest in the earth (Amos 5:7 NKJV).

Thus we can see that, when John mentioned Wormwood, the original readers would have understood he was declaring the apostasy of Jerusalem.

Trumpet 4: Celetial Bodies Disturbed

The fourth trumpet is another obvious parallel to the sixth seal (see Rev. 6:12–14), which uses the same prophetic language explained in *Raptureless* regarding Matthew 24:29. In short, celetial disturbences are used as a prophetic idiom throughout Scripture to point to the destruction of a city.

Trumpet 5: Locusts from the Pit

Let's go back for a moment to our illustration of the painting. As an author, it seems to me like the fifth trumpet of Revelation is like a dark and forboding corner of the painting that is not well understood and is so dark and mysterious that one cannot help but stand and stare in wonder. I will attempt to give what I find to be a reasonable explanation—essentially John was depicting the demonic state into which Jerusalem had devolved before the Roman destruction. Yet I know this will not answer every question for every reader.

But as James Stuart Russell wrote, "With our attention fixed on a single spot of earth, and absolutely shut up to a very brief space of time, it is comparatively easy to read the symbols, and still more satisfactory to mark their perfect correspondence with facts."[3] When we keep in mind that these symbols are about the 70 AD destruction of Jerusalem, it becomes easier for us to find the proper interpretation.

I will start with a quote from *Victorious Eschatology* that I found most helpful:

Some of the most well-known futurist teachers say that these locusts from the bottomless pit are futuristic helicopters that swarm out of the sky and shoot out of their tails a poison that inflicts great pain. Other noted futurists have observed the recent uprising of Islamic terrorists and concluded that the locusts must be the Muslim extremists who will someday attack God's people.

These interpretations of the futurists are interesting because these are the same futurist teachers that claim to be taking the Bible literally. If we take those verses literally, then we have to believe that actual locusts with gold crowns, faces like men, hair like women, teeth like lions, and tails like scorpions will swarm across the earth. Furthermore, if the futurist teachers were taking the Scriptures literally, they would have to say that their helicopters or their Muslim terrorists were coming out of a bottomless pit. Of course, no futurist could reasonably say that. The idea that futurist Christians take the book of Revelation literally is a myth.[4] [It is also interesting to note that the time period mentioned with in fifth trumpet (five months) corresponds with the actual seasonal length of the locusts in that region (May–September).]

We must consider what the first-century Jew would have understood when they heard the description in John's vision. First, they would have connected the locusts to the eighth plague upon Egpyt (see Exod. 10). Second, they would note the plague would be upon the non-Christians, whereas the Christians were "marked" and protected just as Israel was during the Egyptian plagues.

Essentially this picture showed them that Jerusalem had become Egypt in the eyes of Heaven and that the Christians were enacting a new exodus. This theme of a new exodus of Christians exiting Jerusalem and Judaism is developed much more in the coming sections. Suffice it to say that Revelation 11:8 makes it very clear that Jerusalem, *"the city in which our Lord was killed,"* had become *"Sodom and Egypt."* Even here in the fifth trumpet, we find the eighth plague upon Egypt, but we also find language that mirrors the destruction of Sodom.

When he opened the Abyss, smoke rose from it like the smoke from a gigantic furnace (Revelation 9:2a).

> *He looked down toward Sodom and Gomorrah, toward all the land of the plain, and he saw dense smoke rising from the land, like smoke from a furnace* (Genesis 19:28).

One other perspective on the fifth trumpet is that it represented the total demonization of Jerusalem before the destruction by Rome. In fact, Josephus wrote of how evil Jerusalem had become, saying that if Rome hadn't come to destroy them, the earth might have simply opened and swallowed them. This is a very revealing quote from a Jewish non-Christian observer:

> "I am of opinion" he says "that had the Romans deferred the punishment of these wretches, either the earth would have opened, and swallowed up the city, or it would have been swept away by a deluge, or have shared in the thunderbolts of the land of Sodom. For it produced a race far more ungodly than those who were thus visited [i.e., more evil than Sodom].[5]

How could Jerusalem have been truly that evil? Though it may be hard for us to believe, Jesus did declare they would be that evil in Matthew 12:

> *The men of Nineveh will stand up at the judgment with this generation and condemn it; for they repented at the preaching of Jonah, and now something greater than Jonah is here. The Queen of the South will rise at the judgment with this generation and condemn it; for she came from the ends of the earth to listen to Solomon's wisdom, and now something greater than Solomon is here.*

> *When an impure spirit comes out of a person, it goes through arid places seeking rest and does not find it. Then it says, "I will return to the house I left." When it arrives, it finds the house unoccupied, swept clean and put in order. Then it goes and takes with it seven other spirits more wicked than itself, and they go in and live there. And the final condition of that person is worse than the first.* ***That is how it will be with this wicked generation*** (Matthew 12:41–45).

Jesus was not giving a teaching on deliverance or healing. He was declaring that even though His ministry was cleaning up Jerusalem spiritually, once

He was done, the people would quickly refill Jersualem with evil, even seven times worse! And that is exactly what happened historically, which is why Josephus gave such a harsh evaluation of Jerusalem.

Thus the locusts from the pit represent the utter demonization of Jerusalem in preparation for their destruction.

Trumpet 6: Four Angels and 200 Million?

History records that Titus had four military legions stationed at the Euphrates that advanced upon and destroyed Jerusalem. This is pictured in John's vision of four mighty angels who are unleashed to kill and bring destruction.

This trumpet also includes the mysterious number, *"Twice ten thousand times ten thousand."* Many fanciful explanations have been created regarding this number. Some translators have even simply multiplied it and say the army is 200 million. Yet in this passage, we are dealing with prophetic idioms that are two thousand years old, and we must ask, *What would twice ten thousand times ten thousand have meant to the original readers?*

In the Old Testament, *ten thousand* was used to represent an overwhelming and nearly impossible foe. For example, *"Saul has slain his thousands, and David his tens of thousands"* (1 Sam. 18:7, 21:11). So in this passage, we find John declaring ten thousand times ten thousand and twice over! Basically he was saying, "Jerusalem, there is no deliverance for you; you are absolutely and unquestionably doomed!"

The Angel and the Little Scroll

Following the sixth trumpet, Revelation 10 and 11 contain a few important asides before the seventh trumpet. First, John encounters an angel who has him eat a little scroll.

Revelation 10:6 says, *"There will be no more delay!"* In other words, this judgment was about to fall on Jerusalem. John was told he would prophesy to people, kings, and nations about it (see Rev. 10:11). Interestingly, the manner in which John receives this scroll is parallel to Ezekiel 3:1–3, where Ezekiel also receives a scroll that tastes like honey. Not surprisingly, Ezekiel's prophetic message was also about the destruction of Jerusalem.

The Two Witnesses

The second aside in Revelation 10 tells us about the two witnesses. I am not sure why so many of the emails I get from people who have read *Raptureless* focus on my interpretation of the two witnesses. It is not a natural question to jump to after finishing *Raptureless*, yet it seems to be the most common. Clearly, the two witnesses are the subject of great curiousity for many people. For that reason, let's take an indepth look at the passage in question starting at Revelation 11:1.

> *I was given a reed like a measuring rod and was told, "Go and measure the temple of God and the altar, with its worshipers. But exclude the outer court; do not measure it, because it has been given to the Gentiles. They will trample on the holy city for 42 months"* (Revelation 11:1–2).

The first important detail here is the fact that the Temple is standing in the vision. It was utterly destroyed in AD 70. It would be comparable to the Whitehouse, Mount Rushmore, the Statue of Liberty, or some other significant landmark being destroyed. This is yet another proof that Revelation was not written in AD 96. If it was written in AD 96, it makes no sense that John does not ever mention the "past" destruction of Jerusalem and the Temple. Of course, the obvious reason he doesn't mention it as a past event is because it wasn't. Instead, he was prophesying it was about to happen.

Also, it's important to note that forty-two months is three and a half years, the exact length of time the siege of Jerusalem took place, from AD 66–70. It was started by the Emperor Nero (the beast) and ended finally under General Titus.

> *And I will appoint my two witnesses, and they will prophesy for 1,260 days, clothed in sackcloth* (Revelation 11:3).

It is logical that the 1,260 days are the same days that comprise the three and a half years mentioned in the previous verse about the siege of Jerusalem.

> *They are "the two olive trees" and the two lampstands, and "they stand before the Lord of the earth."* [This is a reference from Zechariah 4:3, 11, 14.] *If anyone tries to harm them, fire comes from their mouths and*

> *devours their enemies. This is how anyone who wants to harm them must die. They have power to shut up the heavens so that it will not rain during the time they are prophesying;* [This is a clear reference to Elijah, who called down fire and stopped the rain for three years.] *and they have power to turn the waters into blood and to strike the earth with every kind of plague as often as they want* [This is a clear reference to Moses and the plagues in Exodus 7–11.] (Revelation 11:4–6).

In these first six verses of Revelation 11, the timing of this event and the identities of the two witnesses are revealed. We must keep in mind that Revelation is a book full of symbols. This passage is not talking about the actual Moses and Elijah; rather, Moses and Elijah are the symbols that represent the Law and the Prophets. With that understanding, we can properly interpret what they do in the remainder of the passage:

> *Now when they have finished their testimony, the beast that comes up from the Abyss will attack them, and overpower and kill them. Their bodies will lie in the public square of the great city—which is figuratively called Sodom and Egypt—where also their Lord was crucified* (Revelation 11:7–8).

Here we observe several interesting details. First, in verse 8, John gives us a huge key to interpreting Revelation when he clearly refers to the "great city" as the city where our *"Lord was crucified."* In other words, he tells us plainly that it is first-century Jerusalem, which is figuratively called Sodom and Egypt. Thus when we read in Revelation 17 that the whore of Babylon is the great city, we know the whore was Jerusalem, and when we read that Babylon the great city has fallen, we know it speaks of the destruction of Jerusalem. In this way, Revelation 11:8 is a major key to understanding the theme of Revelation—the judgment of first-century Jerusalem and the establishment of the heavenly Jerusalem. Every time we read "the great city," it is a clear reference to Jerusalem:

> *The* ***great city*** *split into three parts, and the cities of the nations collapsed. God remembered Babylon the Great and gave her the cup filled with the wine of the fury of his wrath* (Revelation 16:19).

> *The woman you saw is the* ***great city*** *that rules over the kings of the earth* (Revelation 17:18).

> *Terrified at her torment, they will stand far off and cry: "Woe! Woe to you,* **great city, you mighty city of Babylon!** *In one hour your doom has come!"...and cry out: "Woe! Woe to you,* **great city,** *dressed in fine linen, purple and scarlet, and glittering with gold, precious stones and pearls!".... When they see the smoke of her burning, they will exclaim, "Was there ever a city like this* **great city**?*" They will throw dust on their heads, and with weeping and mourning cry out: "Woe! Woe to you,* **great city,** *where all who had ships on the sea became rich through her wealth! In one hour she has been brought to ruin!"... Then a mighty angel picked up a boulder the size of a large millstone and threw it into the sea, and said: "With such violence* **the great city** *of Babylon will be thrown down, never to be found again"* (Revelation 18:10, 16, 18–19, 21).

Now let's look back at verse 7, where the two witnesses are killed. The question is, *If the two witnesses represent the Law and the Prophets, how can they be put to death?* I believe the two witnesses (the Old Testament Law and Prophets) were witnessing about Jesus to the Jews before the AD 70 destruction, but ultimately the Law and the Prophets were ignored, rejected, and "killed" by the Jews.

The Law and the Prophets testified as witnesses of Jesus as the Messiah-King and of Israel as the covenant-breaking nation that stood guilty. Even Jesus, during His life on earth, referred to the Old Testament as a witness of Him:

> *You study the Scriptures diligently because you think that in them you have eternal life. These are the very Scriptures that testify about me* (John 5:39).

Later, after His resurrection, Jesus explained to a few of the disciples on the road to Emmaus how the Old Testament had pointed to Him all along:

And beginning with Moses and all the Prophets, he explained to them what was said in all the Scriptures concerning himself (Luke 24:27).

Considering this, I agree with Eberle and Trench's explanation of the two witnesses:

> The Law and the prophets were witnesses against the Jewish people. The Jews had been unfaithful in their covenant with God, and therefore, judgment was coming upon them. However, the Law and the prophets were also the authoritative witnesses of the early

Church. As Christians witnessed to the Jews about Jesus Christ, they did not have a New Testament from which to preach. They spoke from the Law and the prophets, convincing many that Jesus was the Christ. Again, we see how the Law and the prophets were sounding throughout the streets of Jerusalem.[6]

This idea is even more fully exemplified in the next two verses:

For three and a half days some from every people, tribe, language and nation will gaze on their bodies and refuse them burial. The inhabitants of the earth will gloat over them and will celebrate by sending each other gifts, because these two prophets had tormented those who live on the earth (Revelation 11:9–10).

In other words, the AD 70 world was happy to see Jerusalem destroyed and, with it, all the Old Testament rules, regulations, sacrifices, and ceremonies. As Eberle and Trench put it:

In what way were the Law and the prophets put to death? When Jerusalem was destroyed by the Roman army, it appeared that everything in which the Jews had put their trust had failed. All had ended. How could they ever rise again? It seemed impossible. While the two witnesses were silent, the people throughout the Gentile world rejoiced because the Law and the prophets also bore witness against them and their sins.

After the dust from Jerusalem's destruction had settled, "the breath of life from God" came back into the two witnesses (Rev. 11:10). The voice of the Law and the prophets rose again. Then the two witnesses were called back into heaven (Rev. 11:12), but at that same time "there was a great earthquake" (Rev. 11:13). As we have discussed before, in apocalyptic language earthquakes represented a demolition or transfer of authority. Indeed, two witnesses were taken to heaven, but the Law and the prophets continued to sound through the Church. The voices of two witnesses were transferred to the Church, and hence, the Law and the prophets continue sounding forth the voice of God even today.[7]

Thus the testifying, death, and resurrection of the two witnesses symbolize the transition between the Old and New Covenants. Here is the culmination:

> *But after the three and a half days the breath of life from God entered them, and they stood on their feet, and terror struck those who saw them. Then they heard a loud voice from heaven saying to them, "Come up here." And they went up to heaven in a cloud, while their enemies looked on* (Revelation 11:11–12).

The Kingdom of Jesus revived the Old Testament witness, and instead of a religion full of rules in the earthly Jerusalem, Jesus formed Christianity on the foundation of the Old Covenant, enabling His followers to partake of the heavenly Jerusalem.

Maybe you have been taught to read the Book of Revelation with flat literalism rather than as a symbolic book that would have made sense to the original readers. Maybe you have been taught the Book of Revelation is about your future. If so, it is likely you have heard one of the many interpretations of the two witnesses that are much more fanciful and dramatic than what I have just explained. Those explanations may be exciting, but we must ask ourselves this all-important question: *What was the Holy Spirit actually trying to show John?*

I believe John and the original readers would have clearly and easily seen the two witnesses as representations of Elijah and Moses, the Law and the Prophets, essentially the Old Testament Scriptures. They would have understood that Rome was waging war on the Law-and-Prophet system of Jerusalem and that Rome thought it had killed Judaism. Yet dead Judaism transformed and resurrected as the heavenly Jerusalem, which is Christianity.

All this culminates in the seventh trumpet.

Trumpet 7: Jesus Wins

At the seventh trumpet, Jesus is declared the victor, and the Ark of the Covenant is shown to permanently reside in Heaven.

The original Ark of the Old Covenant had gone missing hundreds of years earlier. Now, John watched this vision, he saw an Ark in Heaven! This is not that old Ark; it is the Ark of the New Covenant. The New Covenant is between the Father and the Son; therefore, the Ark that contains the

New Covenant resides in Heaven.

VISION 4

FOLLOWERS OF THE LAMB OR THE BEAST

REVELATION 12:1-15:4

Now that John has spoken of the seals and the trumpets, in this next section he approaches the destruction of Jerusalem with a whole new set of pictures. In the following vision, he covers the birth of Jesus, His ascension to the heavenly throne, and the persecution of the Church by Nero (the sea beast) and the Temple rulers (the land beast). Also he again sees Jesus as the Lamb and the 144,000 Christians on top of Mount Pella avoiding the first-century destruction, as well as a great harvest of souls. All of this is covered in Revelation 12–14, which we will now unpack a little more.

Chapter 12 begins with the woman giving birth. We have a major clue to help us determine who this woman is—she gives birth to Jesus! There is no scholarly debate regarding her son mentioned in verse 5: He *"will rule all the nations with an iron scepter"* (Rev. 12:5), which is a direct quote of Psalm 2:9 regarding Jesus (see also Psalm 110).

Although there are differing opinions as to the identity of this woman, in the bigger picture, it does not matter which of the following interpretations is correct. It does not effect the interpretation of the rest of the visions. Personally, I believe the woman represents the godly remnant of Israel, which Jesus was born from. Yet other commentators have taken this more literally and say she represents the Virgin Mary or Eve the mother of all the living. It is inconsequential to debate this, so we will continue onward.

The next character that John points out is the dragon. Thankfully, John interpretes this one for us in verse 9a: *"The great dragon was hurled down—that ancient serpent called the devil, or Satan, who leads the whole world astray."*

The dragon attacks the woman, but she is given protection during the three-and-a-half year destruction of Jerusalem. How is this woman both the one who gave birth to Jesus *and* the Church that proceeded from Jesus? As the woman, she represents godly Israel who brought forth Jesus and then also responded to the gospel.

The Beast of the Sea

Chapter 13 introduces us to the two beasts, the beast of the sea and the beast of the earth. Nothing in Revelation has been subject to as much speculation and misinformation as the beast from the sea. This has been the source of the modern paranoia regarding implanted microchips and barcodes. The type of interpretation that takes place regarding the mysterious number 666 reminds me of the following humorous example:

> Literary scholar Kathryn Lindskoog sent the following to her friends via the Internet to show how almost anyone or anything can be made to read 666.
>
> Given: Barney is a cute purple dinosaur
>
> Prove: Barney is really the Antichrist in disguise
>
> 1. Start with the given: CUTE PURPLE DINOSAUR
>
> 2. Change all the U's to V's (which is proper Latin anyway): CVTE PVRPLE DINOSAVR
>
> 3. Extract all Roman Numerals in the phrase: CVVLDIV
>
> 4. Convert these into Arabic values: 100 5 50 500 1 5
>
> 5. Add the numbers together: 666[1]

Ultimately, we must go back to a proper form of interpretation. *What would John's original readers have understood this beast to be?* With absolute certainty, I say they would have seen the beast from the sea as Nero and the Roman Empire. I have examined the beast" at great length in Chapter 6 of *Raptureless*. It may be helpful to turn back and reread Chapter 6 before you proceed. I will simply give one additional point regarding the beast.

The apostle John refers to the number 666 and says in verse 18, *"This calls for wisdom. Let the person who has insight calculate the number of the beast, for it is the number of a man. That number is 666."* When we read this verse, we must keep the following details in mind:

1. John was expecting his readers to be able to calculate this number and all arrive at the same conclusion.

2. John was not writing to readers thousands of years in the future but to his immediate contemporaries, and he expected them to arrive at the right interpretation.

3. John was not referring to a deep, profound mystery but to natural knowledge when he said, "this calls for wisdom" and "insight [to] calculate." He said this because the number code he used was the ancient Hebrew and not the concurrent Greek language of the day.

4. When the Jewish readers saw what John wrote, they would have mentally translated the numericle value into its corresponding Hebrew letters and spelled out Nrwn Qsr, or as we would pronounce it, Nero Caesar.

5. Some varients of the text say the number is 616 [check the margin of your Bible], which simply spells out Nero's name in a secondary manner, further solidifying this interpretation. (For more on that, see Kenneth Gentry's book, *The Book of Revelation Made Easy*.)

The Beast of the Earth

The beast from the earth is more accurately translated as the beast from the land (*ge*), which is the land of Israel. Nero was called the beast that arose from the sea because, if one was standing on the shore near Jerusalem looking out to sea, Rome was the major city directly across the sea. By contrast, this beast arose from within the land of Israel.

To the early Church reading John's vision, the beast that had arisen in the local region of Jerusalem was the Temple rulers, the preistly aristocracy that operated under the power and in the presence of the sea beast as a delegated authority (see Rev. 13:12).

After describing these two beasts, in Revelation 14, the scene changes again, and John sees Jesus (as the Lamb) standing with the Christians (the 144,000) who escaped the destruction by fleeing to the safety of Mount Pella. At the same time, below the mountain the three angels fly over Jerusalem (Babylon) declaring her destruction below.

The Great Harvest

A lot of prophets and preachers declare there will be a great end-time harvest of souls, with a billions being swept into the Kingdom of God. While I am for this idea and would love to see it happen, I also realize they are declaring this based on a misinterpretation of Revelation 14. While I agree that the Kingdom of God will continue growing and expanding and filling the whole earth (see Dan. 2; Matt. 13:31–33), I also know Revelation 14 is not about an end-time revival.

Revelation 14:17–20 speaks of the harvester angels reaping a harvest, which is thrown into the winepress of God's wrath, not into a revival!

If we back up and look at a parallel declaration from Jesus, this will begin to make sense. In Matthew 13, Jesus spoke of the approaching harvest. Jesus even indicated it would happen at the end of the age (*aion*), which was at AD 70.

> *He answered, "The one who sowed the good seed is the Son of Man. The field is the world, and the good seed stands for the people of the kingdom. The weeds are the people of the evil one, and the enemy who sows them is the devil. The harvest is* ***the end of the age,*** *and the harvesters are angels. As the weeds are pulled up and burned in the fire, so it will be at* ***the end of the age****"* (Matthew 13:37–40).

Jesus spoke of good seed and bad seed. Revelation 14:4 speaks of the Christians as the firstfruits, the good seed. In Revelation 14:14–20, it speaks of the bad seed being harvested and judged. Thus in neither Matthew 13 nor Revelation 14 can we find proof of an end of the world harvest of souls!

VISION 5

THE SEVEN BOWLS OF WRATH

REVELATION 15:1-16:21

We've looked at the seals and the trumpets. Now let's look at the bowls of wrath. Many modern readers tend to jump directly into the symbols of the plagues and want literal interpretations. Yet again we must back up from the picture in front of us and consider the context of the plagues.

To the first-century Jewish readers, the plagues of Revelation 15–16 would have immediately brought to mind the only other biblical occurance of plagues as judgment—Exodus 7–11. In fact, we can find some stunning direct parallels between the two lists of plagues. For example, the second and third bowls are about water turning to blood, which happened to the Nile during the plagues of Egypt (see Exod. 7:20). And the fifth bowl covers the land with darkness just like the ninth plague of Egypt (see Exod. 10:21–29). In the sixth bowl judgment, an army rises from the river and brings destruction; in Exodus, the Egyptian armies pursued the Hebrews, and the water swallowed them up so the Hebrews were delivered.

In other words, the basic concept in Revelation 15–16 is a clear reversal of the Exodus story. We found in Revelation 11:8 that first-century Jerusalem was considered by God to be Egypt and Sodom. Now the picture expands, and the Christians are making their exodus out of Jerusalem, as represented by the 144,000 marked of the Lord who go to the nearby mountain of Pella. As the Christians leave, behind them Jerusalem is engulfed in the plagues sent by God. Jerusalem is Egypt. Egypt is Jerusalem.

This will seem very challenging the first time you read it; I understand that. Take a moment to read the beginning of Revelation 15:

> *I saw in heaven another great and marvelous sign: seven angels with the seven last plagues—last, because with them God's wrath is completed. And I saw what looked like a sea of glass glowing with fire and, standing beside the sea, those who had been victorious over the beast and its image and over the number of its name. They held harps given them by God and sang the song of God's servant Moses and of the Lamb:*
>
> *"Great and marvelous are your deeds, Lord God Almighty. Just and true are your ways, King of the nations. Who will not fear you, Lord, and bring glory to your name? For you alone are holy. All nations will come and worship before you, for your righteous acts have been revealed"* (Revelation 15:1–4).

Here it's important for us to notice that they sing the song of Moses. This was the song the Hebrews sang right after the Egyptian army was killed in the Red Sea. In Revelation 15, the Christians sing the song of Moses as they are delivered from the new Egypt, first-century Jerusalem. That is what John was conveying to his readers. He goes on:

> *After this I looked, and I saw in heaven the temple—that is, the tabernacle of the covenant law—and it was opened. Out of the temple came the seven angels with the seven plagues. They were dressed in clean, shining linen and wore golden sashes around their chests. Then one of the four living creatures gave to the seven angels seven golden bowls filled with the wrath of God, who lives for ever and ever. And the temple was filled with smoke from the glory of God and from his power, and no one could enter the temple until the seven plagues of the seven angels were completed* (Revelation 15:5–8).

The tabernacle of the covenant Law was opened, and out of the Temple came the plagues upon Jerusalem (Egypt). These verses give us the Just Cause for why Jerusalem had become Egypt and deserved the plagues. Their own disasterous disobedience and rebellion toward the covenant

Law brought judgment upon them. If they had accepted Jesus as their Messiah King and His offer of a New Covenant, all the curses and plagues of the Old Covenant would not have fallen upon them.

Now, let's look at the bowls. I will be brief, as at this point they are quite repetitive of the seal and trumpet judgments. First, here's the outline:

- Bowl 1: Judgment comes on those who took the mark of Nero.
- Bowl 2: The seas turn to blood.
- Bowl 3: The rivers and springs turn to blood.
- Bowl 4: The sun burns the land.
- Bowl 5: Celetial bodies are darkened.
- Bowl 6: The armies are coming from the Euphrates.
- Bowl 7: The Great City is divided into three parts and hailstones fall.

In the first bowl, festering sores break out on those who took the mark of Nero. The seven plagues are reminiscient of the plagues upon Egypt in Exodus; thus, this first bowl is a parallel of the sores and boils inflicted on the Egyptians.

In the second and third bowl judgments, we find the incredibly obvious parallel to the Nile and all the water of Egypt turning into blood at the command of Moses.

In the fourth and fifth bowls, we again find celestial bodies being affected, which is our continual reminder that John was speaking of the destruction of a city or region. This is also a reverse parallel to the plague of darkness in Exodus. In the fourth bowl, it is the exact opposite; it is so much sun that the land is burned. Then in the fifth bowl, the skies go dark.

In the sixth bowl, we learn of Jesus coming (in the AD 70 judgement) as a thief in the night, which is a parallel of First Thessalonians 5:2 and Matthew 24:43. As I have proven in *Raptureless*, those passages are about the AD 70 destruction, so here we have a verse that anchors Revelation 16 with the same first-century event.

In the seventh judgment, we find the city divided in three. This is exactly how ancient Jerusalem was structured. It consisted of three successively higher portions and was invaded by the Romans in stages as each portion was destroyed and the next was seiged.

This bowl also mentions hailstones weighing specifically one talent. Josephus records that the Roman armies lobbed white limestones weighing exactly one talent from their catapults, thus destroying the defenses of Jerusalem in what would have appeared to be a hailstorm of white rocks weighing the exact amount recorded in this prophecy. Josephus wrote:

> The stone missiles weighed a talent and traveled two furlongs or more, and their impact not only on those who were hit first, but also on those behind them, was enormous. At first the Jews kept watch for the stone—for it was white—and its approach was intimated to the eye by its shining surface as well as to the ear by its whizzing sound.[1]

If we keep in mind that the Old Covenant was the veil and that the removal of the veil was the revealing or revelation of Jesus Christ, then we can look upon this tramatic time—when the Old Covenant world was being stoned to death for its unfaithfulness to its covenant partner—with gladness that we live fully in the New Covenant. We are in a New Covenant of forgiveness that contains no wrath. As Revelation 15:1 says: *"Then I saw another sign in heaven, great and amazing, seven angels with seven plagues, which are the last, for with them the wrath of God is finished"* (ESV). God poured out His wrath upon the Old Covenant of wrath until it was no more, and then He welcomed us into the New Covenant of forgiveness, which contains no wrath at all, because all sin is forgiven, and God remembers our sin no more.

VISION 6

THE BABYLONIAN HARLOT

REVELATION 17-19:21

Many questions and wild theories have arisen around Revelation's most mysterious symbol—Babylon the Harlot. Yet I believe David Chilton has beautifully excavated a clue to interpreting the symbols of Sodom, Babylon, and the Whore in the Book of Revelation. That clue is the reoccurring term *the Great City*. In its first occurrence, the text tells us that the Great City is figuratively called Sodom and Egypt, yet literally speaking, this was the city where Jesus was crucified. Therefore, the Great City is Jerusalem. *"Their bodies will lie in the public square of* ***the great city****—which is figuratively called Sodom and Egypt—where also their Lord was crucified"* (Rev. 11:8).

With this key in hand, we can begin to see that Revelation 16–18 speaks of the first-century Jerusalem as not only Sodom and Egypt but also as Babylon and the Great Whore that fornicated with the kings of the earth. After all, the Jews said at Jesus' trial, *"We have no king but Caesar!"* (John 19:15), firmly rejecting their Messiah, their Bridegroom, and joining themselves in adultery with the Roman government.

Ancient Jerusalem was made up of three sections built at different elevations. Therefore, the destruction in AD 70 actually occurred in three parts as the lower to the higher sections were progressively demolished.

Here is how John words his prophecy of the coming destruction of the Great City, Jerusalem, the Harlot City:

> *The* **great city** *split into three parts, and the cities of the nations collapsed. God remembered Babylon the Great and gave her the cup filled with the wine of the fury of his wrath* (Revelation 16:19).

The great city is also said to rule over the kings of the earth:

> *The woman you saw is the* **great city** *which rules over the kings of the earth* (Revelation 17:18a).

Jerusalem's fulfillment of this rulership over the kings of the earth is not obvious unless we consult history, where we discover it was one of the most important financial centers of the world at that time. This is also why the merchants mourned its fall in Revelation 18.

> *Terrified at her torment, they will stand far off and cry: "Woe! Woe to you,* **great city, you mighty city of Babylon!** *In one hour your doom has come!"....and cry out: "Woe! Woe to you,* **great city,** *dressed in fine linen, purple and scarlet, and glittering with gold, precious stones and pearls!... When they see the smoke of her burning, they will exclaim, "Was there ever a city like this* **great city?"** *They will throw dust on their heads, and with weeping and mourning cry out: "Woe! Woe to you,* **great city,** *where all who had ships on the sea became rich through her wealth! In one hour she has been brought to ruin!"...* [The Finality of Babylon's Doom] *Then a mighty angel picked up a boulder the size of a large millstone and threw it into the sea, and said: "With such violence* **the great city** *of Babylon will be thrown down, never to be found again"* (Revelation 18:10, 16, 18–19, 21).

The part of this vision I find most fascinating is John's dual perspectives of the destruction of Jerusalem. He gives the human perspective from planet earth in Revelation 18, and then he gives God's perspective from Heaven in Revelation 19. This was recorded so the Church on earth could know what God's perspective was and not get caught up in the earthly mourning over Jerusalem (Babylon).

> *After this I heard what sounded like the roar of a great multitude in heaven shouting: "Hallelujah! Salvation and glory and power belong to our God, for true and just are his judgments. He has condemned the great prostitute who corrupted the earth by her adulteries. He has avenged on her the blood of his servants."*
>
> *And again they shouted: "Hallelujah!*
>
> *The smoke from her goes up for ever and ever."*
>
> *The twenty-four elders and the four living creatures fell down and worshiped God, who was seated on the throne. And they cried: "Amen, Hallelujah!" Then a voice came from the throne, saying: "Praise our God, all you his servants, you who fear him, both great and small!"*
>
> *Then I heard what sounded like a great multitude, like the roar of rushing waters and like loud peals of thunder, shouting: "Hallelujah! For our Lord God Almighty reigns* (Revelation 19:1–6).

This was Heaven's perspective on the judgment of Jerusalem. Immediately following it, John tells us about the great wedding feast between Jesus and His Bride.

I used to believe the marriage supper of the Lamb was a far distant future event, but our only picture of the timing is in Revelation 19:7, *"Let us rejoice and be glad and give him glory! For the wedding of the Lamb has come, and his bride has made herself ready."* According to this verse, the marriage happened right after Heaven rejoiced over the AD 70 destruction of Jerusalem. It happened right before the beast, the false prophet, and those who took the mark of the beast were all judged in Revelation 19:11–21.

For many, this may require a shift in thinking. The Church is not a lonely fiancé withering away and wondering when her wedding will be. The Church is already married to Christ; we are in the New Covenant, and we remain in Him, and He remains in us (see John 15:4). In other words, the two have become one, and those who are joined to the Lord are one spirit with Him (see 1 Cor. 6:17).

VISION 7

THE NEW HEAVENS AND THE NEW EARTH

REVELATION 20:1-22:11

Part 1 (Revelation 20)

I have studied the many views regarding this passage, and as of yet, I found none of them to be perfectly satisfying. Even David Chilton, the scholar who wrote the 750-page masterpiece, *The Days of Vengeance,* also concluded that his was a mixture of two of the main views of the millennium.[1] Rather than getting into the theological terms and their definitions, I will simply say I agree with Chilton's blending, which has no particular name per se. Now let's jump into examining the text:

> *And I saw an angel coming down out of heaven, having the key to the Abyss and holding in his hand a great chain. He seized the dragon, that ancient serpent, who is the devil, or Satan, and bound him for a thousand years. He threw him into the Abyss, and locked and sealed it over him, to keep him from deceiving the nations anymore until the thousand years were ended. After that, he must be set free for a short time* (Revelation 20:1–3).

The Figurative Nature of the Millennium

These three verses have been the source of countless debates, divisions, novels, and poor quality Christian movies! Nowhere else in Scripture is a thousand-year time period specifically mentioned. In fact, to the Jewish people, the number one thousand simply meant "a whole lot."

For example, look at the song in First Samuel 18, *"Saul has slain his thousands, and David his tens of thousands"* (1 Sam. 18:7). This sounds impressive, except that David had only killed Goliath. With this example, we see it's important to remember the Jewish approach to numbers was not the same as the modern literalism we have been taught.

Another example is the claim that God owns the cattle on a thousand hills (see Ps. 50:10). Actually God owns all the cattle on all the hills of the planet, yet to the Jewish reader, using the number *one thousand* was not limiting God's cattle ownership!

A third example is in this verse: *"Better is one day in your courts than a thousand elsewhere..."* (Ps. 84:10). If understood literally, this verse would mean 1,001 days elsewhere *would* be better than a day in the house of God. Clearly, that was not the psalmist's message.

Pastor Bill Johnson of Bethel Church in Redding, California, said this regarding Revelation 20:

> We have statements in scripture concerning the beasts and the thousand years. For example, it says that the dragon will be bound with chains and cast into a bottomless pit for a thousand years. Now I don't want to take away your millennium... I just want to suggest that we might not know what we are talking about because there are only a couple of verses in the Bible on the subject!
>
> Then Bill Johnson begins to ask questions of the audience:
> Bill Johnson: The Dragon, literal or figurative? Is it a real dragon?
> Audience replies: Figurative
> Bill Johnson: The Chains, literal or figurative? Is it actual chains?
> Audience replies: Figurative
> Bill Johnson: The Bottomless pit, literal or figurative?
> Audience replies: Figurative
> Bill Johnson: The Millennium, literal or figurative?
> To this question, the audience replies only with stunned silence.[2]

Bill then goes on to speak about how we have allowed our interpretation of the millennium and other passages to cancel out our responsibility to demonstrate the Kingdom of God in the present—as if many of the Bible's promises are not for today.

To that I say, "That's a good word, Bill!"

During the Millennium

Now let's look at what the Bible says will happen during the millennium:

> *I saw thrones on which were seated those who had been given authority to judge. And I saw the souls of those who had been beheaded because of their* **testimony about Jesus and because of the word of God.** *They had not worshiped the beast or its image and had not received its mark on their foreheads or their hands. They came to life and reigned with Christ a thousand years* (Revelation 20:4).

The English translation of this passage makes it seem like there are two groups of people in view here, yet in the Greek it is clear that John was describing one group of people, the same group from Revelation 6:9–11:

> *When he opened the fifth seal, I saw under the altar the souls of those who had been slain because of the* **word of God and the testimony** *they had maintained. They called out in a loud voice, "How long, Sovereign Lord, holy and true, until you judge the inhabitants of the earth and avenge our blood?" Then each of them was given a white robe, and they were told to wait a little longer, until the full number of their fellow servants, their brothers and sisters, were killed just as they had been."*

In chapter 6, we find these martyrs under the throne crying out for justice, but in chapter 20, the same martyrs are given thrones of their own to reign in judgment upon! I know this because of the next verse:

> *(The rest of the dead did not come to life until the thousand years were ended.) This is the first resurrection.*

This phrase, *"**The rest** of the dead,"* makes it clear that this group of people is a select number from among the dead. To find out what separates these ones who reign on thrones from "the rest," we need to look at the passage right before chapter 20 begins:

> *But the beast was captured, and with it the false prophet who had performed the signs on its behalf. With these signs he had deluded those who had received the mark of the beast and worshiped its image. The two of them were thrown alive into the fiery lake of burning sulfur.* ***The rest*** *were killed with the sword coming out of the mouth of the rider on the horse, and all the birds gorged themselves on their flesh* (Revelation 19:19–21).

The ones in question, *"**The rest** of the dead,"* were those who died in the AD 70 destruction, the non-believing Jews. We know this to be true because the time indicator in Revelation 19:20 tells us this happened at the same time as the destruction of the Beast and the False Prophet, that is Nero and the Jewish Rulers.

Thus far, this is what we have found in Revelation 20:

- A time period that is very long, symbolized by the number *one thousand*
- First-century martyrs sitting on thrones and passing judgment
- First-century Jewish non-believers being judged
- The dragon (devil) being bound in his ability to deceive the nations

Importantly, we have not found any of the following popular ideas:

- A rebuilt temple in Jerusalem
- The reestablishment of the Old Covenant system
- Jesus reigning physically upon the earth

These concepts that are not found in Revelation 20 have been injected by the system Darby founded in the most abusive form of eisegesis (reading one's own ideas into a text). Darbyists construct their view of the thousand years by taking passages from Jeremiah, Zechariah, Ezekiel, and Isaiah and tearing them out of context in order to make them fit with Revelation 20.

If I were to simply paraphrase my understanding of Revelation 20, I would explain it this way: The thousand years represents the Kingdom of God. When Jesus came to earth, He bound the devil (the strong man, as in Matthew 12:28–29), and the devil could no longer deceive the nations (see Rev. 20:3). This paved the way for the disciples to disciple all nations (see Matt. 28:18–20). The first-century martyrs were given thrones to reign upon in the Kingdom; this occurred in Revelation 11, when Jesus was declared the King over the kingdoms of the earth (see Rev. 11:15) and the first resurrection was indicated (see Rev. 11:17–18). We now live inside the Kingdom of God on the earth, which is growing as the mustard seed and as the leaven going through the loaf (see Matt. 13:31–33). We are in the millennial reign, which is a spiritual Kingdom that is bringing Heaven into the earth progressively (see Matt. 6:10). Someday in the future, the Kingdom will have advanced so far that the only thing remaining to do will be to finally and completely judge the devil. He will be released from his chains to gather up whoever still resists the Kingdom, and the lot of them will be thrown into the lake of fire.

Why the Difficulty?

As we have seen, the Book of Revelation contains weird and mysterious symbols throughout that require interpretation. Comprehending these symbols becomes easier when we understand the symbols are based mainly on the Old Testament and point to the shift from the Old Covenant into the New Covenant.

Yet when we reach Revelation 20, it seems like a dozen interpretations appear, and each interpretation has many credible adherents. Why is Revelation 20 so difficult?

As I worked on writing this section, I had about twenty commentaries open on a table in Starbucks. Each of the books I had brought in my box came from what I consider to be the optimistic perspective. Yet they still held a lot of various answers regarding Revelation 20. Comparing them all, I have determined that, in my opinion, the perspective of James Stuart Russell is most sensible regarding this passage.

I must take a moment to clarify that I do not adhere to James Stuart Russell's beliefs as a whole. His remarkable work, *The Parousia*, published in 1878, is still a magnum opus proving all this end-times stuff has already happened and isn't about our future. The problem is that Russell goes too far and says Jesus isn't coming back and there is no future judgment or resurrection. This is in direct contradiction to what I believe, as I have laid out clearly in *Raptureless* in Chapter 14, "The Big Three." Russell's belief is commonly referred to as full preterism.

Russell's understanding of Revelation 20 is very helpful and insightful, yet it is what he says about this passage that actually causes the purist full preterists to reject Russell and claim he is not a true full preterist.

Russell starts by disagreeing with his collegues (the full preterists):

> Some interpreters indeed attempt to get over the difficulty by supposing that the thousand years, being a symbolic number, may represent a period of very short duration, and so bring the whole within the prescribed apocalyptic limits; but this method of interpretation appears to us so violent and unnatural that we cannot hesitate to reject it.[3]

He is referring to the fact that the full preterist claims the one thousand years is figurative and refers to AD 30–70. Even one hundred years after Russell wrote this, many full preterists still make this claim. I, of course, find it unconvincing and agree with Russell on that. He continues:

> The act of binding and shutting up the dragon does indeed come within the "shortly" of the apocalyptic statement, for it is coincident, or nearly so, with the judgment of the harlot and the beast; but the term of the dragon's imprisonment is distinctly stated to be for a thousand years, and thus must necessarily pass entirely beyond the field of vision so strictly and constantly limited by the book itself.[4]

I agree with Russell's interpretation that the dragon (devil) was bound in the bottomless pit in the first century by the work of the cross. Yet by stating this very large number of years (the metaphor *one thousand years*), John passed beyond the immediate AD 70 destruction that, until that point, has been the main focus of the text of Revelation. In this one instance, we have passed outside the bounds of events shortly to come to pass.

> We believe, however, that this is the solitary example which the whole book contains of this excusion beyond the limits of "shortly;" and we agree with [the famous commentator] [Moses] Stuart that no reasonable difficulty can be made on account of this single exception

> to the rule. We shall also find as we proceed that the events referred to as taking place after the termination of the thousand years are predicted as in a prophecy, and not represented as in a vision.[5]

Russell makes a very strong point here; the rest of the Book of Revelation is a visionary experience, yet in this passage, John is not seeing a vision but begins to declare a prophecy. He has moved from operating as a seer with a vision to interpret, and he has started operating as a prophet speaking declaratively regarding the future.

> This act of seizing, chaining, and casting into the abyss is represented as taking place under the eye of the Seer, being introduced by the usual formula, "And I saw." It is an act of conptemporaneous, or nearly so, with the judgments executed on the other criminals, the harlot and the beast. This part of the vision, then, falls within the proper limits of apocalyptic vision....[6]

Once I saw Russell's explanation, this passage began to make sense to me. Ninty-nine percent of Revelation is a vision with symbols to interpret regarding the destruction of the Old Covenant world and the establishment of the New Covenant. Yet there is one percent of the Book of Revelation found in chapter 20 that passes outside the time and space restrictions of the rest of the book and speaks of the distant future. This is clearly shown by the figurative use of the one thousand years idiom.

After the Millenium

All of the main views of the endtimes (premillenial, postmillenial, amillenial, partial preterist, futurist, historicist, and idealist), except for a few teachers on the fringe (full preterists), believe that the Great White Throne judgment of Revelation 20:11–15 is a future event at the end of human history. While Revelation is the revealing and unveiling of Jesus Christ and His New Covenant—which removed the Old Covenant veil—the following verses *were not* fulfilled in AD 70.

> *When the thousand years are over, Satan will be released from his prison and will go out to deceive the nations in the four corners of the earth—Gog and Magog—and to gather them for battle. In number they are like the sand on*

the seashore. They marched across the breadth of the earth and surrounded the camp of God's people, the city he loves. [The city He loves is not the natural Jerusalem, which was being judged, but the heavenly Jerusalem.] *But fire came down from heaven and devoured them. And the devil, who deceived them, was thrown into the lake of burning sulfur, where the beast and the false prophet had been thrown. They will be tormented day and night forever and ever.*

Then I saw a great white throne and him who was seated on it. The earth and the heavens fled from his presence, and there was no place for them. And I saw the dead, great and small, standing before the throne, and books were opened. Another book was opened, which is the book of life. The dead were judged according to what they had done as recorded in the books. The sea gave up the dead that were in it, and death and Hades gave up the dead that were in them, and each person was judged according to what they had done. Then death and Hades were thrown into the lake of fire. The lake of fire is the second death. Anyone whose name was not found written in the book of life was thrown into the lake of fire (Revelation 20:7–15).

The famous Bible scholar, Milton Terry, wrote a stunning statement about this period of time we live within:

> How long the King of kings will continue His battle against evil and defer the last decisive blow, when satan shall be "loosed for a little time," no man can even approximately judge. It may require a million years.[7]

Part 2 (Revelation 21–22)

While working on my doctorate of theology, I wrote a report on *Navigating the Book of Revelation* by Kenneth Gentry, which opened my eyes to see Revelation 21–22 like never before! Gentry teaches that, although popular teaching says Revelation 21–22 describes Heaven, Heaven is not the primary message of the passage. Yes, Heaven is in view, but it is not the main point.

He starts with four reasons why he does not place Revelation 21–22 as the final and eternal consummate order. They are as follows:

1. The time texts of Revelation (see Rev. 1:1, 3; 22:6) indicate the entire book was imminent [minus Revelation 20:7–15, as noted above].

2. Revelation is filled with bold symbolism that should not be interpreted with rigid literalism.

3. The chronology of this section shows it should be taken in a more symbolic manner.

4. The flow of Revelation shows an expectation that Revelation 21–22 should immediately follow 1–20. No massive time gap is indicated.[8]

Gentry then shows that John's immediate source material for writing Revelation 21–22 was Isaiah 65:17–20. As Gentry states, "Isaiah was not speaking of the consummate order, for he includes aspects of the present fallen order in his description."[9] For example, consider this passage from Isaiah 65:

> *Never again will there be in it an infant who lives but a few days, or an old man who does not live out his years; the one who dies at a hundred will be thought a mere child; the one who fails to reach a hundred will be considered accursed* (Isaiah 65:20).

The descriptions here make it clear that his passage cannot be referring to our eternal state in Heaven since we know people will not be born or die in Heaven. Gentry says the same is true of Revelation 21–22, arguing it is not a picture of Heaven but of new covenant Christianity. To this end, he highlights nine points in chapters 21–22 that point to our current reality in Christ, which I have paraphrased here:

1. Revelation 22:1 speaks of the water of life. This represents God's offer of salvation, which Jesus speaks of in John 4:10–14 and John 7:37. We are invited to come to Him and drink.

2. Revelation 21:14 speaks of the twelve foundations with the apostles names upon them. Paul also wrote of the Church being built upon the foundation of the apostles and prophets (see Eph. 2:20).

3. Revelation 21:16 speaks of the city as a cube, with each side measuring 12,000 stadia. In modern terms, that is approximately 1,400 miles. Gentry then shows that if one were to measure from Rome to Jerusalem (east to west) and from the northern edge to the southern edge of the Roman Empire, it would add up to 1,400 miles by 1,400 miles, with the isle of Patmos exactly at the center of this measurement.

4. Revelation 21:22 tells us no temple exists in the New Jerusalem. This is because the work of the cross removed the necessity of the previous temple.

5. Revelation 21:24 says, *"the nations shall walk by its light."* This suggests nations still exist as separate national entities, leading us to conclude this is a present-temporal condition rather than an eternal condition. It refers to Jesus' establishment of the Church as the *"light of the world"* (Matt. 5:14).

6. Revelation 21:25b tells us the gates never close, illustrating the temporal work of ongoing evangelism.

7. Revelation 21:27 describes those who are *"unclean"* and those who *"practice abomination and lying"*; here again we see evidence of a pre-final-judgment setting. A description of Heaven would not include people of this sort.

8. Revelation 22:1–2 says the tree of life has leaves for the *"healing of the nations,"* indicating the nations have not yet been healed.

9. Revelation 22:15 includes the existence of *"dogs and sorcerers and the immoral persons and the murderers and idolaters and everyone who loves and practices lying,"* showing yet again this cannot be about Heaven after the final judgment. (This point was simply a recapitulation of points 6 and 7 combined.)[10]

Gentry then describes the state of gradual growth that characterizes the new creation:

> The principle of gradualism is important to understand as we look into the idea of the present new creation process. Gradualism recognizes that God generally works His will incrementally over time rather than catastrophically all at once. We see this in God's method in the progress of redemption in time (Gen 3:15; Gal 4:4), in Israel's gradual conquest of the Promised Land (Ex 23:29–30; Dt 7:22), in God's unfolding of His revelation in history (Isa 28:10; Heb 1:1–2), and in the expansion of Christ's kingdom to the end (Mk 4:26–32; Isa 9:6–7).[11]

I find Revelation 21:5 to fit well with Gentry's presupposition, *"…I am making all things new…."* Jesus did not declare, *"I have made all things new"* but that there is a process of *making* all things new. Thus we see that interpreting Revelation 21–22 not as a description of a perfected Heaven but as the beginning of the "making new" process, though it is little-known, is a contextually accurate interpretation. Gentry concludes his book with this summary:

> In Revelation, John details Christ's judgment upon Israel (Rev 1:7, cp. 3:10) and the collapse of the temple and the old covenant order (Rev 11:1–2, 19). Christianity is born out of Judaism, and for its first forty years functions as a sect of Judaism. But once the temple collapses (Hebrews 8:13; 12:20-28), Christianity is finally and forever freed from its mother and the constraints involved in that previous association (cf. Mk 2:21–22; Jn 4:20–24). John is picturing the glory of new covenant Christianity, which arises from the ashes of collapsed Judaism (cp. Mt 8:11–12; 21:43; 22:1–10). Christ promises victory over Israel and her resistance: "Truly I say to you, that you who have followed Me, in the regeneration when the Son of Man will sit on

His Glorious throne, you also shall sit upon twelve thrones, judging the twelve tribes of Israel" (Mt 19:28).[12]

Although Revelation may have some significance regarding what Heaven is like, Gentry has clearly demonstrated that Revelation 21 and 22 are primarily concerned with describing the New Covenant world that replaced the Old Covenant world. The establishment of the New Covenant began with the Marriage supper, and the New Covenant age continues on as we are colaboring with Him to make all things new.

THE EPILOGUE

REVELATION 22:12-21

As I mentioned previously, the introduction and the epilogue are a beautiful frame to the content of the Book of Revelation. As with the introduction, let's look briefly at the text of the epilogue to see how it frames the rest of the book.

> *Look,* ***I am coming soon!*** *My reward is with me, and I will give to each person according to what they have done. I am the Alpha and the Omega, the First and the Last, the Beginning and the End* (Revelation 22:12–13).

When Napoleon Bonaparte wrote that he would attack *soon,* he didn't mean in *our* future. When Abraham Lincoln wrote of ending slavery *soon*, he wasn't referring to *our* future. So why would we think Jesus was talking about *our* future when He said *soon*? Only by doing violence and disrespect to the text can we reinterpret *soon* to mean *not soon.* The destruction of Jerusalem was soon for the original readers of Revelation, and Jesus was exactly right in declaring it was soon.

> *Blessed are those who wash their robes, that they may have the right to* ***the tree of life and may go through the gates into the city.***

Outside are the dogs, those who practice magic arts, the sexually immoral, the murderers, the idolaters and everyone who loves and practices falsehood (Revelation 22:14–15).

In the first century, individuals had two Jerusalems to pick from. If they accepted Jesus as their Lord and Messiah, they spiritually went through the gates and entered into the heavenly Jerusalem, that is, the Bride of Christ, the Church. In contrast, if they chose not partake in the heavenly Jerusalem, they chose the earthly Jerusalem, which was filled with evil and about to be judged, by default.

I, Jesus, have sent my angel to give you this testimony **for the churches.** *I am the Root and the Offspring of David, and the bright Morning Star* (Revelation 22:16).

The churches on earth had been through nearly forty years of incredible persecution since Jesus had left, and it was time for an update from Heaven. As Jerusalem stood on the eve of incredible tragedy, Jesus gave an update to His followers on earth.

The Spirit and the bride say, "Come!" And let the one who hears say, "Come!" Let the one who is thirsty come; and let the one who wishes take the free gift of the water of life.

I warn everyone who hears the words of the prophecy of this scroll: **If anyone adds** *anything to them, God will add to that person the plagues described in this scroll. And* **if anyone takes words away** *from this scroll of prophecy, God will take away from that person any share in the tree of life and in the Holy City, which are described in this scroll.*

He who testifies to these things says, "Yes, **I am coming soon."** *Amen. Come, Lord Jesus. The grace of the Lord Jesus be with God's people. Amen* (Revelation 22:17–21).

Verses 18 and 19 are quite interesting and have been many times quoted through the ages. My simple thought is this: If people in the first century changed the context and content of this prophecy regarding the impending destruction of Jerusalem (see verse 20), others could easily misinterpret and misunderstand the text. That would result in Christians being trapped inside Jerusalem during the destruction. It was absolutely imperative for the whole content of Revelation to remain intact simply because it was Jesus' directions to the churches in the first century for how to avoid the destruction. (I also noted a parallel between Revelation 22:17–21 and Deuteronomy 4:2 in Part 2, "Naming the Painting." In both cases, these passages are typical of historical covenant treaties, thus pointing to the fact that Revelation is a book about covenant.)

As we know from *Raptureless*, every single Christian in the first century understood the Olivet discourse and the Book of Revelation; thus Albert Barnes records, "Not one Christian perished in the destruction of that city [Jerusalem]."[1] Because they knew the passages were about their near future, they knew when to flee to the nearby mountains. The Book of Revelation was an invaluable blessing in the first century, but as time passed and the events of the first century and AD 70 faded into the distant past, people ceased to understand Revelation's purpose for those living right before the AD 70 destruction. This is the correct way to understand this seemingly mysterious book.

THE CONCLUSION

IS REVELATION STILL RELEVANT?

Many untrained students have stood in front of a work of art and asked themselves, *Does paint smeared on a canvas really have any continuing value or relevance?* To the untrained, it does not. Instead, it is just a mess and a mystery. The same is true of the Book of Revelation. But for students trained in art history, the art before them has incalculable value because the artist, the context, the purpose, the location, and the timeframe are all understood and appreciated.

In response to what we've discussed in this book, some may wonder whether Revelation still holds value for modern readers. For many, this is a troubling idea. In fact, Watchman Nee used that same question as an argument against this particular view of Revelation:

> The period when Revelation was written constitutes a serious problem, in part because some Rationalistic teachers have advocated an earlier date for its composition—they assert that probably it was at the time of the reign of the Roman Emperor Nero. They have formulated this particular time frame in order to establish the theory that the serious proclamations recorded in the book of Revelation were all fulfilled after the infamous and devastating fire that took

> place in Rome in Nero's time. According to this theory, what the book prophesied actually pointed only to the persecutions of the Christians of old and destruction of Jerusalem together with events, which occurred at that very period of Roman History. The prophecy concerning the beast or the Antichrist simply has reference to the tyranny and evil deeds, which were perpetrated by Caesar Nero. And thus the contents of the entire book have been completely fulfilled by the events, which occurred around the time of Nero. For these advocates, Revelation is now only a book of already fulfilled prophecies. And hence it has no future spiritual value for us Christians. It merely forms a special part of Roman history and/or ancient Church History. But if that is true, then will not Revelation be quite a meaningless book for us Christians today?[1]

Here we see that, according to Nee's perspective, to understand Revelation from this point of view is to remove all lasting value or purpose. I disagree. If I could dialogue with Nee, this is what I would say:

> According to your logic, how does the Old Testament have lasting value? It was written about events that have already occurred!
> How does the story of the first Christmas have lasting value? It was written about events that have already occurred!
> How does the gospel record have lasting value? It was written about the events of Jesus' life that have already occurred!
> How does the story of the crucifixion have lasting value? It was written about events that have already occurred!
> How do the letters of Paul, Peter, James, and John have lasting value? They were written to Christians who have long since died!

The fact is, the entire Bible has continuing value and relevance, regardless of whether or not particular passages are about past events! The fact that Revelation is not a mysterious jigsaw puzzle to be fiddled about and dissected by each generation does not mean it has less relevance.

Rather, from Revelation we learn many things of value. Here are five of the most significant lessons we can learn from Revelation *despite* the fact that it does not prophecy events in our future:

1. We have been fully established in the New Covenant with our Bridegroom, King Jesus.

2. All wrath has been poured out on the Old Covenant system and never has to be repeated.

3. We are working with the King to *make all things new.*

4. There is no reason to fear a future one-world government run by the beast.

5. Jerusalem is not to be an idol for the modern Christian.

Now that you clearly see *The Art of Revelation*—the total removal of the Old Covenant and the beautiful display of the New Covenant that we live in—it's time to get back to work and make all things new!

A Word to Charismatics

The Bible is the ultimate test for all teachings and revelations. As I have traveled and taught, I have seen an atrocity committed countless times—mainly by charismatic Christians. That atrocity is the thought that experience trumps the Bible.

Although it would never be stated in such a way, many place more value and respect upon a "spiritual experience" than upon "theological training." Theology (the study of God) is spoken of in derogatory terms, such as *head knowledge*, whereas spiritual experience is more highly valued as *heart knowledge.* I believe that all Christians should value experiential knowledge, as no one can even be a Christian without having had the supernatural experience of being born again. Yet all experiences are subject to being tested and evaluated by the Word of God. That is the challenge I desire to remind my fellow charismatics of. We must not believe every prophet, spirit, or prophecy; the Bible clearly tells us they must be tested and evaluated.

> *"Do not treat prophecies with contempt but test them all; hold on to what is good"* (1 Thessalonians 5:20-21).

> *"Above all, you must understand that no prophecy of Scripture came about by the prophet's own interpretation of things. For prophecy never had its origin in the human will, but prophets, though human, spoke from God as they were carried along by the Holy Spirit"* (2 Peter 1:20-21).

> *"But even if we or an angel from heaven should preach a gospel other than the one we preached to you, let them be under God's curse"* (Galatians 1:8).

> *"Dear friends, do not believe every spirit, but test the spirits to see whether they are from God, because many false prophets have gone out into the world"* (1 John 4:1).

In the field of end-time teachings, our movement has displayed an incredible lack of discernment and deep gullibility. For example, one Charismatic TV preacher claims he knows his end-time teachings are right because he prays in tongues while studying. I have heard countless stories of brother so-and-so or sister-whoever who had a vision of the rapture, the antichrist, or a coming Great Tribulation. While it is possible this person did have a vision, this does not automatically mean it was from the Lord.

One of the biggest disagreements I run into when speaking with charismatics regarding the endtimes is a prophetic experience that someone had. Whether it is based on the stories of a beloved grandmother, a respected prophet, or an eight-year-old child who had a near death experience, charismatics are too often leaning their doctrine on experience rather than the study of the Word. But what happens when one eight-year-old child has a vision of the endtimes that disagrees with another eight-year-old child's vision of the endtimes? Then where do the charismatics turn?

Hopefully, they will be like the Bereans and study the Word rather than simply believing the experiences of others (see Acts 17:11). Whichever eight-year-old's experience aligns with the Word and sound doctrine—believe that one! (The other one may have had a vision from the devil or from the cheese eaten before bed. Or, as is the case in many of these stories, the vision was interpreted wrongly by the adult listeners. For example, the child may have seen a great battle, and the adult listener interpreted this as an end-time battle when perhaps the Lord was simply showing the child the great spiritual conflict we are currently engaged in as believers.)

It is time for a revival of evaluating prophecy by the infallible truth of the Word.

Raptureless was written with the deepest respect for the Word of God and a passion for the Holy Spirit. I expect it will be revised many times in my lifetime as I continue to learn. Yet I believe the fundamental presuppositions laid out in the Statement of Faith are sound and hold up against the test of Scripture. Let us have the balance of knowing the Scripture and the power of God, that we might not go into error (see Matt. 22:29).

Sincerely,
Jonathan Welton

The Return of the Nephilim

Recently, there has been a lot of talk in the air regarding Nephilim. Here I will address some of these ideas. First, I will say that I have always been fascinated by mysterious topics. I love thinking about dinosaurs, UFOs, deep-sea creatures, unsolved mysteries, Nephilim, and the pre-Adamic race. I am not writing to put down these topics.

Now let's look at the word *Nephilim*, which appears in only two verses of the Bible:

> *The* **Nephilim** *were on the earth in those days—and also afterward—when the sons of God went to the daughters of humans and had children by them. They were the heroes of old, men of renown* (Genesis 6:4).

> *We saw the* **Nephilim** *there (the descendants of Anak come from the* **Nephilim**). *We seemed like grasshoppers in our own eyes, and we looked the same to them* (Numbers 13:33).

From these two verses we learn that the Nephilim were simply the race of giants that existed in the Old Testament. It is important to recognize how little, beyond their identity as giant, these verses actually say about the Nephilim. These two verses tell us almost nothing, yet much speculation, extrapolation, and exaggeration has come from them.

Most of the modern preaching about the Nephilim has come from a passage in the New Testament, which some say alludes to their return:

> *As it was in the days of Noah, so it will be at the coming of the Son of Man. For in the days before the flood, people were eating and drinking, marrying and giving in marriage, up to the day Noah entered the ark; and they knew nothing about what would happen until the flood came and took them all away. That is how it will be at the coming of the Son of Man* (Matthew 24:37–39).

Some have used this passage to create wild fantasies about Nephilim spirits from Genesis 6 returning to subvert the world system and bring about the end of the world. Due to a lack of sound exegetical methodology, many are preaching, based on this passage, the return of the Nephilim in our future (or perhaps even in our present, depending on how paranoid the preacher is). The modern preachers have turned the original Nephilim (giant people) into the modern Nephilim (a breed of super-soldier demons ushering in the end of the world). This is completely unbiblical. In Matthew 24:37, *Jesus was not predicting a return of the Nephilim.*

I don't believe there is *any* validity to the modern Nephilim teachings. I am always careful to be respectful of Scripture, and I am saddened when I see leaders who have been in the ministry for decades take a handful of verses and speculate, extrapolate, and exaggerate them to the point that they have no cultural or historical relevance to the original hearers. We must not buy into this hype and paranoia. Jesus was *not* predicting super-solider demons in our future.

Rather, Jesus was simply saying the time of His coming would be like the days of Noah. As we've already discussed, in Matthew 24 Jesus was speaking of the AD 70 destruction of Jerusalem. In other words, He was saying that period of time preceding His coming in judgment against Jerusalem (AD 30–70) would be like the days of Noah. This was true in those days. Noah preached to the culture around him, and people did not repent of their evil ways; rather, they perished in the flood. This mirrors the way in which over 1.1 million Jews did not heed the voice of the early Church and, instead, perished in the destruction. Also, Noah and his family were perfectly protected in the ark, and not one Christian died in the destruction of Jerusalem. Clearly this passage has already been fulfilled in history and relates, in no way, to the supposed future return of the Nephilim.

The Coming of Elijah

Much excitement is found in declaring something amazing is about to come and in telling people if they hungrily pursue something they lack, they might find it. I feel an increasing frustration with such nonsense. Yet it is not as popular or profitable to tell people they already have what they need and certain Scriptures have already been fulfilled. If we have already been given what we need—through the finished work of the cross—and if certain passages have been fulfilled, then the weight of responsibility is upon our shoulders. We must rise up and do something with what we have already been given.

With this thought in mind, I will address the idea of a future coming of the so-called spirit of Elijah. I have been hearing a lot about a coming movement of the Holy Spirit, sometimes called the spirit of Elijah. (Simply type "the spirit of Elijah" in the Youtube.com search to find myriad examples.) This idea comes from a few passages that have been plucked out of context and thrown a few thousand years into the future, resulting in a future prophecy for us. When preachers cherry-pick passages and don't follow sound rules of biblical interpretation, they can make exciting sermons but not healthy disciples. Healthy teaching produces healthy disciples.

This teaching on the spirit of Elijah revolves around a passage in Malachi, which says:

> *See, I will send the prophet Elijah to you before that great and dreadful day of the Lord comes. He will turn the hearts of the parents to their children, and the hearts of the children to their parents; or else I will come and strike the land with total destruction* (Malachi 4:5–6).

When Malachi prophesied these words, he was speaking about events that were future to him—but they are *not* future to us! Rather, the great and dreadful day that this passage speaks of is a reference to the destruction of Jerusalem in AD 70.

With this understanding, we can recognize that John the Baptist fulfilled Malachi's prophecy regarding the spirit of Elijah. In fact, even before he was born, an angel prophesied to Zechariah that his son, John the Baptist, would fulfill the prophecy from Malachi:

And he will go on before the Lord, in the spirit and power of Elijah, to turn the hearts of the parents to their children and the disobedient to the wisdom of the righteous—to make ready a people prepared for the Lord (Luke 1:17).

Further, when the disciples asked Jesus about the prophecy from Malachi regarding the spirit of Elijah, Jesus said it had been fulfilled through John the Baptist:

And they asked him, "Why do the teachers of the law say that Elijah must come first?" Jesus replied, "To be sure, Elijah does come first, and restores all things. Why then is it written that the Son of Man must suffer much and be rejected? But I tell you, **Elijah has come,** *and they have done to him everything they wished, just as it is written about him"* (Mark 9:11–13).

The disciples asked him, "Why then do the teachers of the law say that Elijah must come first?" Jesus replied, "To be sure, Elijah comes and will restore all things. But I tell you, **Elijah has already come,** *and they did not recognize him, but have done to him everything they wished. In the same way the Son of Man is going to suffer at their hands"* (Matthew 17:10–12).

Jesus said it even more clearly in Matthew 11:

For all the Prophets and the Law prophesied until John. And **if you are willing to accept it, he is the Elijah who was to come.** *Whoever has ears, let them hear* (Matthew 11:13–15).

I find it amazing how Jesus clarified the fulfillment of this prophecy. First He said, *"If you are willing to accept it, he is the Elijah who was to come."* In other words, Jesus knew His first-century listeners were going to have a hard time with His declaration that Malachi 4 had been fulfilled. Even today, many preachers are not *"willing to accept it."* Then He told those who had ears to hear (willingness to hear) to listen. Again today, many do not have ears to hear.

Malachi 4 has been fulfilled and completed; this prophecy has no future fulfillment. The spirit of Elijah is not something we are looking for or waiting for. We have the privilege of living inside Christ, who is greater than Elijah. As Jesus put it:

> *Truly I tell you, among those born of women* **there has not risen anyone greater than John** *the Baptist;* **yet whoever is least in the kingdom of heaven is greater** *than he* (Matthew 11:11).

Now that is truly exciting! And it puts the responsibility squarely upon our shoulders! We are not awaiting a future event; we have already been given all we need to live fruitful and fulfilling lives. Now it is time to show up the Old Testament saints!

Statement of End-Time Beliefs

I believe in the optimistic view of the Kingdom of God being present and growing, as was taught and believed before the Darbyism of the 1830s became popular.

I believe when the New Testament writers spoke of the last days they were referring to the end of the Old Covenant Age, not the end of the world.

I believe when Jesus spoke of His *coming*, He was using Old Testament apocalyptic language to describe His *coming* in judgment upon Jerusalem in AD 70.

I believe Daniel's prophecy of seventy weeks was referring to Christ and completed by Christ. I do not believe Daniel 9 teaches a future seven-year Tribulation.

I believe the destruction of Jerusalem in AD 70 fulfilled the Great Tribulation, the day of vengeance, and the time of Jacob's trouble.

I believe in the return of Christ, the resurrection of the dead, and the final judgment. I do not believe in a secret rapture of Christians prior to the return of Christ.

I believe *antichrist* is a first-century name for Gnosticism and perhaps other false teachings. I do not believe the Bible prophesies a future one-world ruler.

I believe the Beast of Revelation is a reference either to the person of Nero or the Roman Empire (depending on the context).

I believe the Israel of God, the *Ekklesia,* is and always has been the true inheritor of His covenant promises. This is not based on race but faith.

I believe the Kingdom of God arrived with Jesus' first coming and will fill the whole earth in preparation for His final return.

Recommended Reading

I have categorized the following books so that you can find more information about any specific end-time topic. I hope you have enjoyed my book as a clear and concise introduction. I am not endorsing everything in each of the following books, but for the most part, each of them has been of benefit to me in my journey. Swallow the meat, spit out the bones. God bless!

A Good Overview and Introduction

The Last Days According to Jesus by R.C. Sproul
Last Days Madness by Gary DeMar

Understanding Matthew 24

Is Jesus Coming Soon? by Gary DeMar
Victorious Eschatology by Harold Eberle and Martin Trench
Matthew 24 Fulfilled by John L. Bray
The Great Tribulation by David Chilton
The Olivet Discourse Made Easy by Kenneth Gentry

The History of the Modern View

Whose Right It Is by Kelley Varner
10 Popular Prophecy Myths Exposed and Answered by Gary DeMar

Israel's Place in the Endtimes

Exploding the Israel Deception by Steve Wohlberg (Jewish Christian author)
Israel and Bible Prophecy by John L. Bray
10 Popular Prophecy Myths Exposed and Answered by Gary DeMar
Zion's Christian Soldiers? by Stephen Sizer

Ezekiel 36–38 (Gog and Magog)

Why the End of the World Is Not in Your Future by Gary DeMar

Zechariah 12 and 14

One chapter in *Last Days Madness* by Gary Demar

Dating the Writing of the Book of Revelation

Before Jerusalem Fell by Kenneth Gentry

The Early Church and the End of the World by Gary DeMar and Francis Gumerlock

The Destruction of Jerusalem

Josephus: The Complete Works

The Destruction of Jerusalem by George Peter Holford

The Early Church Understanding of the Endtimes

The Early Church and the End of the World by Gary DeMar

The Antichrist

The Man of Sin of 2 Thessalonians 2 by John L. Bray

The Beast of Revelation Identified by Kenneth Gentry

Commentaries on the Book of Revelation

The Great Tribulation by David Chilton

Days of Vengeance by David Chilton

Commentary on Revelation by Gordon Fee

The Book of Revelation Made Easy by Kenneth Gentry

Navigating the Book of Revelation by Kenneth Gentry

Revelation for Everyone by N.T. Wright

ENDNOTES

RAPTURELESS

Chapter 1: How Did We Get Here?

1. Gary DeMar, *Last Days Madness* (Atlanta, GA: American Vision, 1999. 4th edition), 289.
2. It is important to note that Luther was misusing those titles, which belonged in their first-century fulfillment. But also Ribera did not represent the dominant historical view. Whenever doctrine is not formed out of deep study, considerable debate, much prayer, and the leading of the Holy Spirit, it stands suspect. This is especially true when doctrine is thrown together as a reactionary and defensive response. The dominant end-time view before the 1500s was that the majority of prophecies in the New Testament had been fulfilled by the AD 70 destruction. Some modern day teachers try to counter this truth by saying that a Catholic Priest named Luis Del Alcazar was the first one to create this point of view as a reaction to Luther. It is true that Luis wrote a book about AD 70 fulfilling prophecy, but this was simply encapsulating the standard and dominant view into a solid book. This *was not* written as a new invention, whereas the book that Ribera wrote actually was a new and reactionary writing. See Kelley Varner, *Whose Right It Is* (Shippensburg, PA: Destiny Image, 1995), Chapter 7, "A Fresh Historical Look at Dispensationalism."
3. Fr. Stephen Lourie, "Origin of Rapture Idea," *Saint George Orthodox Church* (2011); stgeorgepa.net/2011/05/origin-of-rapture-idea/. Also see Kelley Varner, *Whose Right It Is* (Shippensburg, PA: Destiny Image, 1995).

4. Kenneth Boa, "Starting Over: Cultic Christianity—Reinventing the Faith," *Bible.org*; http://bible.org/seriespage/starting-over-cultic-christianity-reinventing-faith.
5. Ralph Woodrow, *Great Prophecies of the Bible* (Riverside, CA: Ralph Woodrow Evangelistic Association, 1971), 148.
6. DeMar, 236.
7. *Ibid.*, 412–413.
8. Pamela Starr Dewey, "Edgar Whisenant's 88 Reasons," *Field Guide to the Wild World of Religon* (2011); http://www.isitso.org/guide/whise.html.
9. *Ibid.*
10. Hal Lindsey, The 1980s: *Countdown to Armageddon* (NYC, NY: Bantam Books, 1982), 8.
11. Charles Ryrie, *Dispensationalism* (Chicago, IL: Moody Publishers, New Edition, 2007), 63
12. *Ibid.*, 65.
13. F.F. Farrar, *The Early Days of Christianity* (1882), quoted in Brian Simmons, *Behind the Veil of Moses* (Camarillo, CA: Xulon Press, 2009), 460.
14. John Bray, *Matthew 24 Fulfilled* (Powder Springs, GA: American Vision, 5th Edition, 2008), 148.
15. Alan Hajek, "Pascal's Wager," *Stanford Encyclopedia of Philosophy* (2008); http://plato.stanford.edu/entries/pascal-wager/.
16. Gary DeMar, "I Can Agree With These Atheists (Up to a Point)" *American Vision* (May 2, 2011); http://americanvision.org/4414/i-can-agree-with-these-atheists-upto-a-point/.

Chapter 2: The Rapture

1. In this passage, the word translated as "rise" is the same Greek word that is often translated "be resurrected."
2. Matthew Henry, *Matthew Henry Commentary on the Whole Bible* (1706), 1 Thessalonians 4.
3. Adam Clarke, *The Adam Clarke Commentary* (1832), 1 Thessalonians 4.
4. Gary DeMar, *Last Days Madness,* 218.
5. John Walvoord, *The Revelation of Jesus Christ* (Chicago: Moody, 1966), 103.

6. Timothy LaHaye, *No Fear of the Storm* (Colorado Springs, CO: Multnomah Books, 1994), 69.
7. H.A. Ironside, *The Mysteries of God* (New York: Loizeaux Brothers, 1908), 50.

Chapter 3: The Great Tribulation

1. Eusebius, *Ecclesiastical History*, III:7.
2. Eusebius, *The History of the Church: From Christ to Constantine* (1965), 69.
3. Albert C. Outler, ed., *The Works of John Wesley, Volume 2* (Nashville, TN: Abingdon Press, 1985).
4. Manlio Simonetti, ed., *The Ancient Christian Commentary on Scripture: Matthew 14-28* (IVP Academic, 2002), 191.
5. Charles Haddon Spurgeon, *Spurgeon's Popular Exposition of Matthew* (Grand Rapids, MI: Baker Publishing Group, 1979), 211.
6. John Lightfoot, *A Commentary on the New Testament from the Talmud and Hebraica,* 4 vols. (Oxford University Press, [1658-1674] 1859), 2:320.
7. Phillip Doddridge, *The Family Expositor; or, A Paraphrase and Version of the New Testament; with Critical Notes, and a Practical Improvement of each Section*, 6 vols. (Charlestown, MA: Ethridge and Company, 1807), 1:377.
8. Thomas Newton, *Dissertations on the Prophecies, Which Have Remarkably Been Fulfilled, and at This Time Are Fulfilling in the World* (London: J. F. Dove, 1754), 377.
9. *Adam Clarke's Commentary*, Vol. 3 (Nashville, TN: Abingdon Press, 1810), 225.
10. John Calvin, *Commentary on a Harmony of the Evangelists, Matthew, Mark, and Luke, Volume 3* (Grand Rapids, MI: W.B. Eerdmans, 1949), 151.
11. N.T. Wright, *Jesus and the Victory of God* (Minneapolis, MN: Fortress Press, 1997), 321.
12. R.C. Sproul, from the Foreword to *The Parousia* by James Stuart Russell (Grand Rapids, MI: Baker Books, 1983), ix.

13. George Peter Holford, *The Destruction of Jerusalem* (1805); www.bible.ca/pre-destruction70AD-george-holford-1805AD.htm. The Covenant Media Foundation has given the author, Jonathan Welton, permission to print and use this updated version of George Peter Holford's written work (www.cmfnow.com). For the author's original footnotes to his booklet, view the online version. I have omitted them here for simplicity and readability.
14. J. Marcellus Kirk, *Matthew Twenty-Four Exposition* (Philadelphia, PA: Presbyterian and Reformed, 1948), 93.
15. Henry Alford, *The New Testament for English Readers* (Chicago, IL: Moody Press, n.d.), 163.
16. Edward Hayes Plumptre, "The Gospel According to St. Matthew," *Ellicott's Commentary on the Whole Bible*, ed. Charles John Ellicott, 8 vols. (London: Cassell and Company, 1897), 6:146.
17. Seneca, *Ad Lucilium Epistulae Morales*, translated by Richard M. Gummere, vol. 2 (London: 1920), 437. Quoted in Jonsson and Herbst, *The "Sign" of the Last Days-When?* (Atlanta, GA: Commentary Press, 1987), 75.
18. David Chilton, *The Great Tribulation* (Fort Worth, TX: Dominion Press, 1987), 29–31.
19. Philip Doddridge, *The Family Expositor*, 6 vols. (Charlestown, MA: S. Etheridge, 1807), 2:365, Quoted in Gary DeMar, *Last Days Madness*, 89.
20. Gary DeMar, *Ten Popular Prophecy Myths Exposed and Answered* (Powder Springs, GA: American Vision, 2010), Chapter 8, "The Myth that the Gospel Has Yet to be Preached in the 'Whole World.'"
21. Quoted in John L. Bray, *Matthew 24 Fulfilled*, 5th ed. (Powder Springs, GA: American Vision, 2009), 54.
22. *Ibid.*
23. Albert Barnes, *Barnes' Notes on the New Testament* (1832), Matthew 24.
24. Eusebius, *The History of the Church*, 111. Quoted in John L. Bray, *Matthew 24 Fulfilled*, 62–63.
25. Albert Barnes, *Barnes' Notes on the New Testament* (1832), Matthew 24.
26. John Gill, *John Gill's Exposition on the Entire Bible* (1908), Matthew 24.
27. William Whiston, note b in Josephus, *Wars of the Jews*, 2:19:6, 631–632.

28. Harold R. Eberle and Martin Trench, *Victorious Eschatology* (Yakima, WA: Worldcast Publishing, 2006), 15.
29. DeMar, 120.
30. John Forster, *The Gospel-Narrative* (London: John W. Parker, 1847), 307.
31. DeMar, 145.
32. Eberle and Trench, 60.
33. Chilton, 15.
34. Eberle and Trench, 61–62.
35. DeMar, 175.
36. John F. Walvoord, *Matthew: Thy Kingdom Come* (Chicago, IL: Moody, 1974), 191–192.
37. Chilton, 25.
38. DeMar, 193–194.
39. Chilton, 14–15.

Chapter 4: The End of the World

1. David Chilton, *The Great Tribulation*, 17–18.
2. John Broadus, *An American Commentary on the New Testament: Gospel of Matthew* (American Baptist Publishing Society, 1886), 482.
3. George Hill, "Predictions Delivered by Jesus," *Lectures in Divinity* (New York: Robert Carter, 1847) 103–104.
4. Gary DeMar, *Last Days Madness,* 192.
5. Maimonides, *The Guide for the Perplexed* (Philadelphia, PA: Empire Books, 2011), 204.
6. Josephus, *Antiquities of the Jews*, Book 3, Chapter 7.
7. James Stuart Russell, *The Parousia* (Grand Rapids, MI: Baker Books, 1983), 289–290.
8. Charles H. Spurgeon, *Metropolitan Tabernacle Pulpit*, Vol. 37 (Banner of Truth Publications, 1970), 354.

Chapter 6: The Antichrist

1. "John is…writing shortly before the Roman attack on Jerusalem and the destruction of the temple, sometime in the 60s AD." Peter J. Leithhart, *The Epistles of John Through New Eyes: From behind the Veil* (Potosi, WI: Athanasius Press, 2009), 9.

2. "There were three stages of Gnostic development. The pre-Christian drew its inspiration from Greek, Jewish and eastern sources. In the second stage, a still mainly heathen Gnosticism used Christian ideas to fill up gaps—Jesus, for example, appearing as the agent of man's redemption. The third stage presented Christianity modified by Gnosticism to make it acceptable to religiously-minded, intellectual pagans, and in this form was heretical and a real danger to orthodox Christian belief.... This version of Gnosticism was a variety of Docetism (from the Greek *Dokeo* = I seem) which, arising from the Gnostic dislike of matter and suffering as associated with God, taught that Jesus's body was not a real one." David Christie-Murray, *A History of Heresy* (London: Oxford University Press, 1976), 22, 25.
3. Matthew Henry, *Matthew Henry Complete Commentary on the Whole Bible* (1706), Daniel 9.
4. Information about John Levi in this section is gathered from *The Man of Sin of 2 Thessalonians 2* by John L Bray (Lakeland, FL: John L. Bray Ministry, 1997). For easier reference, all instances of John Levi in Holford's *The Destruction of Jerusalem* have been put in boldface.
5. *Ibid.*
6. Josephus, *The Jewish War*, 313.
7. F.W. Farrar, *The Early Days of Christianity,* 471–472.
8. "Emperor Nero," *The Preterist Archive*; http://preteristarchive.com/Rome/Monarchs/nero.html.
9. "Revelation 13:18: Number of the Beast," *The Preterist Archive*; http://preteristarchive.com/BibleStudies/ApocalypseCommentaries/revelation_13-18.html.
10. N.T. Wright, *Revelation for Everyone* (Louisville, KY: Westminster John Knox Press, 2011), 121.
11. Richard Anthony, "The Mark of the Beast," *Ecclesia.org*; www.ecclesia.org/truth/beast.html.
12. R.C. Sproul, *The Last Days According to Jesus* (Grand Rapids, MI: Baker Books, 1998), 186–187.

Chapter 7: The Persecution Mindset

1. Glenn Penner, "Is the Blood of the Martyrs Really the Seed of the

Church?" *Persecution.net*; http://www.persecution.net/download/seed.pdf.
2. Jonathan Welton, *Eyes of Honor* (Shippensburg, PA: Destiny Image, 2012), 105–107.

Chapter 8: The Israel of God

1. Brian L. Martin, *Behind the Veil of Moses*, 334.
2. Thomas Ice of the Pre-Trib Research Center and Randall Price have said, "There are no Bible verses that say, 'there is going to be a third temple.'" *Ready to Rebuild: The Imminent Plan to Rebuild the Last Days Temple* (Eugene, OR: Harvest House, 1992), 197–198.
3. Gary DeMar, *Last Days Madness,* 398.
4. Harold R. Eberle and Martin Trench, *Victorious Eschatology,* 251.

Chapter 9: The Kingdom Transition

1. Brian L. Martin, *Behind the Veil of Moses*, 234.
2. Matthew Henry, *Matthew Henry Complete Commentary on the Whole Bible,* Daniel 9.
3. Gary DeMar, *Last Days Madness*, 95.
4. David Chilton, *The Great Tribulation*, 45–46.

Chapter 10: The Kingdom Without Wrath

1. Many have pointed to Isaiah 53 to support a doctrine of the Father beating the Son to death, which violates every Old Testament shadow of lamb sacrifice leading to Jesus' death. Also, Isaiah 53:4b is quite revealing, *"We saw his suffering and thought God was punishing him."* Isaiah is clearly prophesying about how we would misunderstand what was happening to Jesus at the cross. Those who try to hold up their argument with Isaiah 53 literally prove Isaiah's prophecy about *not* understanding the cross.
2. There will be a Final Judgment, a dividing of individuals before God's throne, yet this will not take place on earth.
3. Note also that Hebrews 10:27 says *"but only a fearful expectation of judgment and of raging fire that will consume the enemies of God."* This was in reference to the burning of Jerusalem, not a reference to

hell. According to many theologians, hell doesn't consume; it tortures, but it does not consume. If that is true, then we can easily see that the consuming fire here has more in common with the burning to the ground of the Holy City in AD 70.

Chapter 11: The New Covenant of Light

1. David Chilton, *The Days of Vengeance* (Dallas, GA: Dominion Press, 1987), 572–573.
2. *Ibid.*, 571.

Chapter 12: The Kingdom Now

1. F.W. Farrar, *The Early Days of Christianity*, 464.

Chapter 13: The Kingdom Advancing

1. Ernest Hampden Cook, *The Christ Has Come* (1895), xvi.
2. The historical data in the two sections prior is paraphrased from Harold R. Eberle, *Christianity Unshackled, Are You a Truth Seeker?* (Shippensburg, PA: Destiny Image, 2009), 264–267.
3. George Weigel, "Christian Number-Crunching Reveals Impressive Growth," (2011), *Catholic Education Resource Center*; www.catholiceducation.org/articles/facts/fm0146.htm.
4. James Rutz, *Mega Shift, Igniting Spiritual Power* (Colorado Springs, CO: Empowerment Press, 2005), 25–27.
5. Weigel.
6. "Global Christianity: A Report on the Size and Distribution of the World's Christian Population," (Dec. 19, 2011) *The Pew Foundation*; www.pewforum.org/Christian/Global-Christianity-exec.aspx.
7. Center for the Study of Global Christianity, www.gordonconwell.edu/resources/CSGC-Resources.cfm.
8. "Global Christianity...," *The Pew Foundation.*
9. *Ibid.*
10. Weigel.
11. David B. Barrett, et al., *World Christian Encyclopedia: A Comparative Study of Churches and Religions in the Modern World*, (New York: Oxford University Press, 2001), 236.

Chapter 14: The Big Three

1. "The Nicene Creed"; http://www.creeds.net/ancient/nicene.htm.

Chapter 15: The Apostolic Mission

1. John A.T. Robinson, *Redating the New Testament* (SCM Press, 2012).
2. Gary North, preface to David Chilton, *The Days of Vengeance* (Dallas, GA: Dominion Press, 1987), xvi.
3. "Tables for Finding Holy Days," *The Book of Common Prayer* (1662).
4. *The Works of John Wesley* (Nashville, TN: Abingdon Press, Volume 2, 1985), 499.
5. *The Works of Jonathan Edwards* (London, England: Banner of Truth Trust, 1974), 488.
6. Henry Davenport Northrop, *Life and Work of Charles Haddon Spurgeon* (Chicago: Monarch Book Company, 1890), 4:210.
7. Bill Johnson and Randy Clark, *The Essential Guide to Healing* (Bloomington, Minn: Chosen Books, 2011), 116–117.

THE ART OF REVELATION

Part 1: Building the Picture Frame

1. Eberle and Trench, 127.
2. Gordon D. Fee and Douglas Stuart, *How to Read the Bible for All Its Worth* (Grand Rapids, MI: Zondervan, 2003), 74.
3. *Strong's Concordance*, s.v. "Ge" (Greek #1093); www.studylight.org/lex/grk/gwview.cgi?n=1093.
4. *Strong's Concordance*, s.v. "Kosmos" (Greek #2889); www.studylight.org/lex/grk/gwview.cgi?n=2889.

Vision 1: The Seven Churches

1. David Chilton, *Days of Vengeance*, 86–89.
2. *Ibid.*, 134.

Vision 2: The Seven Seals

1. Robert Mounce, *The Book of Revelation* (Grand Rapids, MI: Eerdmans, 1977), 155.

Vision 3: The Seven Trumpets

1. David Chilton, *Days of Vengance,* 16–17.
2. *Ibid.*, 238–239.
3. James Stuart Russell, *The Parousia*, 411.
4. Eberle and Trench, 155.
5. James Stuart Russell, *The Parousia*, 412.
6. Eberle and Trench, 163.
7. *Ibid.*, 163–164.

Vision 4: Followers of Lamb or Beast

1. Gary DeMar, *Last Days Madness,* 233.
2. W.F. Farrar, *The Early Days of Christianity*, 471–472.
3. "Emperor Nero," *The Preterist Archive*; http://preteristarchive.com/Rome/Monarchs/nero.html.
4. "Revelation 13:18: Number of the Beast," *The Preterist Archive*; http://preteristarchive.com/BibleStudies/ApocalypseCommentaries/revelation_13-18.html.
5. N.T. Wright, *Revelation for Everyone* (Louisville, KY: Westminster John Knox Press, 2011), 121.
6. Richard Anthony, "The Mark of the Beast," *Ecclesia.org*; www.ecclesia.org/truth/beast.html.
7. R.C. Sproul, *The Last Days According to Jesus* (Grand Rapids, MI: Baker Books, 1998), 186–187.

Vision 5: The Bowls of Wrath

1. Quoted in Chilton, *Days of Vengeance*, 417.

Vision 7: The New Heaven and New Earth

1. David Chilton, *The Days of Vengeance*, 493–494.
2. Bill Johnson, "Mission Possible," CD (15:30 minute mark – 17:05 minute mark).

3. James Stuart Russell, *The Parousia*, 514.
4. *Ibid.*
5. *Ibid.*
6. *Ibid.*, 515.
7. Milton Terry, *Biblical Apocalyptics* (Whitefish, MT: Kessinger Publishing, 2009), 451.
8. Kenneth Gentry, *Navigating the Book of Revelation* (Fountain Inn, SC: GoodBirth Ministries, 2009), 178–179.
9. *Ibid.*, 179.
10. *Ibid.*, 180–182.
11. *Ibid.*, 182.
12. *Ibid.*, 184.

Epilogue

1. Albert Barnes, *Barnes' Notes on the New Testament* (1832), Matthew 24.

Conclusion

1. Watchman Nee, *Aids to Revelation* (Fort Washington, PA: Christian Literature Crusade, 1983), 17–18.